THE PE COACH

The Private Equity Coach

A Novel Playbook for Compounding Value Creation Through Talent and Discipline

First Edition

Mohamad Chahine

MeriTIP

MeritIP Publishing

Copyright

Gender Neutrality

This book is written using a gender-neutral approach. All references to the **Coach** as a metaphor for leadership, and to **CEOs** and operating executives in portfolio companies, are intended to be inclusive of all genders. The language, examples, and coaching moments are designed to reflect the diverse styles of high-performance leadership found in private equity and across business.

Taxonomy and Jargon

This book uses a simple taxonomy to reduce jargon and keep the reader focused on execution.

The core role in this playbook is the operating leader inside a portfolio company. You will see this person described interchangeably as the **PE-Backed CEO, OpCo CEO,** or **PortCo CEO.** For simplicity, the book may use **PE CEO** or simply **CEO** to refer to the executive accountable for growth, operational excellence, and value creation in a private equity-backed business, whether serving in a full-time, interim, or fractional capacity.

To avoid confusion, we will state this clearly: **PE-Backed CEO does not refer to the chief executive of a private equity general partner (GP).** This playbook is about the leadership of the operating company, not the management of the investment firm.

You will also see repeated references to **the Coach**. In this book, the Coach is not a motivational speaker and not a "helper on the sidelines." The Coach is a practical leadership force-multiplier: someone who creates clarity under pressure, installs operating discipline, strengthens decision quality, and builds the conditions for performance to compound. Sometimes the Coach is an operating partner. Sometimes it is the board chair. Sometimes it is a seasoned CEO advisor. And sometimes it is the CEO themselves adopting the coaching stance.

This playbook is crafted for **CEOs, operating partners, functional leaders, and founders** operating in the high-intensity environment of PE-backed companies. My 25+ years in private equity informs the patterns, practical moves, and real-world situations throughout. This is not a technical manual on deal-making. It is an execution blueprint for leaders who need tested ways to drive outcomes, build durable teams, and create value that holds up at exit.

Author's Quote

"In private equity, true leadership starts after the deal. Beyond the spreadsheets and boardroom dynamics is the real game: leading people, building something durable, and earning performance when the pressure is highest. The best leaders give more than they take. And the best Coaches make others better without needing the spotlight. Be genuine: soft as a rose, firm as its thorns."

The Coach

*"In the game of business, winning is not measured by capital deployed. It is measured by leadership that converts adversity into momentum. The most important part of any investment is the person running it. You can tell how fit that leader is by watching three things: they **train to play, play to win, and win with others**. That is the Coach standard."*

Introduction

Private equity has evolved. Financial engineering alone no longer generates superior returns. The difference between a good investment and a great one is execution. Execution is a human endeavor.

I have been in this industry for three decades. I have seen hundreds of deals. The pattern is consistent: the investments that compound are the ones where someone bridges the gap between the spreadsheet and the operating floor. Someone who understands both the economics and the people. Someone who can translate a thesis into behavior, and behavior into results.

I have always aspired to be that someone.

I have worked with CEOs struggling under PE pressure and helped them find their footing. I have installed disciplines that transformed chaotic organizations into execution machines. I have coached leadership teams through crises that could have destroyed value but instead became turning points.

This book captures what I have learned over many years. It is not theory. It is practice, distilled into principles that work.

The PE Coach is not a luxury. In an industry where the margin between success and mediocrity is measured in basis points of IRR, coaching is a necessity. The companies that have it outperform. The companies that lack it leave value on the table.

Read this book. Apply it. Your returns will thank you.

Contents

Who This Book Is For

This book serves three distinct audiences, each with different needs.

If you are an Operating Partner or board member, this book will multiply your impact. You will learn how to coach execution rather than manage it, how to install disciplines that compound value, and how to turn oversight into acceleration. You will get frameworks for the first 90 days, tools for navigating CEO transitions, and the language to bridge capital and operations.

If you are a CEO in a PE-backed company, this book will help you decode your environment and exceed expectations. You will understand how PE economics shape board behavior, what "good" looks like in your sponsor's eyes, and how to build credibility that buys you time and trust. You will get tactical playbooks for cash discipline, decision velocity, and exit readiness.

If you are a sponsor or investor, this book will sharpen your lens on portfolio operations. You will see why great investment theses fail in execution, how coaching infrastructure creates alpha, and what separates portfolio companies that outperform from those that underperform. You will learn to ask better questions and recognize operating capability when you see it.

One warning: this is a practitioner's manual, not an academic treatise. The ideas here come from operating floors, boardrooms, and crisis situations. Not from research papers. The numbers are real. The dynamics are real. The failures and successes are real. If you are looking for theory, read something else. If you want tools you can use Monday morning, keep reading.

How This Book Works

This book is built on a simple premise: **the investment thesis is only as good as the human system that executes it.** Capital structure, strategic insight, and market timing matter. But without disciplined execution by aligned, capable people, none of it translates into returns.

The PE Coach is the person who makes that translation happen.

The book is structured as an operating system, not a narrative. You can read it cover to cover or jump to what you need now:

Part I: Foundation. Why coaching matters and the operating system that makes it repeatable.

Part II: Relationships. Building trust with sponsors, CEOs, and boards. Establishing standards that enable speed.

Part III: The Craft. Performing under pressure, driving decision velocity, navigating the first 90 days.

Part IV: Operating Rhythm. Installing the cadence of execution: meetings, cash discipline, accountability.

Part V: Value Creation. Translating PE economics, building infrastructure, treating plans as hypotheses.

Part VI: Exit Readiness. Building sellability from day one, crafting narratives that command premiums.

Part VII: The Canon 50. The numbers, rules, and heuristics that anchor the coaching practice.

Part VIII: Field Clinics. Tactical playbooks for weak teams, cash stress, stale plans, and the re-rate imperative.

Each chapter ends with three tools:

- **Coach Cards Referenced**: Key frameworks and metrics used in that chapter.
- **Field Drills**: Actions you can execute immediately.
- **Clinic Questions**: Questions that surface truth about your situation.

Take what is useful. Apply it. Adapt it to your context. The work begins now.

Why This Book Exists

I have spent my career in the gap between capital and operations.

On one side, the financial engineers: sponsors, investors, board members who see the world through returns, multiples, and thesis validation. On the other side, the operators: CEOs, leadership teams, frontline managers who see the world through customers, products, and people.

Both sides are essential. Neither side is sufficient.

The financial engineer can model a value creation plan with precision but cannot make it happen. Cannot install the behaviors, build the culture, or navigate the human complexity that converts strategy into execution.

The operator can run a business but may not understand how PE economics work, how boards think, or how today's actions connect to exit value three years from now.

The gap between these worlds is where value is created or destroyed.

I have watched exceptional investment theses fail because no one could translate them into operating reality. I have watched talented operators struggle because no one helped them understand the PE context. I have watched sponsors and CEOs talk past each other, each speaking a language the other did not fully grasp.

And I have watched a different outcome when someone bridges the gap. When someone helps the CEO understand the economics, helps the sponsor understand the operations, installs the disciplines that create consistency, and coaches the human beings through the pressure that PE ownership creates.

That someone is the PE Coach. This book is my attempt to codify what I have learned about that role.

Three Beliefs That Shaped This Book

First: The PE industry is under-investing in human engineering while over-investing in financial engineering. The deals that underperform are rarely failures of capital structure or strategic insight. They are failures of execution, leadership, alignment, and truth-telling. They are failures of the human systems that must carry the thesis from PowerPoint to reality.

Second: CEOs in PE-backed companies deserve better support. They operate at a pace and intensity most executives never experience. They are held to unforgiving standards. They carry weight that is often invisible to those around them. A skilled coach can help them succeed where they might otherwise struggle or burn out.

Third: The numbers are not arbitrary. The 13-week cash forecast, the Rule of 40, the 70% decision threshold, the 100-day plan. These are coaching tools that shape behavior. They translate PE economics into operating discipline. They create the guardrails within which execution happens.

What You Will Not Find Here

This book will not teach you how to model an LBO or structure an investment. It will not give you industry-specific turnaround strategies. It will not resolve governance debates or provide legal advice on board composition.

This book assumes you already understand PE fundamentals. It assumes you know how to read a financial model, understand basic accounting, and comprehend how returns are generated. If you need those foundations, start elsewhere.

What You Will Find Here

You will find an operating system for creating value through coaching. A framework for installing disciplines that compound. A language for bridging capital and operations. Tools for the first 90 days, for cash discipline, for decision velocity, for exit readiness.

You will find 50 rules that anchor the practice. Field clinics for situations you will face. Questions that surface truth. Drills you can execute immediately.

Most importantly, you will find **practice refined into principles**. Not theory abstracted from reality, but reality distilled into repeatable patterns.

The ideas here are synthesized from decades of work, countless conversations, hundreds of board meetings, and the accumulated wisdom of practitioners who came before me. Much of what I know came from unnamed sources: a comment in a meeting, an observation on a plant floor, a late-night conversation with a struggling CEO. I have tried to organize this knowledge into something coherent and actionable.

A Note on Use

If you are reading this, you are probably already in the arena. You know the pressure. You know the stakes. You know how hard it is to translate intent into outcome.

My hope is simple: that this book makes you better at the work. That it gives you tools you can use Monday morning. That it helps you see situations more clearly and act more effectively. That it makes the companies you touch more successful and the people you work with more capable.

The work of the PE Coach is the work of building value through people. It is demanding, often invisible, and profoundly important.

Welcome to the practice.

The PE Coach Oath

Before we begin, a commitment.

The work of the PE Coach is consequential. Careers depend on it. Families depend on it. Capital depends on it. The companies we touch employ thousands. The decisions we influence shape outcomes for years.

"I will never let a problem age. I will never mistake motion for progress. I will always tell the truth, even when it is expensive. I lead beyond the deal, because value is built on trust, and trust is built on proof."

This work demands a standard.

The Five Commandments of the PE Coach

To live the Oath, a coach must adhere to these five non-negotiables:

1. **Truth Over Optics.** My job is not to make the Board feel comfortable; it is to make the business capable. I will report the "Red" before it becomes a crisis.
2. **Velocity Over Activity.** I value decision speed over meeting volume. I will fight the "theater of work" and focus ruthlessly on the vital few levers that move the needle.
3. **Ownership Over Blame.** I am not a spectator. If the Quarterback fails, I have failed to prepare them. I own the outcome of my coaching.
4. **Soft is Not Kind.** I will maintain radical candor and high standards because allowing a leader to underperform is the most unkind thing I can do for their career and the fund.

5. **Exit-Back Integrity.** I will build a company that is not just "sale-ready," but truly "buy-worthy." I will never trade long-term durability for a short-term multiple.

The PE Coach Infographic

THE PRIVATE EQUITY COACH

A definitive guide to value creation through discipline and talent

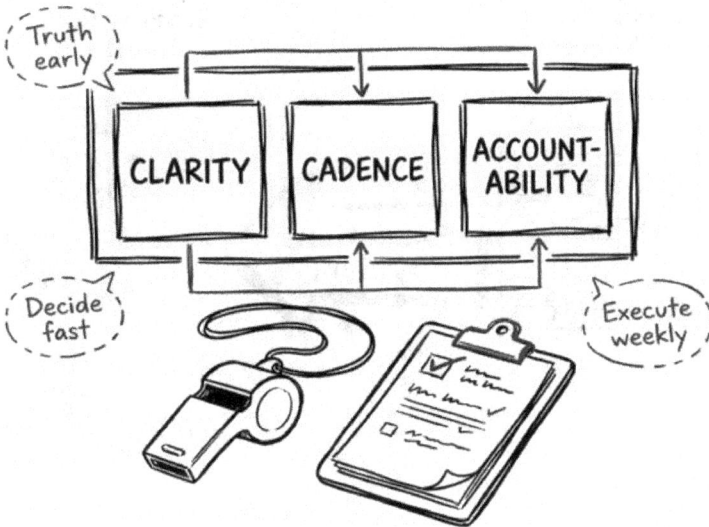

Truth early

Decide fast

Execute weekly

CLARITY CADENCE ACCOUNT-ABILITY

- Turn pressure into performance
- Replace heroics with repeatable rhythm
- Make reality discussable (facts > stories)
- Build decision-quality, not slide-quality
- Coach the system, not personalities
- Win with others, not alone

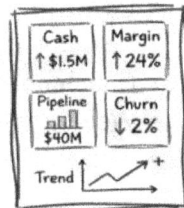

Cash ↑$1.5M   Margin ↑24%
Pipeline $40M   Churn ↓2%
Trend

After the Deal Is the Real Game

Deals set intent.
Execution determines outcomes.

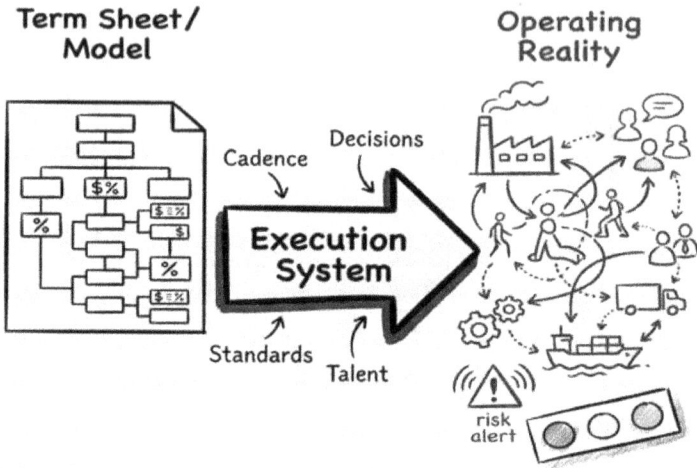

Term Sheet/ Model

Operating Reality

Decisions

Cadence

Execution System

Standards

Talent

risk alert

- Capital doesn't create value, performance does
- Operating drift quietly destroys returns
- Speed + discipline reduces risk
- Coaching closes the intent-to-reality gap
- Weekly truths beat quarterly surprises
- The exit is built in ordinary weeks

The Coach Role

Force multiplier, not an extra management layer

DO	DON'T
• Clarify priorities (few, not many)	• Run functions or replace leaders
• Install cadence and operating rhythm	• Micromanage or become the hero
• Raise standards + enforce accountability	• Create theatre or "pretty reporting"
• Improve decision velocity and decision quality	• Drown teams in frameworks
• Surface truth early ("no surprises")	• Chase perfection instead of traction
• Upgrade the team (right people in seats)	• Confuse advice with ownership
• Translate strategy into weekly execution	

TRUST IS THE OPERATING CURRENCY
No surprises beats perfect news

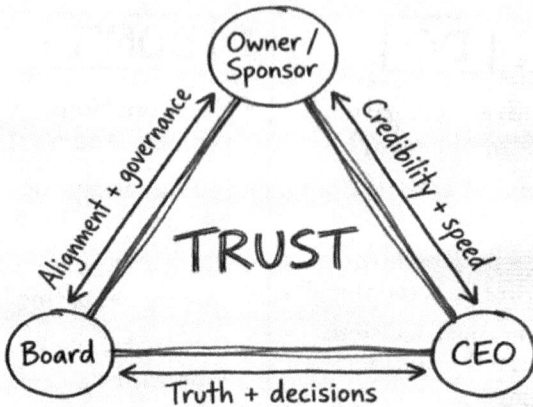

- Surprises destroy momentum and optionality
- Bad news early is competence, not weakness
- Truth speed beats narrative management
- Pre-wires prevent ambushes
- One-page fact packs beat long decks
- Coach protects relationships under stress
- Fix trust first, then fix strategy

48h fact pack

Cadence Runs the Company

Meetings are the interface of execution

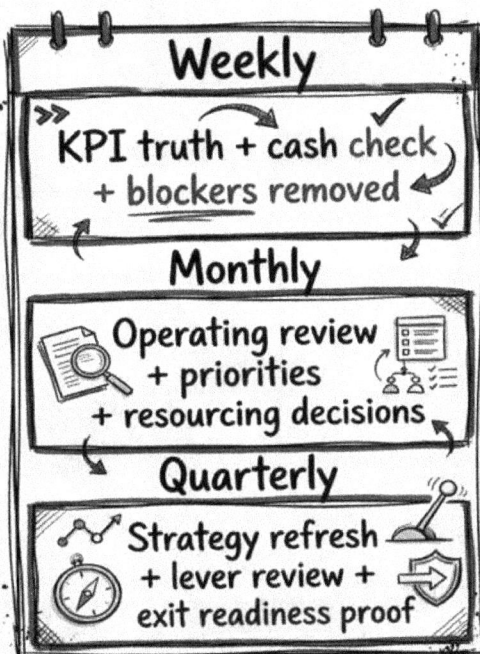

Weekly

KPI truth + cash check + blockers removed ✓

Monthly

Operating review + priorities + resourcing decisions

Quarterly

Strategy refresh + lever review + exit readiness proof

Rules

- Start with truth (numbers first)
- End with decisions (owners + dates)
- If it's not actionable, remove it

- Cadence reduces drama and surprises
- Clear rhythm creates execution speed
- Weak cadence turns leadership into firefighting

- Great cadence makes performance repeatable
- Weekly wins compound
- Consistency beats intensity

KPI dashboard
$ Rev | Growth %
CAC | NPS

Decision Log

Decision Velocity Wins

Speed comes from clarity + decision rules

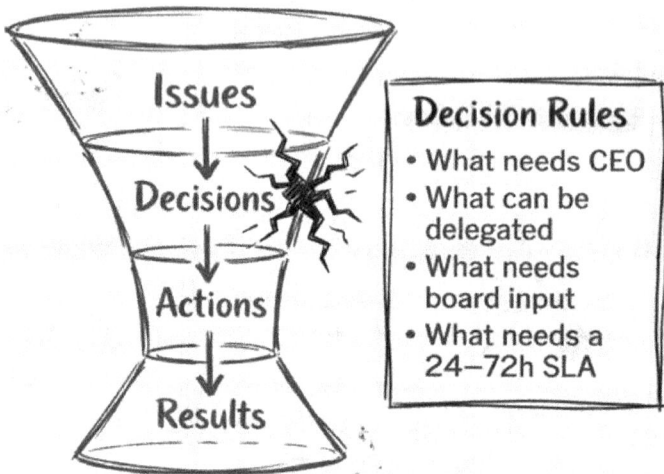

Issues → Decisions → Actions → Results

Decision Rules
- What needs CEO
- What can be delegated
- What needs board input
- What needs a 24–72h SLA

- Slow decisions are hidden costs
- Clarity reduces politics and rework
- Good decisions come from clean facts
- Pre-wire decisions before group meetings
- Commitments beat discussions
- One owner per action
- Review outcomes, not intentions

SLA clock:
24h surface,
72h decide,
7d implement

CASH IS TRUTH

Visibility beats optimism

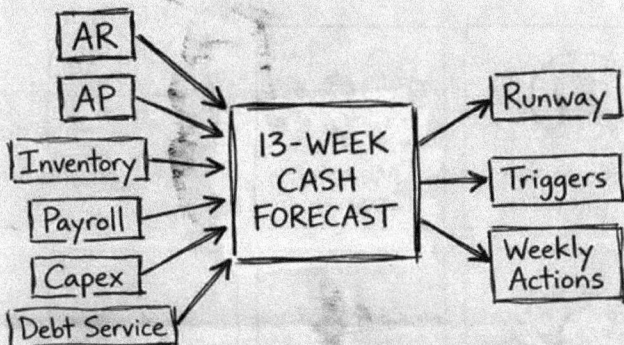

AR → 13-WEEK CASH FORECAST
AP →
Inventory →
Payroll →
Capex →
Debt Service →

13-WEEK CASH FORECAST → Runway
13-WEEK CASH FORECAST → Triggers
13-WEEK CASH FORECAST → Weekly Actions

Red: < 10 weeks	Yellow: 10–16 weeks	Green: runway > 16 weeks

- Cash removes debate and storytelling
- Growth without cash is fragile
- Forecast is only useful if it drives actions
- Weekly collections war room beats monthly regret
- Working capital discipline is leadership discipline
- Escalate early, not late
- Protect optionality by protecting liquidity

Value Creation Levers
Focus on what moves enterprise value

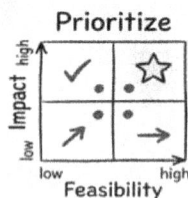

Revenue growth

Margin expansion

Prioritize

Smart acquisitions

Debt paydown

Multiple expansion

- Pick the few that matter now
- Assign owners and measurable outcomes
- Separate "busy work" from value work
- Review weekly: progress + blockers
- Kill initiatives that don't move value
- Don't confuse activity with results
- Align levers to capacity and talent
- Make tradeoffs explicit

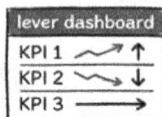

lever dashboard
KPI 1
KPI 2
KPI 3

Build the Exit from Day One
Buyers pay for durability and proof

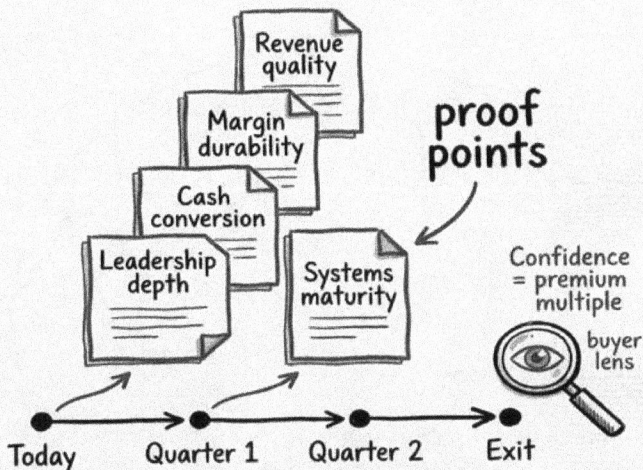

Revenue quality

Margin durability

Cash conversion

Leadership depth

Systems maturity

proof points

Confidence = premium multiple

buyer lens

Today — Quarter 1 — Quarter 2 — Exit

- Exit is not an event, it's a build
- Diligence gets easier if you prepare quarterly
- Repeatability beats heroics
- Risk reduction expands the multiple
- Clean data increases buyer trust
- Leadership depth reduces key-person risk
- Narrative must be evidence-backed

QoE-ready

The Coach Loop
Repeatable behavior beats one-time heroics

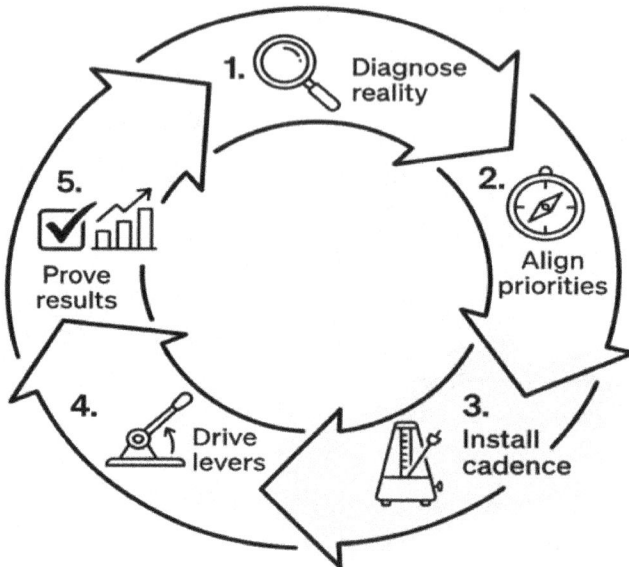

1. Diagnose reality

2. Align priorities

3. Install cadence

4. Drive levers

5. Prove results

- Diagnose with facts, not opinions
- Align roles and decision rights
- Convert goals into weekly commitments
- Track variance, not just progress

- Remove blockers fast
- Upgrade the team continuously
- Build proof points quarterly
- Repeat until performance compounds

Field Drills

TRANSLATE VALUE INTO BEHAVIOR

Make the numbers actionable for humans

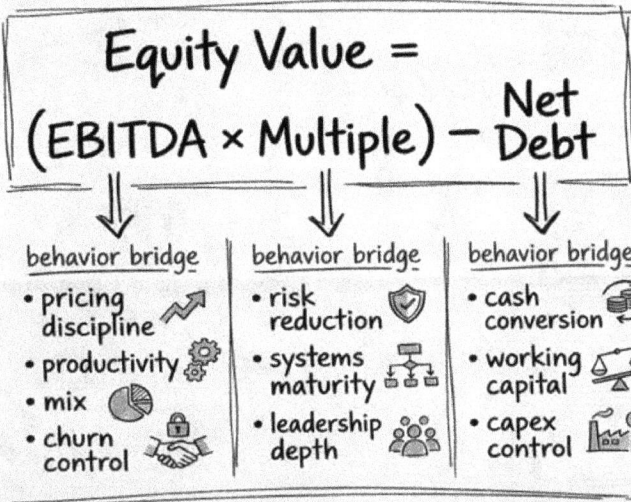

$$Equity\ Value = (EBITDA \times Multiple) - Net\ Debt$$

behavior bridge	behavior bridge	behavior bridge
• pricing discipline	• risk reduction	• cash conversion
• productivity	• systems maturity	• working capital
• mix	• leadership depth	• capex control
• churn control		

- Teams execute behaviors, not formulas
- If it can't be measured weekly, it drifts
- Link initiatives to 1–2 KPIs only
- Replace vague goals with thresholds
- Build "numbers as guardrails"
- Talk tradeoffs openly
- Prove value with evidence, not adjectives

translation table

Initiative
↓
KPI
↓
Owner
↓
Timeline

TALENT IS A VALUE LEVER

Right people, right seats, right standards

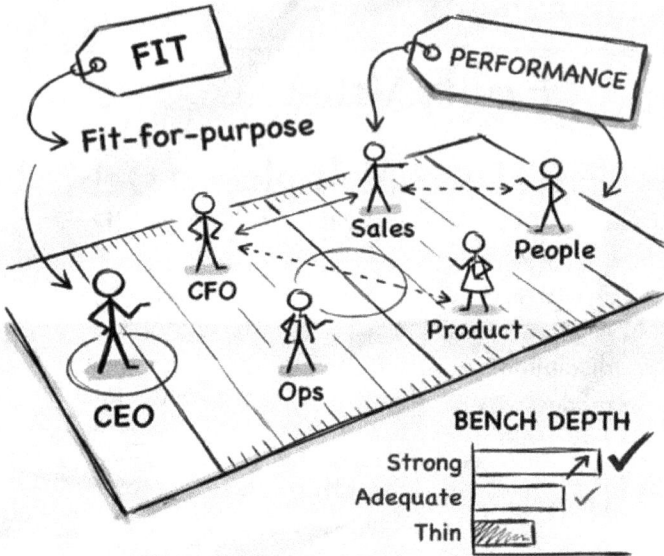

FIT

PERFORMANCE

Fit-for-purpose

Sales

People

CFO

Product

CEO

Ops

BENCH DEPTH

Strong ✓

Adequate ✓

Thin

- Strategy fails when seats are wrong
- A-players raise the standard silently
- Underperformers create hidden tax
- Coaching is clarity + courage
- Upgrade talent early (first 90 days)
- Make accountability humane and direct
- Build a second line of leaders
- Culture is the system of behaviors

hiring funnel

coaching 1:1

performance contract

Focus Beats Volume

Prioritize the few moves that matter now

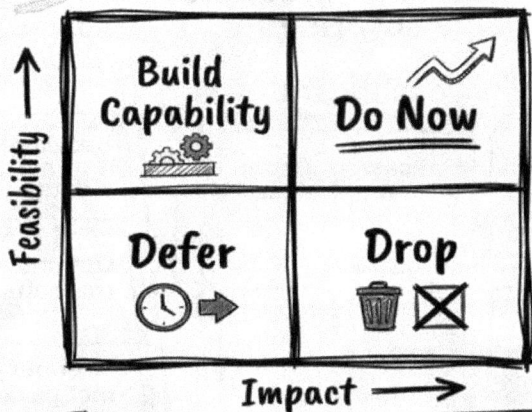

Feasibility ↑

| Build Capability ⚙ | Do Now 📈 |
| Defer 🕐➡ | Drop 🗑 ☒ |

Impact →

Simplification = Focus

✓ Too many initiatives equals no initiative
✓ Capacity is a strategic constraint
✓ Tradeoffs are leadership, not weakness
✓ Pick 3 priorities per cycle, not 12
✓ Assign owners + milestones
✓ Review weekly, reset monthly
✓ Stop doing work that doesn't move value

Stop / Start / Continue

⊗ STOP — Busy work
⇨ START — High Impact
↻ CONTINUE — Momentum 🚀

Prioritization Sketch - Oct 26

Run the Company on Signals

Early detection prevents expensive surprises

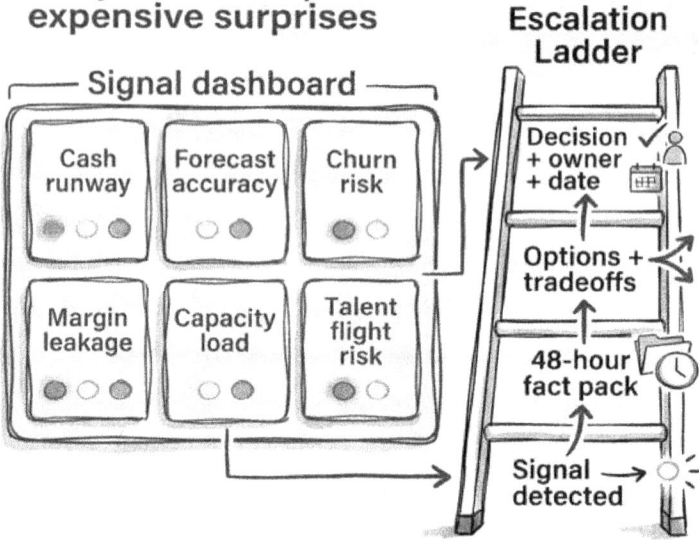

Escalation Ladder

Signal dashboard

Cash runway	Forecast accuracy	Churn risk

Margin leakage	Capacity load	Talent flight risk

Decision + owner + date

Options + tradeoffs

48-hour fact pack

Signal detected

- Lagging metrics are too late
- Watch leading indicators weekly
- Escalate fast, calmly, fact-first
- Risks become crises when ignored
- Owners love transparency, not spin
- Coaching creates psychological safety for truth
- Fix root causes, not symptoms

no surprises

The Coach Conversation

Direct, calm, specific, action-oriented

1. Reality
Here's what the numbers say...

2. Standard
This is what good looks like...

3. Commitment
By Friday, we will...

- Talk about facts before feelings
- Name the standard, not the person
- Make tradeoffs explicit
- End with commitments (owner + date)
- Avoid blame, insist on ownership
- Repeat the cadence until it sticks
- Praise truth-tellers publicly
- Coach the system, not the drama

commitment log

Action	Owner	Date	Status
---	---	---	✓
---	---	---	---

PART I

THE COACHING FOUNDATION

Why Private Equity Needs Coaches and How They Operate

Chapter 1

The Coaching Mandate

Why Private Equity Needs Coaches Now

The deal closed six weeks ago. The thesis was crisp: consolidate a fragmented regional services market, professionalize the sales function, and grow EBITDA from twelve million to twenty-two million within four years. The investment committee approved it unanimously. The CEO came with the business, a founder who had built something real over two decades. The operating partner assigned to the deal had done three similar transactions. Everyone was experienced. Everyone believed.

Now the CFO is on the phone with the lender explaining why cash came in two million dollars below the rolling forecast. The CEO is in a conference room telling the sales team that the new CRM will go live next month, which is the same thing he said last month. The operating partner is staring at a board pack that shows pipeline coverage at 1.2x when the plan assumed 3x. Nobody in the room can explain exactly where the gap is or who owns fixing it.

This is the moment that separates investments that compound from investments that stall. The thesis was sound. The numbers were modeled correctly. The people are capable. But something is not translating. The plan exists on slides. Execution exists in fragments. The space between strategy and action is filled with meetings, reports, and polite optimism. Not with the disciplined conversion of intent into outcome.

That space is where coaching lives.

The Incomplete Model

Private equity was built on an elegant logic: buy good businesses, apply financial discipline, create strategic clarity, and sell at a higher value. The model works when markets cooperate, when management teams are perfectly matched to the challenge, and when execution happens automatically.

Execution never happens automatically.

The traditional PE operating model assumes that capital, governance, and strategic direction are sufficient. Provide the money. Set the targets. Install the board. Review the numbers. Management will figure out the rest.

This assumption is dangerously incomplete.

The real world introduces friction that spreadsheets do not capture. People carry agendas that conflict with the plan. Processes contain inefficiencies that nobody mapped during diligence. Cultures resist the pace of change that PE ownership demands. Politics distort priorities in ways that never appear in KPI dashboards. External events arrive without warning, forcing adaptation that the original thesis did not anticipate.

A CEO who thrived running a founder-led business may struggle with the reporting intensity of PE ownership: monthly board meetings, weekly cash forecasts, quarterly thesis validation. A brilliant strategist may freeze when forced to make decisions with only seventy percent of the information. A strong operator may avoid the hard conversation with an underperforming sales leader for months, watching pipeline erode while hoping the problem resolves itself.

These are not failures of intelligence. They are failures of translation. The investment thesis describes what must happen. Coaching is the mechanism that helps it actually happen.

Consultant vs. Coach

In private equity, advice is cheap. Execution is expensive.

A consultant stands on the sideline. They analyze the game, hand you a 100-page playbook, and leave before the whistle blows. Their success metric is the delivery of the report.

A PE Coach stands on the sideline, but wears the headset. The Coach does not just hand you the play. The Coach watches you run it, corrects your stance in real time, and owns the result on the scoreboard. The success metric is EBITDA growth.

Consultants sell answers. Coaches build capability. Consultants love complexity. Coaches demand clarity.

This book is not for consultants. It is for leaders who have skin in the game.

CHAPTER 1

The Coaching Mandate

PE performance is human execution more than financial engineering

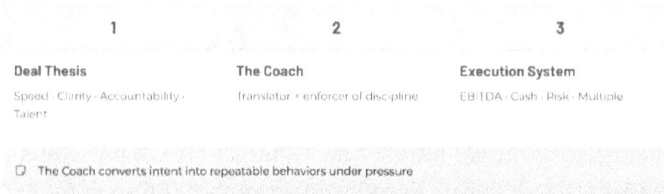

1	2	3
Deal Thesis	**The Coach**	**Execution System**
Speed · Clarity · Accountability · Talent	Translator + enforcer of discipline	EBITDA · Cash · Risk · Multiple

☐ The Coach converts intent into repeatable behaviors under pressure

The Translation Problem

Every PE investment is a set of hypotheses dressed in conviction. We believe we can grow revenue by expanding into adjacent markets. We think we can improve margins by professionalizing procurement. We expect to integrate two bolt-on acquisitions and extract synergies. We assume the management team can execute at a pace they have never sustained before.

The moment the deal closes, these hypotheses collide with human systems.

The sales team does not clear the backlog because they disagree about which opportunities deserve priority. Procurement savings stall because middle managers protect suppliers they have known for years. The integration playbook sits in a shared drive while the acquired company's best people start interviewing elsewhere. The CEO says the right things in board meetings but avoids making the organizational changes the plan requires.

This is not a failure of planning. It is a failure of conversion.

The operating partner can calculate a target return and build a 13-week cash forecast. But someone must translate those targets into the daily decisions, weekly rhythms, and personal accountabilities that produce results. Someone must notice when the CEO is stuck, when the CFO is hiding bad news, when the commercial leader is managing the dashboard instead of managing the business. Someone must create the conditions where truth travels fast, where decisions happen at the right pace, and where the plan evolves as reality teaches the team what works.

That someone is the PE Coach.

What Coaching Actually Means

Coaching in this context is not therapy. It is not cheerleading. It is not the soft counterpart to hard financial engineering.

Coaching is the systematic conversion of strategic intent into operating behavior. It is the discipline of making sure the right things happen at the right time, repeatedly, until they become culture.

The Coach sets standards. We will run a 13-week cash flow forecast every week, updated by Friday, reviewed by the leadership team Monday morning. No exceptions. No excuses about being too busy. When a CFO says, "We don't have time for weekly cash updates," the Coach responds: "You don't have time not to. A surprise in week ten costs ten times what a conversation in week three would have cost."

The Coach instills cadence. We will meet every Monday for ninety minutes to review the five metrics that matter. Every quarter we will step back and assess whether the plan still fits reality.

The Coach uses numbers as guardrails. If the Rule of 40 falls below threshold, we will decide whether to cut costs or accelerate growth. We will not drift. We will choose.

The Coach creates urgency through timeboxes. The first 100 days will focus on five initiatives, each with a single owner and a clear deliverable. By day 100, we will know which hypotheses are working and which need revision.

The Coach holds leaders to their commitments. You said you would have the pipeline rebuilt by the end of Q2. It is now July. What happened, and what changes this week?

The Coach celebrates progress when it is earned. The working capital improvement released three million dollars of cash in sixty days. That is real. That matters. Now let us talk about the next lever.

This is not abstract. This is operational. Coaching is the bridge between the investment thesis and the human system that must execute it.

The Economics of Coaching

Skeptics view coaching as a luxury, a soft intervention when budgets allow and feelings need managing. This view misses the economics entirely.

Consider the cost of missing a debt covenant. The lender accelerates or renegotiates. Pricing increases by 50 to 150 basis points. Control shifts. In severe cases, the sponsor faces a forced sale at precisely the wrong moment. A single covenant breach can cost more than the entire value creation plan was supposed to deliver.

Consider the cost of a misaligned leadership team. The CEO pulls in one direction. The COO pulls in another. The CRO is running a sales process that the CFO cannot forecast accurately. Six months pass while everyone works hard on initiatives that conflict. The market moves. Competitors advance. The window for value creation narrows. That is six months of EBITDA growth you will never recover.

Consider the cost of losing top talent because communication broke down. The VP of Product leaves because she felt blindsided by the board's decision to cut R&D. She takes institutional knowledge with her. Two other strong performers follow. The product roadmap stalls. Customer satisfaction dips. Churn increases by 200 basis points. Revenue softens. The exit story weakens.

Coaching prevents these costs by preventing the misalignments and execution failures that create them. It also accelerates the upside. An aligned team can move faster. An organization that surfaces problems early can solve them before they metastasize. A CEO who receives honest feedback improves faster than one surrounded by deference.

The return on effective coaching often exceeds the cost by an order of magnitude. Not because coaching is magic, but because the leverage on human behavior in a PE-backed company is enormous. Small improvements in decision velocity, alignment, and execution discipline compound into large differences in EBITDA, cash, and exit multiple.

The Coach's Lens

The Coach notices patterns that others miss because they are too close to the business.

What the Coach notices: The CEO who nods in board meetings but does not follow through. The CFO who buries bad news in variance explanations. The sales leader who blames marketing instead of owning pipeline. The leadership team that debates in public and commits in private (the reverse of what works).

What the Coach reinforces: Fast escalation of problems. Decisions made at 70% information with a clear fallback plan. Leaders who own outcomes, not activities. Meetings that end with documented decisions, not more meetings.

What the Coach shuts down: "We're still working on it" without a timeline. "That's not my department" when customers or cash are at risk. Presentations that explain failure instead of proposing fixes. Optimism unsupported by evidence.

The Coach might say: "You've told the board you're 'on track' for three months. Your pipeline says otherwise. What does 'on track' actually mean?" Or: "You're avoiding the conversation with your CRO. Every week you wait costs pipeline. Have the conversation by Friday or I will sit in it with you."

This is not cruelty. It is care expressed through standards.

Human Engineering

If financial engineering is about structuring capital, human engineering is about structuring behavior.

A successful value creation plan requires three ingredients: capital to fund the transformation, a disciplined operating system to coordinate the work, and human energy to execute day after day under pressure. The first two get abundant attention in PE. The third is often assumed rather than managed.

The Coach focuses relentlessly on human energy. Not motivation in the abstract, but the specific behaviors that produce results.

How does the CEO make decisions? Too fast, too slow, or in the zone where velocity matches the stakes?

How does the leadership team communicate? Do they surface problems or hide them? Do they debate in private and commit in public, or do they undermine decisions in hallway conversations?

How does the organization respond to pressure? Does it accelerate, freeze, or fragment?

These questions matter because human systems under pressure often behave in ways that destroy value. Fear slows decisions. Defensiveness blocks feedback. Politics distort resource allocation. Avoidance allows small problems to become crises.

The Coach intervenes in these patterns. Not by lecturing, but by installing disciplines that make better behavior the default. The weekly cash huddle forces truth about liquidity. The Monday operating review surfaces blockers before they calcify. The 100-day plan creates urgency without panic. The 70% decision rule prevents paralysis on reversible choices.

Coaching is human engineering in action.

Culture Under Pressure

Culture is how people behave when nobody is watching. In a PE-backed company, culture is stressed by the pace of change. The company is asked to grow faster, cut costs, adopt new systems, integrate acquisitions, and prepare for exit, all within a compressed timeline. The old culture may not survive this pressure.

Some elements of the existing culture are assets. A commitment to customer service, an engineering discipline around quality, a sales intensity that closes deals. These must be protected even as everything else changes.

Other elements of the existing culture are liabilities. A tolerance for missed commitments, a tendency to avoid hard conversations, a belief that the company is special and therefore exempt from standard metrics. These must be dismantled, deliberately and without apology.

The Coach helps leaders navigate this distinction. What do we keep? What do we change? How do we move fast enough to create value but carefully enough to avoid destroying what made the company worth buying in the first place?

Culture cannot be changed by memo. It changes through repeated actions, reinforced consistently, modeled from the top. The Coach holds leaders accountable for modeling the behaviors they want to see. The Coach notices when words and actions diverge. The Coach ensures that the culture shift is real, not performative.

The Time Horizon Problem

PE operates within a defined time horizon. The fund has a life. The investment has a target hold period. There is no infinite runway.

This creates urgency, which is useful. It also creates risk, because short-term fixes can undermine long-term value. Cutting R&D may boost EBITDA this year and kill the product roadmap for the next owner. Stretching payables may improve working capital this quarter and destroy supplier relationships that take years to rebuild.

The Coach brings balance to this tension. The Coach pushes for early wins because momentum matters and because credibility with the board is earned through delivery. But the Coach also protects against moves that mortgage the future. The Coach asks: If we do this, what happens in year three? What happens when the next buyer looks under the hood?

The goal is to build a company that can be sold at a premium because it is genuinely excellent, not because it has been dressed up for the transaction. The Coach keeps the exit in view while ensuring that the company would thrive even if the exit never happened.

The Hypothesis Mindset

Every investment thesis is a hypothesis waiting to be tested. The Coach treats it exactly that way.

The thesis says we can grow EBITDA by ten million dollars through a combination of pricing, procurement, and commercial expansion. The Coach asks: What evidence will prove this? When will we know? What do we do if the evidence says we were wrong?

This is not skepticism. It is rigor. The Coach is not attached to being right about the original plan. The Coach is committed to creating value, whatever form that takes.

If pricing increases cause more churn than expected, the Coach pushes for root cause analysis. Why are customers leaving? Is the price wrong, or is the value proposition weak? What must change?

If procurement savings are slower than planned, the Coach presses for specifics. Which categories are ahead? Which are behind? Where are the blockers? Who owns the fix?

If commercial expansion is not producing the pipeline the model assumed, the Coach insists on confronting reality. Is the market smaller than we thought? Is the sales team under-resourced? Is the product missing features that customers require?

The hypothesis mindset keeps the team honest. It prevents the slow drift into denial that kills so many PE investments. It ensures that the plan evolves as the team learns, rather than becoming a static document that everyone pretends to follow while the business moves in a different direction.

The Ripple Effect

Coaching cascades through an organization in ways that compound over time.

When the CEO learns to make decisions faster, the COO begins modeling the same behavior. When the CFO implements a rigorous cash forecast, the finance team starts thinking about cash in everything they do. When the board sees the CEO accepting feedback and acting on it, they trust management more and step back from micromanagement. When the CEO shows vulnerability in a coaching conversation, the leadership team begins opening up about their own challenges.

This ripple effect builds a culture of learning and accountability. It transforms the organization from a collection of individuals protecting their positions into a system that naturally surfaces problems and solves them.

That is the ultimate return on coaching. Not a single intervention, but a self-improving machine. A company that gets better at getting better.

The New Frontier

Private equity has mastered financial engineering. Leverage, capital structure, transaction mechanics, tax optimization. These disciplines are well understood and widely practiced.

The next frontier is human engineering.

The PE Coach sits at the intersection of people, process, and performance. The Coach takes the plan off the page and turns it into lived experience. The Coach ensures that the thesis evolves from hypothesis to execution. The Coach understands that numbers like the 13-week cash forecast, the Rule of 40, and the 100-day plan are not just metrics. They are coaching tools that shape behavior and drive accountability.

The Coach holds leaders to a higher standard while building them up. The Coach keeps the board aligned with the field. The Coach converts strategy into action and action into value.

The coaching mandate is not optional. It is the new necessity for generating consistent returns in an industry where financial engineering alone is no longer enough.

Coach Cards Referenced

- **13-Week Cash Forecast:** A weekly discipline that forces the team to confront liquidity reality before it becomes a crisis.
- **100-Day Plan:** A timebox that transforms the investment thesis into urgent, actionable steps with clear ownership.
- **Rule of 40:** A growth-profit balance indicator that reveals when to lean into expansion and when to prioritize efficiency.

- **70% Decision Rule:** A reminder that waiting for perfect information usually costs more than making a well-informed bet and adjusting.
- **30/60/90 Plan:** An onboarding and integration framework that structures early momentum for new leaders and acquisitions.

CHAPTER 1

What the Coach Does vs Doesn't

A clean boundary chart that prevents confusion and politics

Coach DOES	Coach DOESN'T
Clarifies priorities	Run functions
Installs cadence	Replace CEO
Raises standards	Play hero
Surfaces truth early	Create slideware
Upgrades decisions	Micromanage

○ Coaching is a force multiplier, not an extra layer of management

Field Drills

- **Run a Reality Check Meeting:** Bring your leadership team together to examine the gap between your investment thesis and current performance. Identify three hypotheses that need immediate testing.
- **Implement a 13-Week Cash Forecast:** Assign clear ownership and begin updating it every Friday. Use it to drive substantive conversations about working capital and investment priorities.
- **Draft a 100-Day Agenda:** Even if you are past the first 100 days, define the next 100. Limit yourself to five initiatives with one owner each.
- **Adopt the 70% Rule in Meetings:** Challenge yourself and your leaders to make decisions when you have roughly 70% of the information you would like. Commit, execute, and adjust.

- **Schedule a Coach Conversation:** If you are an Operating Partner, establish a standing coaching session with your CEO. Make it inviolable.

Clinic Questions

- When you examine your investment thesis, which assumptions remain untested? How are you actively testing them?
- Where is your execution slowest? Is the bottleneck a lack of information, fear of being wrong, or unclear ownership?
- What metrics do you review each week? Are they telling you the truth about cash, pipeline, and customer health?
- How often do you revisit your value creation plan? Is it a living document or a relic from the deal deck?
- When did your CEO last have a candid conversation about their blind spots?
- If you had to coach yourself, what would you tell yourself to stop doing and start doing in the next 30 days?
- What part of your culture is at risk because of the pace and pressure of the hold period?

Chapter 2

The PE Coach Operating System

Infrastructure for Repeatable Excellence

The previous chapter made the case for coaching. This chapter answers the harder question: how does coaching actually work at scale?

An operating system, in the computing sense, is invisible infrastructure. It manages memory, schedules tasks, and provides services to applications. Without it, hardware is just expensive metal. The PE Coach Operating System works the same way: it manages the flow of information, decisions, behaviors, and feedback in a PE-backed company. Without this OS, a company cannot execute a value creation plan effectively, no matter how elegant that plan appears in a board presentation.

The OS is what makes coaching repeatable. It transforms good intentions into consistent behavior. It replaces heroics with habits. It makes excellence systematic rather than accidental.

The Ad Hoc Problem

Many PE firms approach portfolio operations with good intentions but weak systems. They have experienced CEOs and capable functional leaders. They have playbooks, frameworks, and dashboards filled with metrics. They have weekly reports and monthly board decks.

Peel back the layers and you often find ad hoc processes masquerading as discipline.

Meetings happen irregularly. They get cancelled when things get busy, which is precisely when they are needed most. Metrics are inconsistent across functions, making comparison meaningless. Project owners are unclear, leading to diffusion of responsibility. Decision rights are fuzzy, resulting in either paralysis or uncoordinated action.

The result is unpredictable performance. Some companies outperform despite the chaos, usually because of an exceptional individual carrying more than their share of the load. Others underperform because no one is carrying it at all. Neither outcome is repeatable. Neither outcome is scalable.

The PE Coach Operating System converts chaos into rhythm. It makes the implicit explicit. It ensures that value creation is not dependent on any single heroic performer.

The Six Components

The PE Coach OS operates as a continuous loop with six components:

Diagnose. Align. Install Cadence. Drive Levers. Prove with Numbers. Re-rate to Exit.

This loop keeps spinning throughout the hold period. It is not a linear sequence you complete once and file away. You revisit each component repeatedly as the business evolves, as market conditions shift, and as the team matures.

The OS is alive or it is useless.

Diagnose: Fast Truth, Not Slow Consensus

Diagnosis is about understanding what is actually happening. Not what the deck says should be happening. Not what management wishes were happening. What is actually happening.

The Coach begins by gathering truth. This means examining cash balances with clear eyes, conducting margin analysis without defensiveness, collecting customer feedback without filters, assessing team capability without politics, and mapping cultural dynamics without denial.

A good diagnosis is ruthless. It calls out the good, the bad, and the ugly with equal clarity.

The tools of diagnosis are concrete. A 13-week cash forecast forces truth about liquidity. A deep dive into gross margin by product and customer reveals where profit is actually coming from. A listening tour with employees and customers surfaces signals that never appear in dashboards.

Speed matters enormously. In PE, the cost of delay compounds daily. If it takes six months to recognize that a product launch is failing, you have burned time, money, and credibility that cannot be recovered. The rule: diagnose within the first 30 days, not the first 90.

The Coach drives a fast diagnostic cycle. Weekly huddles surface red flags before they grow. Monthly reviews connect actions to outcomes. Hypotheses get tested early, before they calcify into assumptions that no one questions.

Without clear diagnosis, everything else in the OS becomes guesswork dressed as strategy.

What the Coach notices: The CFO who describes "timing issues" instead of structural problems. The CEO who blames the market for what is actually a sales execution failure. The leadership team that cannot agree on which three metrics matter most.

What the Coach says: "Show me the 13-week cash. Not the narrative. The numbers." Or: "You've explained why the forecast missed. Now tell me what changes next week."

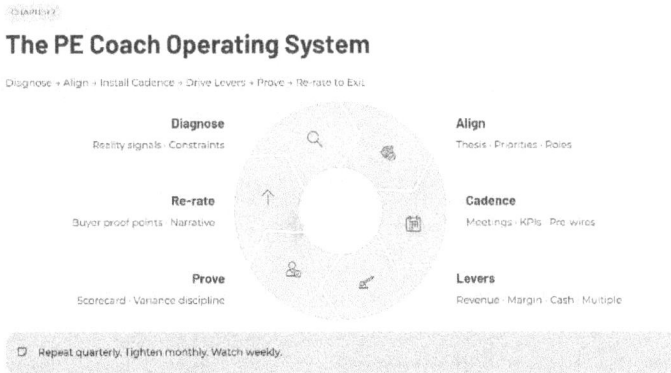

The PE Coach Operating System

Diagnose → Align → Install Cadence → Drive Levers → Prove → Re-rate to Exit

Diagnose — Reality signals · Constraints
Align — Thesis · Priorities · Roles
Re-rate — Buyer proof points · Narrative
Cadence — Meetings · KPIs · Pre-wires
Prove — Scorecard · Variance discipline
Levers — Revenue · Margin · Cash · Multiple

Repeat quarterly. Tighten monthly. Watch weekly.

Align: Sponsor, Board, CEO, and Team

Alignment is the art of getting everyone on the same page. In many portfolio companies, misalignment is the biggest silent killer of value.

The board wants aggressive growth while management craves stability. The sponsor pushes for an early exit while the CEO wants to build a legacy. Functional leaders do not understand how their departmental goals connect to the value creation plan. Or they understand and simply do not believe the plan is realistic.

Alignment is not about forcing agreement on every detail. That is neither possible nor desirable. It is about ensuring that everyone understands the destination, the constraints, and their specific role in the journey.

The Coach facilitates alignment conversations. The Coach helps the CEO pre-wire the board 48 hours before major decisions so that surprises are eliminated. The Coach teaches leaders how to disagree in private and commit in public. The Coach ensures that frontline managers understand how their work connects to the investment thesis.

Alignment is particularly critical when plans change. A shift in market conditions may require a strategic pivot. A key assumption may prove wrong. A new opportunity may emerge that was not in the original thesis.

If alignment erodes during these transitions, friction builds and trust degrades. The Coach uses the OS to check alignment repeatedly. When the pulse weakens, the Coach intervenes before misalignment becomes dysfunction.

What the Coach reinforces: The CEO who calls the sponsor before a board meeting to preview a miss. The functional leader who translates their budget request into EBITDA impact. The team that debates vigorously, then aligns publicly.

What the Coach shuts down: Board surprises. Hallway undermining. "That's above my pay grade" when a decision needs an owner.

What the Coach says: "If the board is going to hear about this problem, they need to hear it from you first. Not in the meeting. Before the meeting."

Install Cadence: Meetings Plus Metrics Equals Culture

Cadence is the heartbeat of the organization. It is a predictable rhythm of meetings and metrics that maintains alignment and enforces accountability.

Without cadence, organizations drift. With it, they move with purpose.

The Coach helps the CEO design and enforce this rhythm:

Daily stand-ups catch small issues before they grow. Fifteen minutes, same time each day, same format. What did you accomplish yesterday? What will you accomplish today? What is blocking you?

Weekly huddles review KPIs and unblock projects. Ninety minutes, structured agenda, decisions documented. The CEO runs it. The Coach observes and intervenes only when patterns emerge that the CEO is not seeing.

Monthly operations reviews connect actions to financial outcomes. Half-day session, deep dive into one or two topics, forward-looking rather than backward-explaining.

Quarterly board meetings debate strategy and re-evaluate the thesis. Prepared in advance, pre-wired with the sponsor, focused on decisions rather than presentations.

Annual planning sessions reset priorities and prepare for the year ahead. Off-site when possible, two days minimum, honest assessment of what worked and what did not.

This cadence is not busywork. It is the structure that enables speed without chaos. It creates predictability in an inherently unpredictable environment.

Metrics are the feedback loop within the cadence. The Coach insists on a clear dashboard with five to twelve KPIs that reflect the thesis. Revenue growth rate. Gross margin. Working capital days. Customer churn. Net promoter score. Employee turnover. These metrics must be updated consistently and discussed openly.

The distinction between leading and lagging indicators is crucial. Lagging indicators like revenue and EBITDA tell you what happened. Leading indicators like pipeline velocity, product development throughput, and employee engagement tell you what will happen.

The Coach teaches teams to focus on leading indicators because they can still be influenced. By the time lagging indicators arrive, the story is already written.

What the Coach notices: The meeting that consistently starts late or runs over. The dashboard that shows all green while cash tightens. The weekly huddle that becomes a status report instead of a decision forum.

What the Coach says: "This meeting has become a report. Reports can be emailed. Meetings are for decisions. What decision are we making today?"

Drive Levers: The Fruitful Five

With cadence installed, the Coach turns to driving the levers that create value. We call them the Fruitful Five:

Grow Revenue through pricing, product, channels, and market expansion.

Expand Margins through procurement, operations efficiency, and product mix optimization.

Execute M&A through disciplined acquisition and integration.

Accelerate Debt Paydown through working capital optimization and cash generation.

Expand Exit Multiple through risk reduction, story building, and quality of earnings.

Each lever has sub-levers. Pricing strategy breaks into list price, discount governance, and value-based segmentation. Procurement breaks into direct spend, indirect spend, and supplier consolidation. M&A breaks into target identification, diligence, and integration.

The Coach ensures these levers are not buzzwords on slides but real projects with owners, timelines, resources, and consequences.

For example, growing revenue might involve launching into a new market segment. The Coach helps the team define concrete success metrics: monthly recurring revenue targets by month three, customer acquisition cost below a specific threshold, retention rate above 85% at month six. The Coach ensures the project owner has genuine authority and adequate support. The Coach helps structure 30/60/90 milestones. The Coach anticipates risks before they materialize: channel conflict, competitor response, internal resource competition.

CHAPTER 7

The Coach's Toolkit Map

Tools are not the system. They plug into the system.

13-Week Cash Liquidity visibility and runway tracking	**30/60/90** Credibility-building execution phases	**Meeting Architecture** Cadence system for decisions
Decision Rules Clarity on who owns what	**Value Creation Plan** Hypothesis-driven lever prioritization	**Digital Signals** Leading indicators and dashboards
Exit Readiness Buyer confidence proof points		

Use tools when they solve problems. Retire them when they don't.

The levers become real work, not slogans. That transformation is where value creation actually happens.

What the Coach reinforces: Lever owners who report outcomes, not activities. Teams that quantify their initiatives in EBITDA terms. Leaders who kill projects that are not working instead of defending them.

What the Coach shuts down: "We're making progress" without numbers. Lever ownership that is shared (which means unowned). Initiatives that have been on the plan for three quarters without measurable movement.

Prove with Numbers: Evidence and Confidence

Numbers are the language of private equity. They distinguish genuine progress from wishful thinking. They create confidence with sponsors and future buyers.

The Coach insists on quantifying the impact of every initiative. If you cut procurement costs, what happened to gross margin and cash? If you changed pricing, what happened to volume and churn? If you expanded the sales team, what happened to pipeline and close rates?

The Coach teaches teams to build models and track actuals against projections. Not as an exercise in precision, but as a discipline of accountability. When projections miss, the team learns why. When projections hit, the team knows what drove success.

Numbers serve a deeper purpose than reporting. They are input signals, not just output scorecards.

A 13-week cash forecast is a leading indicator of liquidity risk. If the forecast shows a covenant squeeze in week nine, the team has eight weeks to act. If the team discovers the problem in week eight, they have days.

A drop in net promoter score predicts future churn. A change in working capital days signals operational efficiency shifts or customer payment behavior changes. A decline in employee engagement scores predicts turnover that will show up in six months.

The Coach teaches teams to treat their numbers as a dashboard for navigation, not a scoreboard for judgment. Numbers are tools for learning and adjustment.

What the Coach notices: The initiative that has been "in progress" for two quarters without quantified results. The metric that moved in the wrong direction but nobody mentioned it. The variance explanation that explains without proposing a fix.

What the Coach says: "That's a good explanation of why we missed. Now tell me what we're changing. Specifically. This week."

Re-rate to Exit: Constant Upgrading

The final component is re-rating. This is the deliberate process of making the company more valuable in the eyes of potential buyers.

A premium exit story is built throughout the value creation journey. It is not invented in the final months before a process. It accumulates through consistent performance, risk reduction, and narrative clarity.

Re-rating involves strengthening strategic position. Demonstrating quarter after quarter of reliable performance. Building a deep talent bench that does not depend on any single leader. Proving that systems and processes can scale. Reducing customer concentration (no single customer above 15% of revenue). Diversifying revenue streams. Improving compliance. Creating clean legal and financial structures.

The Coach guides the team to build these attributes proactively. Not as exit preparation, but as ongoing discipline. The Coach reminds leaders that everything they do must make the company more attractive to the next owner.

Re-rating is also about narrative. Buyers pay for confidence. A company that demonstrates consistent performance, clear levers, and a credible story of future growth commands a higher multiple than one that merely delivers good numbers. The numbers must be packaged in a story that buyers can believe and extend.

The Coach ensures the company can articulate its story succinctly and authentically. The Coach prepares management for quality of earnings reviews, management presentations, and due diligence. The Coach helps the CEO tell the truth compellingly.

What the Coach reinforces: Teams that track quality of earnings metrics from year one. CEOs who can articulate the investment thesis in 90 seconds. Organizations where buyers would find no surprises.

What the Coach says: "If a buyer walked in tomorrow, what would they find? What would make them nervous? Fix that before they arrive."

The Flywheel Effect

When the PE Coach OS operates properly, it creates momentum that builds on itself.

Clear diagnosis enables alignment. Alignment enables cadence. Cadence enables disciplined lever execution. Lever execution produces numbers that build evidence and confidence. Evidence and confidence enable re-rating. Re-rating increases motivation and attracts investment in the next phase of growth, which surfaces new issues requiring fresh diagnosis.

The flywheel builds energy rather than consuming it. It transforms a static plan into a dynamic system. It moves the organization from reactive to anticipatory. It reduces dependency on heroic individuals and institutionalizes excellence.

But flywheels do not spin themselves. They need initial force and continuous energy. The Coach provides that. The Coach keeps the OS alive when inertia threatens. The Coach pushes when complacency creeps in. The Coach slows the pace when the team approaches burnout.

The OS is not a template you complete and file. It is a living practice that requires constant attention.

A Case in Action

A consumer services company was acquired by a mid-market fund. The thesis was straightforward: optimize pricing, streamline operations, and expand through acquisitions.

The leadership team was experienced but had never operated under PE ownership with its reporting intensity and accountability expectations.

The Coach began with diagnosis. The truth was uncomfortable. Margins were lower than reported because of unrecognized discounts buried in customer contracts. Cash was tighter than anyone admitted because of mismanaged receivables (DSO had crept from 42 to 58 days without anyone noticing). The culture was paternalistic and resistant to the pace of change PE ownership required.

The Coach moved to alignment. Board and management came together around a new reality: cash came first. Everything else was secondary until liquidity was stabilized. They agreed to implement a weekly 13-week cash forecast and daily pipeline review. These were non-negotiable commitments that would have seemed excessive weeks earlier.

The Coach installed cadence. Monday cash huddles. Wednesday sales huddles. Monthly operations reviews. Quarterly strategic planning sessions. The rhythm became the culture.

The Coach helped drive levers. Renegotiating supplier contracts released 180 basis points of margin. Rationalizing the product portfolio eliminated complexity (cutting 40% of SKUs that contributed only 8% of gross profit). A 30/60/90 customer retention campaign addressed the real reasons customers were leaving.

The Coach insisted on evidence. Tracking gross margin improvement weekly, not monthly. Monitoring working capital days in real time, not at quarter end. Progress became visible. Setbacks became learnable.

The Coach began re-rating early. Building a narrative around superior customer retention (churn dropped from 18% to 11% annually) and operational efficiency that differentiated the company from peers.

When the company went to market three years later, buyers could see the OS in action. The discipline was visible in the numbers, in the management presentations, in the quality of answers during diligence. The company commanded a premium multiple that reflected not just its EBITDA but the confidence buyers had in its systems.

The Integration of Numbers

Throughout this operating system, numbers are not afterthoughts. They are integrated into every component.

The 13-week cash forecast sits at the heart of Diagnosis and Cadence. It forces weekly truth about liquidity.

The 100-day plan anchors Alignment and creates urgency. It ensures that the first phase of ownership is not wasted on drift.

The Rule of 40 influences how the team prioritizes growth versus margin initiatives when driving levers. It provides a framework for tradeoffs.

The 70% decision rule informs how quickly the team moves within Cadence. It prevents waiting for information that will never arrive.

The 30/60/90 integration plan structures new hires and acquisitions. It ensures that additions to the organization are productive fast.

This integration of numbers into behavior is what separates genuine operating discipline from reporting theater. The numbers are not decorations. They are coaching tools that shape decisions and measure progress.

The Backbone of Excellence

An operating system is only as good as the people who use it. The PE Coach OS is not bureaucracy. It is backbone. It supports the body of the business so it can run, pivot, and adapt.

It helps the Coach and CEO manage complexity without paralysis. It ensures the right things happen at the right time. It transforms intentions into outcomes.

The chapters that follow will break down each component further. They will show how to apply the OS in the real scenarios you face every day.

The architecture is here. Now we build.

Coach Cards Referenced

- **13-Week Cash Forecast:** The heartbeat of Diagnosis and Cadence, forcing weekly truth about liquidity.
- **100-Day Plan:** A timebox for early alignment and urgency, preventing drift.
- **Rule of 40:** Shapes how to balance growth and margin initiatives in lever prioritization.
- **70% Decision Rule:** Guides decision velocity within Cadence, preventing analysis paralysis.
- **30/60/90 Plan:** Structures onboarding and integration, creating early momentum.
- **Fruitful Five:** The five primary value creation levers (Revenue, Margins, M&A, Debt Paydown, Multiple Expansion).

Field Drills

- **Map Your Current OS:** Draw out your existing diagnosis, alignment, cadence, levers, numbers, and re-rating activities. Be honest about where the gaps exist.
- **Schedule a Weekly Cash Huddle:** Commit to a specific day and time. Invite finance and operations. Keep it to thirty minutes. Use the 13-week cash forecast as the anchor.
- **Identify Your Fruitful Five Projects:** List one specific initiative for each lever. Assign an owner and a deadline. Review progress weekly.
- **Design Your KPI Dashboard:** Limit yourself to five to twelve metrics. Ensure the mix includes leading indicators. Publish it weekly without fail.
- **Start Your Re-Rating Binder:** Create a folder where you collect proof points. Monthly financials, customer testimonials, process documentation, talent bench charts. You will need them for exit.

Clinic Questions

- How quickly do you surface the truth about your business? What are your genuine early warning indicators?
- Where do misalignments exist between sponsor, board, and management? How are you addressing them?
- Is your meeting cadence predictable? Do meetings start and end on time? Are they driving decisions or just generating reports?
- Which of the Fruitful Five levers are you neglecting? What is the real reason?
- How do you ensure that numbers drive learning rather than just reporting?
- What does your re-rating plan actually look like? Are you building the company you want to sell?
- If a potential buyer visited tomorrow, what would they see? A disciplined system or a team held together by individual heroics?

Chapter 3

How to Use This Book

A Manual for Becoming the Coach Your Company Needs

This book is a blueprint for becoming a more effective PE Coach. Whether you serve as an operating partner, a board chair, a CEO, or an emerging leader in a PE-backed company, these pages are written for you.

The book is intentionally practical and unapologetically opinionated. It marries philosophy with execution. Theory without application is entertainment. Application without understanding is dangerous. This book aims to give you both.

Approach it not as a novel to be consumed but as a manual to be used. Read with a pen in hand. Mark the passages that challenge you. Question the ideas that provoke discomfort. Those are often the ones that matter most.

The Architecture of the Book

The chapters are designed to build upon one another, each layer strengthening the foundation for what follows.

Part I lays the groundwork. It explains why coaching matters in private equity and introduces the operating system that makes coaching actionable and repeatable.

Part II establishes the shapes of value. It addresses the relationships between sponsor, CEO, and Coach. It defines standards and values. It explains how boards create value through questions rather than control.

Part III addresses the coach identity and inner game. It covers coaching under pressure, decision velocity, and the critical first days and weeks of an engagement.

Part IV focuses on cadence and rhythm. Meeting architecture, cash and reality disciplines, translating PE economics for human understanding, and the execution backbone that sustains momentum.

Part V connects coaching directly to value creation. The value creation plan as a hypothesis. Digital, AI, and modern signals. The practical levers that convert strategic intent into EBITDA and cash.

Part VI examines exit-back coaching. Starting with exit readiness on day one. Coaching the narrative that commands premium multiples. Building backward from the outcome you seek.

Part VII delivers the Canon 50 Coach Cards. The numbers, rules, and heuristics that underpin the coaching philosophy.

Part VIII provides clinics for the situations you will inevitably face. Strong CEO with a weak team. Beautiful board pack with ugly reality. Growth that is fine while cash is dying. Plans that have gone stale. Companies that need a re-rate, not just more EBITDA.

Reading in sequence builds the foundation before you tackle specialized scenarios. The progression is deliberate.

Apply Immediately

Do not wait until you finish the book to act.

Each chapter concludes with three sections designed for immediate deployment:

Coach Cards Referenced lists the specific numbers and rules that appeared in the chapter. These are the heuristics that anchor coaching interventions.

Field Drills provides concrete actions you can take within the next seven days. Not abstract suggestions. Specific moves with deadlines.

Clinic Questions offers diagnostic prompts that surface the truth about your situation. Use them in one-on-one conversations, leadership meetings, and personal reflection.

End each chapter by selecting one field drill and executing it within a week. Coaching is a practice, not a theory. Action builds understanding in ways that reading alone cannot.

Use the Coach Cards

Part VII contains the Canon 50, but references to these cards appear throughout the book. These are not trivia. They are coaching instruments.

When you encounter a reference to the 13-week cash forecast, stop and ask: Are we doing this? Who owns it? How frequently do we update it? Is it actually informing decisions, or is it just a reporting exercise that nobody believes?

When you see the Rule of 40, ask: Are we genuinely balancing growth and profitability? What does our Rule of 40 look like this quarter versus last? Should we adjust priorities based on what it reveals?

The cards function as prompts. They interrupt comfortable patterns and force useful thinking.

Print them. Save them in your notes application. Pull them out in meetings when the conversation drifts toward abstraction. Ask which cards are most relevant to the current situation. The answer will change as the business evolves.

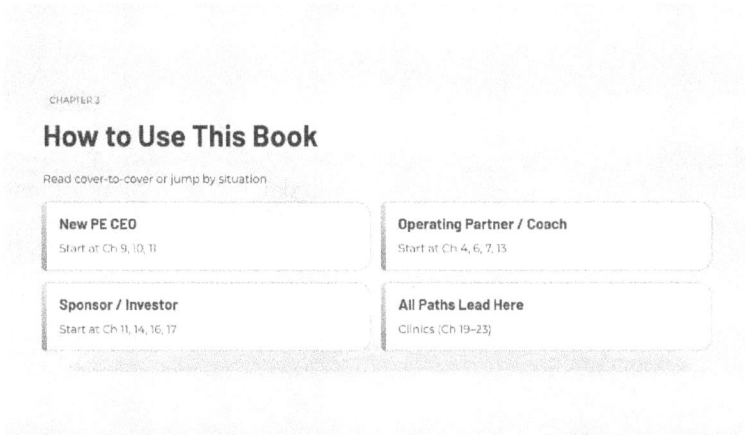

CHAPTER 3

How to Use This Book

Read cover-to-cover or jump by situation

New PE CEO	Operating Partner / Coach
Start at Ch 9, 10, 11	Start at Ch 4, 6, 7, 13

Sponsor / Investor	All Paths Lead Here
Start at Ch 11, 14, 16, 17	Clinics (Ch 19–23)

Execute the Drills

Each chapter provides field drills that range from scheduling a new type of meeting to mapping organizational misalignments to designing a KPI dashboard.

When you execute a drill, you learn how your organization actually responds. You discover who embraces new disciplines and who quietly resists. You expose gaps that spreadsheets hide and strengths that modesty conceals.

Share them with your team. If you are the CEO, delegate ownership of certain drills to your executives. Give them the opportunity to step up and lead. If you are an operating partner, work through these drills alongside your CEOs. The shared experience builds rapport and trust faster than any number of status update meetings.

Drills build muscle that no amount of reading can develop.

Ask the Clinic Questions

The clinic questions are diagnostic instruments designed to be asked and answered with uncomfortable honesty.

Use them in one-on-one coaching conversations, team offsites, and board preparation sessions.

When you ask "What metrics do you review each week?" you may discover that your COO is drowning in data noise without a clear signal.

When you ask "Where are your misalignments?" you may uncover tension between the CRO and VP of Product that everyone senses but no one names.

When you ask "When did your CEO last have a candid conversation about their blind spots?" you may realize that the CEO operates in a bubble of deference that prevents learning.

These questions surface issues quickly. Do not fear uncomfortable answers. Those are the valuable ones. Coaching creates safe space for truth. The sooner you know what is actually happening, the sooner you can act.

Tailor to Your Context

Every PE-backed company is unique. Industry dynamics, company size, market conditions, and leadership personalities create distinct challenges.

The principles in this book are universal. Their application must be tailored.

A SaaS business may rely heavily on Rule of 40, net revenue retention, and customer acquisition cost payback as its primary indicators. A manufacturing company may focus on working capital days, labor productivity, and safety metrics. A healthcare services firm may prioritize regulatory compliance and quality scores.

Adjust the metrics and emphasis to match your business reality. The coaching OS is a framework designed to flex, not a straitjacket that constrains.

Cultural context matters equally. A founder-led business with a strong legacy culture may need intensive coaching on leadership transition and transparent communication. A professionalized team experiencing high turnover may need coaching focused on trust-building and accountability systems.

Use the ethos chapters to assess what kind of culture you need to build and which aspects of existing culture you must protect.

CHAPTER 2

The Learning Flywheel

Turning ideas into behavior

Read
Pick 1 chapter for the month

Drill
Run 1 field drill in a real meeting

Repeat
Re-run with tighter standards

Reflect
Coaching journal: what worked, what didn't

You don't know it until you can do it under pressure

Collaborate with Others

Coaching is not a solo endeavor. Even if you operate as a solo operating partner, you need thought partners and collaborators.

Share this book with your CEOs and leadership teams. Use it to establish common language. When everyone speaks the same vocabulary, alignment becomes dramatically easier. You spend less time explaining concepts and more time applying them.

Invite team members to read a chapter and discuss their reactions. Ask which field drills they are willing to attempt. Use clinic questions as agenda items in your next leadership meeting.

Collective learning accelerates change. Shared vocabulary is an underrated competitive advantage.

Reflect and Iterate

Coaching is an iterative discipline. You will try approaches that work brilliantly and approaches that fail spectacularly. Both outcomes contain information.

Reflect deliberately on your experiments. Did that new meeting cadence improve decision-making or just add noise? Did the 100-day plan create clarity or confusion? Did the clinic question about misalignment reveal something unexpected?

Maintain a journal to capture observations as they occur. Discuss them with peers or mentors. Iterate on your practices.

The operating system is designed as a loop precisely because you will cycle through diagnosis, alignment, cadence, levers, numbers, and re-rating repeatedly. Each pass should be sharper than the last.

Guard Against Overuse

Exercise judgment about when to deploy and when to retire any tool.

A 13-week cash forecast is powerful, but obsessing over cash at the expense of growth investment is its own form of failure. A daily stand-up keeps people aligned, but back-to-back meetings can exhaust a team to the point of diminishing returns. The Rule of 40 is a useful heuristic, but it may not apply cleanly to an early-stage product pivot.

Coaching requires judgment above all else. Use tools when they solve actual problems. Retire them when they no longer serve. Flexibility is as important as discipline.

The mark of a mature coach is knowing which instrument to reach for and which to leave in the case.

The Companion Resources

Several elements accompany this book to support your practice.

The Canon 50 Coach Cards in Part VII serve as a reference you will return to repeatedly. Each card contains a number or rule, its context, when it applies, when it breaks, and the coaching lesson it carries.

The Clinics in Part VIII address specific scenarios you are likely to face. When you find yourself in one of these situations, turn to the relevant clinic for a structured approach.

The Field Drills can be compiled into a personal action plan. Track which drills you have attempted, what you learned, and what you would do differently.

The Clinic Questions can be assembled into a diagnostic protocol for new engagements. When you take on a new portfolio company or a new leadership assignment, work through these questions systematically to surface the truth quickly.

Your Work Begins Now

This book is your companion, but you must do the work.

Read with intention. Reflect with honesty. Apply with courage. Adapt with humility.

The chapters build your foundation. The Coach Cards give you prompts. The Field Drills create momentum. The Clinic Questions reveal truth.

Use them to become the coach your company needs. The one who transforms financial engineering into human engineering. The one who converts strategy into action. The one who creates value sustainably and ethically.

With that, let us turn to the relationships that make or break every PE investment. Beginning with the triangle of trust.

Coach Cards Referenced

- **13-Week Cash Forecast:** A recurring discipline for weekly truth about liquidity.
- **100-Day Plan:** A timebox for creating early momentum and demonstrating execution capability.
- **Rule of 40:** A balanced perspective on the growth-profitability tradeoff.
- **70% Decision Rule:** Encourages decisive action without waiting for impossible certainty.
- **30/60/90 Plan:** Structures new initiatives and integration with clear phase gates.

Field Drills

- **Establish Your Coaching Journal:** Create a dedicated space to record what resonates from each chapter, what you plan to try, and what results you observe. Review it monthly.
- **Share a Chapter with Your Team:** Select the chapter most relevant to your current challenges and facilitate a

discussion. Ask each team member to commit to executing one field drill within the week.

- **Identify Your Top Three Coach Cards:** Determine the three numbers or rules most critical to your business right now. Ensure everyone on the leadership team knows them.
- **Design Your First Clinic:** Choose a scenario from Part VIII that you expect to face soon. Prepare by reviewing the relevant clinic questions and mapping your planned interventions.
- **Schedule a Quarterly Cadence Review:** Block time every quarter to assess how you are using this book. What is working? What needs adjustment?

Clinic Questions

- How do you currently learn best? Through reading, observing, or doing? How will you integrate this book into your learning rhythm?
- Which field drills create the most resistance in you? Why? Is it because they will surface uncomfortable truths?
- Who else in your organization needs to engage with this material? How will you invite them into the process?
- What numbers or rules do you instinctively resist? Why? Do you fully understand their purpose?
- When did you last deliberately reflect on a coaching interaction? What did it teach you?
- How will you measure the impact of coaching on your business? Improved EBITDA, lower turnover, faster product launches, better board relationships?
- Are you ready to release old habits to embrace the operating system?

PART II

THE SHAPES of VALUE

Trust, Values and Value

Chapter 4

The Triangle of Trust

Sponsor, CEO, Coach

The problem usually shows up first in the calendar, not in the numbers.

A board meeting gets pulled forward by a week. A "quick touchpoint" appears between the sponsor partner and the CFO that the CEO did not schedule. The CEO starts asking for your notes in writing, not because they value documentation, but because they want receipts.

Then comes the moment every PE-backed leadership team recognizes.

You are in a pre-board prep with the CEO. The deck is mostly fine. The business is mostly fine. Not perfect, but fine. There is one slide the CEO wants to soften. It is a working capital slide. Inventory is up, receivables are slow, and the cash curve is bending the wrong way.

The CEO says: "We will message this as timing. It is temporary. We are already on it."

Ten minutes later, the sponsor calls you.

"Just level with me. Is this a cash issue or a CEO issue?"

That is the fork in the road.

If you answer in a way that makes you the sponsor's private truth source, you have just weakened the CEO in the eyes of the sponsor. If you answer in a way that protects the CEO at the expense of reality, you have just weakened yourself and made the eventual surprise bigger. If you dodge, you weaken everyone.

The triangle is not about being nice. It is about keeping one shared reality across three parties who are under pressure and who do not have the same incentives.

The sponsor has a fund clock. The CEO has an operating clock. The Coach has a trust clock.

If you let those clocks run in different directions, you will spend the rest of the deal trying to repair alignment instead of creating value.

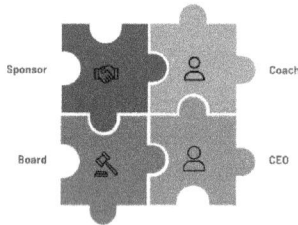

The Triangle of Trust

Why the Triangle Matters More Than the Plan

Most PE deals do not fail because the plan was wrong. They fail because the plan could not travel through the company cleanly.

Plans do not execute themselves. People execute plans. People need clarity, authority, and trust to execute.

The sponsor controls capital and governance. The CEO controls the company. The Coach is supposed to help the CEO and sponsor turn intent into motion without turning the company into a political arena.

When the triangle works, you get speed without chaos. When it breaks, you get activity without progress.

A broken triangle creates predictable operating damage. Decisions slow down because people do not know whose voice matters. Bad news travels late because nobody wants to be the first to say it. Leaders start managing optics instead of managing reality. Talent starts leaving because high performers can smell politics and they hate it. Forecast credibility erodes, which creates more sponsor pressure, which creates more management defensiveness, which creates more politics.

This is the loop that quietly bleeds EBITDA, cash, and multiple.

You will not see "triangle failure" in a KPI dashboard. You will see it in the friction behind the KPIs.

The Central Failure Mode: Two Channels

A strong triangle runs on one channel. A weak triangle runs on two.

Channel one is what gets said in the room. Channel two is what gets said in side calls, text messages, and private recaps.

Two channels are tempting because they feel efficient. Sponsors tell themselves they are just "getting comfortable." CEOs tell themselves they are just "managing stakeholders." Coaches tell themselves they are just "helping."

Two channels always degrade into three things.

Triangulation. The sponsor speaks through the Coach. The CEO speaks through the Coach. The Coach becomes the courier of emotion and subtext that should be spoken directly.

Messaging drift. The board hears one story. The team hears another. The sponsor carries a third version internally. Nobody is lying, but nobody is aligned.

Shadow authority. People start guessing who the real decision maker is. CFOs and functional leaders start routing around the CEO. The CEO starts guarding information. The sponsor starts escalating more often.

Once you have two channels, you are no longer coaching a business. You are managing a system of mistrust.

The fix is not to forbid private conversations. Private conversations happen. The fix is to build rules that keep private conversations from becoming a parallel governance system.

Roles: What Each Corner Owns

You cannot fix the triangle if you are vague about roles. Vague roles produce power games.

The sponsor owns governance and capital outcomes. The sponsor is responsible for stewardship of capital, risk management, and fund outcomes. They have every right to press for performance, insist on truth, and enforce discipline. They also have a responsibility to avoid unintentionally destabilizing management by running around the CEO. A sponsor who bypasses the CEO may feel fast, but it creates slow motion later.

The CEO owns the company. The CEO owns the operating system of the business. The CEO hires, fires, sets priorities, and runs the team. They are the accountable leader. They are not a reporter. They are not a caretaker. They are the builder of the asset.

When the CEO senses that ownership is being diluted, they will either fight or withdraw. Both are expensive.

The Coach owns coherence, cadence, and truth flow. The Coach is not a second CEO. The Coach is not a sponsor proxy. The Coach is a stabilizer of the relationship architecture and an installer of operating discipline.

The Coach notices where reality is being softened, where fear is slowing decisions, where teams are gaming dashboards, where messages are inconsistent, where sponsor pressure is producing defensive behavior. Then the Coach intervenes, not by grabbing authority, but by installing better behavior and tighter rhythm.

The Coach's job is to make the triangle work even when the room is tense.

The Boundary That Protects Everything

There is a version of "helpful" that destroys deals.

It looks like this. The Coach starts giving direct instructions to the CFO, COO, or CRO. The Coach starts being the person the sponsor calls first for the "real story." The Coach starts attending meetings where the CEO is absent and decisions are made. The Coach starts writing the story instead of helping the CEO own the story.

It feels productive. It is not.

It creates dependency. It also creates ambiguity. Ambiguity is one of the fastest paths to execution drag.

A Coach who grabs the wheel becomes a short-term accelerant and a long-term liability. Buyers see it. They price it. Teams feel it. They route around it.

The correct posture is simple. You can be deeply involved without becoming the decision maker. You coach the decision process. You do not become the decision.

What the Coach says: "That is a CEO decision, not a Coach decision. I can help you think through the options, but you own the call."

What Trust Looks Like Inside a Control Environment

Trust in PE is not built by warmth. It is built by reliability.

A sponsor trusts a CEO when reality surfaces early, when decisions are made fast enough, when commitments are honored, when risks are not hidden, when the CEO does not perform for the board.

A CEO trusts a sponsor when the sponsor does not surprise them in public, when the sponsor does not undercut authority through side channels, when the sponsor can be direct without being erratic, when the sponsor's priorities are consistent, when the sponsor respects the line between governance and management.

The Coach builds trust by enforcing behaviors that remove ambiguity. One coherent narrative. Consistent definitions of metrics. Disciplined escalation. Predictable touchpoints. Fast surfacing of issues.

Trust is not a feeling. It is the absence of fear around truth.

One Voice Outward

"One voice outward" is not branding. It is risk management.

The sponsor, CEO, and Coach can disagree privately. They should. That is healthy. But outward, the company needs one coherent set of messages: to the board, to lenders, to the top team, to the broader organization.

If the CEO says one thing to the team and the sponsor signals something else to a functional leader, you create a split brain. The business becomes political. People optimize for protection, not performance.

One voice outward requires a discipline that is small but powerful. Before a board meeting, before a major decision, before a sensitive escalation, the triangle aligns on what is true, what is uncertain, and what the plan is. Not in a two-hour meeting. In a tight touchpoint.

This is where the weekly 15 to 30 minute triangle rhythm becomes the backbone of trust.

The Weekly Triangle Touchpoint

If you do not schedule alignment, you will spend time later repairing misalignment.

A short weekly touchpoint between sponsor, CEO, and Coach has three purposes.

Reality check. What changed this week? What surprised us? What is now a risk?

Decision alignment. What decisions are coming? What are the options? What is the sponsor's threshold? What does the CEO recommend?

Narrative coherence. What are we saying to the team? What are we saying to the board? What is the one sentence message that must be consistent?

This rhythm reduces sponsor anxiety because they are not waiting for board meetings to find out what is happening. It reduces CEO defensiveness because they are not being interrogated at random moments. It reduces Coach risk because it prevents you from being pulled into private side channels.

The weekly touchpoint is a small investment that prevents large political costs.

The 48-Hour Pre-Alignment Rule

Most board friction is not caused by disagreement. It is caused by timing.

A CEO walks into a board meeting thinking one topic is minor. The sponsor walks in thinking it is major. Nobody aligned. The discussion becomes reactive. The CEO feels ambushed. The sponsor feels misled. Trust takes a hit.

The fix is simple. Sensitive topics get aligned 48 hours before they hit the boardroom.

Sensitive topics include: covenant risk and liquidity, a leadership upgrade or termination, a missed quarter, a major customer event, a pricing reset, a strategic pivot, an acquisition pause or acceleration, any item that changes the thesis story.

Pre-alignment is not about controlling debate. It is about ensuring debate happens with shared context, not emotional surprise.

The board meeting is where you decide. Not where you discover.

The 24-Hour Surfacing Norm

A PE-backed company cannot afford slow truth.

When leverage exists, slow truth is expensive. It creates covenant surprises, lender anxiety, rushed fixes, and credibility loss.

A practical rule that works: material issues surface within 24 hours. Not solved. Surfaced.

Material issues include: cash shortfall risk, covenant headroom erosion, a major customer loss or delayed renewal, a serious safety or compliance event, a cyber incident, a leadership failure that will impact results, a supply disruption that will impact delivery and revenue.

Surfacing within 24 hours is not a governance gimmick. It is leadership maturity. It prevents two destructive behaviors. Optimism delay, where the team waits because they hope it will fix itself. Cover delay, where the team waits because they fear consequences.

Both delays create the same outcome: bigger damage, bigger sponsor pressure, more politics.

The Coach enforces this norm by how you react when issues surface. If your reaction punishes truth, you will get slower truth. You can be demanding and still be safe.

What the Coach says: "I do not need you to have it solved in 24 hours. I need to know in 24 hours so we can control it together."

Decision Speed: The 70 Percent Rule Used Properly

The 70 percent decision rule has one job: prevent paralysis on reversible decisions.

In PE-backed companies, leaders often slow down because they want to be defensible in front of the board. They wait for perfect data. They wait for certainty. Meanwhile the business bleeds time.

The Coach's job is to separate decisions into two categories.

Reversible decisions include hiring changes below the top tier, pricing tests, pilot programs, process changes, small capex, go-to-market experiments. On reversible decisions, you do not wait for full information. You decide with what you have, then you correct quickly.

Hard to reverse decisions include acquisitions, divestitures, CEO changes, strategic pivots that change the customer promise, leverage events, long-term commitments that lock cost structure. On hard to reverse decisions, you slow down and do the work properly.

The sponsor and CEO often disagree because they do not agree on whether a decision is reversible. The Coach clarifies the category. That alone speeds execution.

What the Coach notices: The weekly meeting where two decisions have been "pending" for three weeks. The CEO who wants "one more data point" on a hiring decision. The leadership team that debates endlessly instead of testing in market.

What the Coach says: "This is reversible. We are not building a bridge. We are running an experiment. Decide by Friday."

How Triangulation Starts and How to Stop It Early

Triangulation usually starts with one innocent habit: private validation.

The sponsor wants to validate concerns without confronting the CEO directly. The CEO wants to validate fears without confronting the sponsor directly. So they call the Coach.

If you allow yourself to become the emotional outlet for both sides, you will end up carrying subtext that should be spoken directly. That is how silent agenda wars begin.

A Coach stops triangulation with disciplined moves.

Redirect critical messages to the line. When the sponsor says "I am worried about the CFO," you do not say "I agree" or "I will handle it." You say: "Tell me exactly what you are seeing. I will align with the CEO and we will address it in the open." Then you do it quickly. Not next week.

Make escalation explicit. The triangle needs a shared view of what escalates, to whom, and how fast. If escalation is vague, every side conversation becomes an escalation.

Do not carry secrets that create enterprise risk. You can hold confidences. You cannot hold risk. If someone shares information that changes the enterprise risk picture, it must enter the shared reality. The method can be thoughtful. The timing can be calibrated. But it must enter.

Use the weekly touchpoint as the default channel. When people know there is a predictable place to surface concerns, they use side channels less.

The Economics Translation

It is easy to treat triangle work as soft. It is not. It is financial.

Misalignment creates delayed decisions. Delayed decisions create missed pricing windows, slower commercial responses, longer operational cycle times, slower cost actions, slower talent upgrades. Those delays show up as margin leakage and revenue softness. Not because the ideas were wrong, but because the timing was lost. A pricing decision delayed by six weeks can cost 50 to 100 basis points of margin for an entire quarter.

Misalignment creates cash surprises. Cash surprises come from slow truth on working capital, unowned collections discipline, inventory drift without accountability, capex creep, delayed corrective actions. Cash surprises trigger sponsor anxiety and lender concern. That drives reactive governance. Reactive governance drives management defensiveness. Defensiveness slows truth further. Cash gets worse.

Misalignment creates talent flight. High performers hate politics. They will not say it directly. They will leave quietly. When talent leaves, execution weakens. Execution weakness drives sponsor pressure. Pressure increases politics. The business loses both performance and energy. Replacing a VP-level leader costs six to twelve months of productivity.

Misalignment compresses the multiple. Buyers pay for predictability, quality, and control. Misalignment produces inconsistent narratives, surprises in diligence, unclear ownership, dependence on individuals, weak forecasting discipline. That gets priced as risk. Risk is a discount. A half-turn of multiple on a 15 million dollar EBITDA business is 7.5 million dollars of enterprise value.

The triangle is the earliest indicator of control.

Repair: When the Triangle Has Cracked

Even good deals hit moments where trust takes a hit.

A surprise misses the board. A leader hides a problem. A sponsor makes a public comment that undercuts the CEO. A Coach gets pulled into a side channel and does not close the loop fast enough.

Repair requires speed and honesty.

Name the crack. Not emotionally. Factually. "We had two versions of reality last week. That cannot happen."

Reconstruct the shared reality. What did we know, when did we know it, what did we decide, what did we communicate.

Agree on new behavior. What changes next week. A new cadence. A new escalation rule. A new pre-alignment discipline.

Demonstrate quickly. Trust does not rebuild through apology. It rebuilds through consistent behavior.

The Coach's role is to keep repair from turning into blame. Blame creates fear. Fear slows truth. Slow truth kills deals.

CHAPTER 4

Trust Breakdown Diagnostic

A quick heatmap to locate the failure point

Signals	Root Cause	Coach Intervention
Surprise misses	No escalation protocol	Pre-wire discipline
Passive-aggressive meetings	Role ambiguity	Crisp KPIs + role clarity
Decision avoidance	Fear of conflict	Escalation rules
Shadow conversations	Weak governance	Meeting architecture reset

☐ Fix trust before you fix strategy

The Triangle Is a Discipline, Not a Personality

Some leaders believe alignment depends on chemistry. Chemistry helps. Discipline is what carries the deal when chemistry fails.

The triangle becomes reliable when you install: weekly rhythm, 48-hour pre-alignment, 24-hour surfacing, one voice outward, decision classification for speed, explicit escalation.

This is how you create trust inside a control environment. Not by hoping everyone behaves. By designing the system so behavior has fewer places to go wrong.

The Coach's Drill: The "2AM Call" Protocol

The hardest thing about being a PE-backed CEO is the isolation. You cannot tell your employees you are scared. You cannot tell the Board you are unsure.

As a PE Coach, you must be the "Third Place."

The Script: "John, I know the pressure is high. I want you to know: I am your '2AM Call.' If the plant burns down, if you lose your biggest customer, or if you just wake up in a cold sweat about the quarter, call me. I will not judge. I will not panic. We will fix it. But never worry alone."

Why this works: It converts you from an "overseer" (someone who judges) to a "partner" (someone who helps).

Coach Cards Referenced

- **Weekly 15 to 30 minute sponsor, CEO, Coach alignment touchpoint**
- **48-hour pre-alignment before sensitive board topics**
- **24-hour surfacing norm for material risks**
- **One voice outward principle**
- **70% decision rule for reversible calls**

- **Decision classification (reversible versus hard to reverse)**

Field Drills

- **Schedule a recurring weekly 20-minute triangle touchpoint** with a fixed agenda: reality, decisions, narrative.
- **Define what qualifies as a material issue** and adopt a 24-hour surfacing norm. Model the right reaction when issues surface.
- **Create a 48-hour pre-alignment rule** for any sensitive board topic and enforce it for the next board cycle.
- **Audit side channels:** Identify where sponsor or executives are bypassing the CEO and shut it down with a clear redirect.
- **Write a one-page escalation map** that states what escalates, to whom, and within what time window.

Clinic Questions

- Where do we currently run two channels, and what is the cost in speed and trust?
- Do we have one coherent narrative across sponsor, CEO, and management, or are we carrying multiple versions of reality?
- What is our current surfacing speed for bad news, and what behaviors reward or punish truth?
- Which decisions are reversible and should be made faster? Which are hard to reverse and deserve more diligence?
- When the sponsor is anxious, what do they do, and does it strengthen or weaken the CEO's authority?
- When the CEO feels undercut, what do they do, and does it strengthen or weaken transparency?
- What is one behavior we must stop this week to protect the triangle?

Chapter 5

Standards, Values, and the No Surprises Rule

In PE-backed companies, the most expensive sentence is not "we missed the number."

It is "we did not know."

That is the sentence that turns a sponsor from supportive to suspicious, a board from constructive to controlling, and a CEO from confident to defensive. Not because the board enjoys drama. Because leverage punishes uncertainty. Time punishes uncertainty. Buyers punish uncertainty.

The irony is that most surprises are not truly sudden. They are delayed.

They are the outcome of a leadership system that trained people to wait, to soften, to hope, to manage optics, or to avoid discomfort. It is rarely malice. It is usually fear mixed with habit.

The No Surprises Rule is not about perfection. It is about speed of truth.

It is a values statement that shows up as operating behavior.

If you want a clean company, you need clean data. If you want clean data, you need clean reporting. If you want clean reporting, you need clean accountability. If you want clean accountability, you need clean truth flow.

That truth flow does not happen by accident. It happens because leaders build a culture where bad news can travel without becoming a career-ending event.

At the same time, it must not become a culture where bad news becomes entertainment, or where leaders throw raw problems into the room and expect the board to do management's job.

The standard is simple and difficult. Truth moves fast. Ownership moves with truth. Options move with ownership.

That is what "no surprises" means when it is real.

CHAPTER 5

Standards, Values, and the No Surprises Rule

Standards create performance. Values create stability.

Standards	Values	No Surprises Rule
What 'good' looks like · Non-negotiables	How we behave under stress	Bad news early · Facts not spin

☐ Surprises destroy trust faster than misses

What a Surprise Actually Is

Many CEOs misunderstand this at first. They hear "no surprises" and assume it means "no bad news." So they hide bad news.

Then the sponsor finds out anyway. Usually through numbers, through a lender, through an auditor, through a customer, or through a senior leader who is nervous and starts seeking cover.

Then the CEO is shocked at the reaction. "We told you it was fine because we thought we could fix it."

That sentence is how trust dies.

A surprise is not a negative outcome. A surprise is a negative outcome that arrives without context, without warning, without a plan, and without evidence that management saw it early.

The board can tolerate misses. It can tolerate volatility. It can tolerate a tough market.

What it cannot tolerate is a leadership team that looks unaware, unprepared, or optimistic in a way that sounds like denial.

So the No Surprises Rule is a precision tool. It means: if something materially changes the risk picture, the sponsor and board learn about it early enough to help, to adjust, to plan, and to prevent secondary damage.

It also means: when you bring a problem, you bring ownership and options, not just emotion.

This is values in action. This is standards expressed as behavior.

Standards Are Not Soft

There is a confused idea in business that standards are harsh. Real standards are care.

They are the mechanism by which you protect customers, employees, and investors from chaos. They are the mechanism by which you create pride in the work. They are the mechanism by which you build a company that can be sold at a premium because it feels controlled.

In PE-backed leadership, standards are also the mechanism by which you protect the CEO.

If you want CEOs to survive in PE, you do not give them comfort. You give them clarity.

Clarity is a standard.

The Coach must hold this line. The team is not punished for surfacing reality. The team is punished for hiding reality.

That is the trade.

Once that trade is clear, truth speeds up. When truth speeds up, decisions speed up. When decisions speed up, execution becomes possible. And when execution becomes consistent, the company earns trust and value compounds.

The Culture Problem Underneath

The No Surprises Rule fails in three predictable cultures.

Optics culture. This is where leaders believe they are paid to look good. They present green dashboards that everyone knows are yellow. They talk about "headwinds" instead of ownership. They say "timing" when it is not timing. Optics culture is contagious because it feels safe in the moment. It is not safe. It makes the eventual board meeting far worse.

Hero culture. This is where leaders believe they are paid to fix everything alone. They hide problems because they want to solve them first. They treat help as weakness. They treat escalation as failure. Hero culture creates late truth. Late truth creates expensive fixes.

Blame culture. This is where leaders believe bad news is punished. So they hide it. Or they surface it late with excuses. Or they surface it with finger-pointing. Blame culture creates fear. Fear creates silence. Silence creates surprises.

The Coach's job is to break these cultures without turning the company into a therapy session. This is not emotional work. This is operational work.

You create fast truth by installing a system that makes fast truth the rational choice.

The No Surprises Rule as an Operating System

Values only matter if they translate into repeatable behavior.

Here is what "no surprises" looks like as a system.

A weekly cadence where truth is expected. If you do not have a rhythm, you will have surprises. A weekly cadence is not optional in PE-backed businesses. It is the minimum viable operating discipline. The cadence is where leaders learn that issues are surfaced routinely, ownership is assigned routinely, follow-up is tracked routinely. When follow-up is routine, truth becomes safer.

A 24-hour surfacing norm for material issues. This is one of the most practical standards you can install. Material issues surface within 24 hours. Surfacing does not mean solving. It means making the triangle aware so the company does not drift. This single norm prevents the two most common executive failure behaviors: waiting because you hope the issue resolves, and waiting because you fear consequences.

A Coach makes the norm real by how they respond. If your response to bad news is emotional, theatrical, or punitive, you will get slower truth. If your response is calm, direct, and focused on next actions, you will get faster truth.

A 48-hour pre-alignment discipline before sensitive board topics. Most surprises happen in board meetings because the room was not aligned on what mattered. The board meeting should not be where issues are discovered. It should be where issues are decided. So sensitive topics get aligned 48 hours before the board meeting. Not to control debate. To prevent ambush. Ambush creates defensiveness. Defensiveness slows truth. Slow truth creates more surprises.

A 7 to 10 day board pack timing standard. If your board pack arrives late, you are either disorganized or hiding. Neither earns trust. A strong standard: board materials go out 7 to 10 days in advance. That forces a discipline in the organization. Close the numbers. Reconcile key variances. Clarify risks. Align the story. When the board pack goes out on time, the board meeting becomes decision-focused rather than reading-focused.

A cash truth engine anchored by the 13-week discipline. If you want no surprises, you start with cash. In leveraged businesses, cash is the early warning system. Cash is the stress test. Cash is the credibility signal. A rolling 13-week cash forecast is not a finance exercise. It is a leadership standard.

When it is real, it changes behavior. Commercial leaders stop making promises that ignore working capital. Operations leaders stop building inventory without accountability. Finance leaders stop hiding behind accrual. The CEO starts seeing reality before the lender does.

A Coach uses the 13-week cash discipline as a truth audit. If the forecast is wrong repeatedly, it is not a spreadsheet problem. It is an ownership problem.

What the Coach notices: The CFO who updates the forecast but does not discuss variances. The weekly meeting that skips cash because "there is nothing new." The leadership team that talks about revenue without mentioning DSO.

What the Coach says: "Walk me through the cash forecast. Not the summary. The drivers. What changed from last week, and who owns the fix?"

The Coach's Definition of Integrity

Integrity in PE is not about being nice. It is about being consistent with reality.

A Coach looks for one question: do the leaders match their internal story to their external story?

If the internal story is "we are behind on churn fixes" and the external story is "everything is trending positively," that gap will eventually surface.

The market always finds gaps. Lenders find them. Auditors find them. Buyers find them. Employees find them.

The No Surprises Rule is a way of closing the gap before the world forces it.

This is why it is a values chapter, not a process chapter. Process without values becomes gaming. Values without process becomes wishful thinking.

You need both.

How Bad News Should Travel

A PE-backed company needs a clear path for bad news. Not a heroic CEO who magically knows everything. A path.

The path must answer: who needs to know, how fast they need to know, what qualifies as material, what evidence needs to accompany it, what decisions need to be triggered.

A Coach helps the CEO establish a simple protocol.

Define "material" in plain language. Material is anything that changes one of these: cash runway and liquidity risk, covenant headroom, near-term EBITDA trajectory, customer concentration or churn risk, safety, compliance, or cyber exposure, leadership stability in key seats. Material is not "we had a bad sales week."

Material is "we lost a customer that represented 12 percent of revenue" or "we are trending into covenant risk" or "our pipeline conversion collapsed for three weeks."

Surface within 24 hours with a short format. The format matters. The board does not want drama. It wants clarity. A practical format: what happened, why it matters, what we are doing in the next 48 hours, what decisions we may need from the sponsor or board, when the next update will be.

Align the narrative before it becomes public. If the sponsor hears one version and the CEO communicates another to the team, politics begins. So after surfacing, the triangle aligns on the message. One coherent message outward.

Follow up on cadence. Bad news without follow-up becomes noise. Bad news with follow-up becomes credibility. The Coach pushes for one thing: make sure the next update arrives when promised. That is how trust is built, even in tough situations.

What Leaders Say When They Are Hiding

A Coach learns to hear hiding language. Not because leaders are dishonest, but because they are protecting themselves.

The most common hiding phrases include: "It is just timing." "It is mostly under control." "We have a plan, but we are not ready to share it yet." "The number will come back next month." "This is not a big deal."

These phrases may be true sometimes, but in PE they are dangerous because they invite a second question: if it is not a big deal, why are you softening it?

The Coach's job is not to accuse. It is to clarify.

What the Coach says: "What evidence do we have that it is timing? What are the leading indicators that will prove it in two weeks? What is the worst-case scenario and what would trigger escalation? Who owns the fix and what is the first action?"

This shifts the conversation from posture to truth.

Standards as Leadership

Many CEOs dislike "standards" because they associate standards with bureaucracy. That is a mistake.

Standards are the difference between a company that runs on heroics and a company that runs on systems.

Heroics do not sell well. Systems sell well.

A buyer paying a premium multiple is paying for predictability. Predictability comes from standards.

The Coach's job is to help the CEO stop seeing standards as administrative burden and start seeing them as valuation engineering.

Examples of standards that create value: a consistent definition of adjusted EBITDA, monthly close completed within seven business days, working capital metrics reported consistently, one set of KPIs that the entire leadership team uses, board pack delivered on time, issues surfaced within 24 hours, sensitive topics aligned 48 hours before board meetings, owners assigned, actions tracked, follow-up delivered.

These standards do not feel glamorous. They create a company that feels controlled. Control is what the market pays for.

Care With Teeth

If you want to build a performance culture, you must combine two truths.

People need safety to surface reality. People need pressure to perform.

Safety without pressure creates comfort. Pressure without safety creates fear. Both kill performance.

A Coach creates what I call care with teeth.

Care means you listen, you respect context, you avoid humiliation, you help solve.

Teeth means commitments matter, timelines matter, ownership matters, repeated excuses are not accepted.

The CEO must model this. If the CEO is kind but vague, standards collapse. If the CEO is sharp but unsafe, truth slows.

The Coach helps the CEO stay in the narrow lane: direct, fair, consistent.

What the Coach reinforces: The leader who brings a problem with a proposed fix. The CFO who flags a variance before being asked. The team that hits its commitment three weeks in a row.

What the Coach shuts down: "We are still working on it" for the third consecutive week. Explanations that do not include next actions. Updates that sound like press releases instead of operating reviews.

The Economic Cost of Softened Truth

Here is the direct translation.

When truth is softened, decisions are delayed. Delayed decisions mean pricing actions land late, cost actions land late, talent upgrades land late, sales coverage changes land late. Every month of delay is real money. A pricing decision delayed by 60 days costs 50 to 100 basis points of margin for an entire quarter.

When truth is softened, cash gets surprised. Cash surprises trigger lender pressure, sponsor escalation, urgent working capital actions that harm customer service, rushed cuts that damage capability. Cash surprises are not only financial. They are cultural. They train the organization to fear truth.

When truth is softened, credibility gets discounted. Credibility is the invisible currency in PE. When credibility is high, you get flexibility. When credibility is low, you get control. Control slows the company. Slower companies underperform. Underperforming companies sell at discounts.

So softened truth becomes multiple compression.

This is why the No Surprises Rule is a value creation lever.

The Sponsor Side

This is where many sponsors create problems without realizing it.

Sponsors sometimes hold their own concerns privately, discuss internally, then bring them into a board meeting as a surprise to the CEO.

That might feel like governance. It is not. It weakens the CEO and creates defensiveness.

If the sponsor wants a strong CEO, they must treat the CEO with the same discipline they expect from management.

The sponsor should not surprise the CEO in the board meeting with a major shift in confidence, a major shift in direction, or a major concern that could have been raised earlier.

That is how you keep one channel.

The Coach can help by encouraging pre-alignment, by ensuring concerns surface in the weekly rhythm rather than as board theatrics.

This is not about politeness. It is about speed. A defensive CEO is a slower CEO. A slower CEO is an expensive CEO.

CHAPTER 5

The No Surprises Operating Protocol

A simple escalation ladder that prevents panic

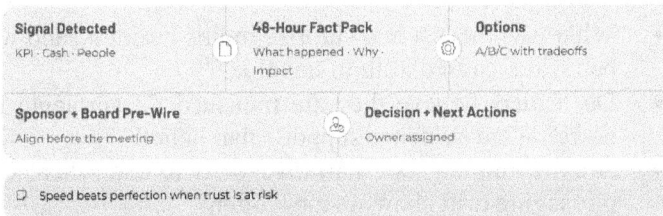

Signal Detected	48-Hour Fact Pack	Options
KPI · Cash · People	What happened · Why · Impact	A/B/C with tradeoffs

Sponsor + Board Pre-Wire	Decision + Next Actions
Align before the meeting	Owner assigned

Speed beats perfection when trust is at risk

Coach Cards Referenced

- **24-hour surfacing norm for material risks**
- **48-hour pre-alignment before sensitive board topics**
- **Weekly sponsor, CEO, Coach cadence to keep one shared reality**
- **Board pack delivered 7 to 10 days in advance**
- **13-week cash forecast as the truth engine**
- **One coherent narrative outward**

Field Drills

- **Define what "material" means for your company** in one page and adopt a 24-hour surfacing norm for those events.
- **Install a weekly 20-minute sponsor, CEO, Coach rhythm** with a fixed agenda: risks, decisions, narrative.
- **Set a board pack timing standard of 7 to 10 days** and enforce it for the next board cycle.
- **Make the 13-week cash forecast a weekly leadership discipline**, not a finance exercise. Require owners for the top cash drivers.
- **For the next sensitive board topic**, run a 48-hour pre-alignment touchpoint and lock one coherent message before the meeting.

Clinic Questions

- What was the last real surprise in this business, and what behaviors caused truth to travel late?
- Do leaders believe they are punished for surfacing bad news? What evidence supports that belief?
- Are we running one narrative or two, and where does messaging drift show up most often?
- Do we have clear thresholds for what escalates within 24 hours, and are those thresholds respected?
- Does our cash discipline reveal reality early, or do we discover cash issues after they become urgent?
- Are board meetings used for decisions or discovery, and what does that say about our operating standards?
- If I asked three executives what our standards are, would I get one answer or three?

Chapter 6

Board Value Is Questions, Not Control

Most board meetings in private equity are not failing because the board is weak. They are failing because the board is noisy.

Noise looks like control. It sounds like involvement. It feels like "we are on top of it."

But noise does not create outcomes. It creates performance theater.

The meeting runs long. The deck is thick. Every function reports. Everyone "updates." The sponsor partner asks ten questions, each one slightly different, because they are trying to find signal inside a story. The CFO answers carefully. The CEO tries to keep the room calm. The operating leaders sit quietly and watch the mood.

Then you leave the room with a vague set of "actions," no real decisions, and a familiar discomfort: we talked a lot, but we did not move much.

That discomfort is the cost of board meetings that confuse control with value.

A board does not create value by acting like management. A board creates value by asking questions that sharpen reality, force clarity, and accelerate good decisions.

The board's product is not advice. It is better thinking under pressure.

And in PE, better thinking shows up as fewer surprises, faster decisions, cleaner accountability, tighter cash discipline, more credible narratives, less politics, higher trust.

All of that translates directly to EBITDA, cash, and multiple.

CHAPTER 6

Board Value Is Questions, Not Control

Boards accelerate value by improving decisions, not running the company

Control Board

- Micromanagement
- Fear driven culture
- Slow execution
- Defensive posture

Question Board

- Clarity on priorities
- Accountability with trust
- Faster decisions
- Lift through inquiry

Coach shapes the questions that matter

The Central Tension

The fastest way to kill candor is to turn the board into a management team.

It usually happens for understandable reasons. The sponsor feels pressure. The numbers are not yet stable. The CEO is new or unproven. The CFO is still building the finance engine. The operating model is not installed. Everyone wants to reduce risk.

So the board starts drifting into management. Board members start prescribing tactics. They start directing functional leaders. They start asking for weekly details in a quarterly forum. They start solving instead of questioning.

The CEO lets it happen because they want support, or because they fear conflict, or because they think "this is what PE is."

Then two things happen.

First, the leadership team stops bringing messy truth. They bring polished updates.

Second, the CEO stops thinking in the room. They start performing.

That is the beginning of board theater.

A board that tries to run the company will get one of two outcomes: a defensive management team that hides risk until it is unavoidable, or a dependent management team that waits for the board to decide everything.

Both outcomes slow execution. Both outcomes create surprises. Both outcomes depress value.

The board is not the engine. The board is the compass.

A compass does not push the car. It makes sure the car goes in the right direction, fast, with fewer crashes.

What the Board Is For

A PE board has three jobs.

Protect the downside. This includes governance, risk, liquidity, covenants, compliance, and leadership stability.

Accelerate value creation. This includes prioritization, decision velocity, capital allocation, and removing obstacles management cannot remove alone.

Engineer an exit-ready story. This includes narrative coherence, proof points, and building buyer confidence long before a banker shows up.

Notice what is not on the list. "Run weekly operations." "Rewrite the org chart in real time." "Debate every tactic." "Catch management on mistakes."

Those behaviors may feel active, but they do not scale. They also do not sell.

Buyers want to see a management team that runs the business with discipline, not a board that substitutes for management.

So the board's value is not control. The board's value is questions that create signal and decisions.

The Difference Between a Bad Question and a Good Question

Bad questions create posture. Good questions create clarity.

A bad question is often a disguised opinion. "Why are you not hiring more salespeople?" "Why are we not cutting costs faster?" "Why are we still missing forecast?" "Why is churn still high?"

These questions often trigger defensiveness because they assume failure without first establishing reality.

A good question is structured to surface truth and choices. "What are the two or three drivers of churn right now, and which one is most economically material?" "What is the constraint in the sales system, and what evidence proves it?" "What decision are we avoiding because we want more certainty, and what is the cost of waiting?" "What would need to be true for this plan to work, and what early signals will tell us if it is failing?"

Good questions do not sound nicer. They sound sharper.

They create a clean path from reality to decision.

This is why the phrase "board value is questions" is not poetic. It is operational. If the board asks better questions, the company runs better.

The Coach's Role

A Coach does not make the board friendly. A Coach makes the board useful.

That starts with a simple shift. Stop treating board meetings as presentations. Treat them as decision workshops.

The workshop mindset changes everything. The deck becomes a tool, not a performance. The board pack becomes a pre-read, not a script. The meeting agenda becomes a set of decisions, not a tour of functions. The CEO becomes a leader in conversation, not a narrator of slides.

The Coach helps the CEO install this shift without triggering sponsor insecurity. Sponsors often equate thick decks with control. You are not trying to remove control. You are trying to convert control into signal.

What the Coach says: "We are going to send the pack earlier, reduce the reading in the room, and spend the meeting on decisions and risks. You will get more signal, not less."

That usually lands if you execute it with discipline.

Board Hygiene

A high-functioning board meeting is mostly won before it happens.

There are three simple disciplines that separate great boardrooms from noisy ones.

The board pack goes out 7 to 10 days before the meeting. If you send the pack late, you force the board to read in the room. Reading in the room produces one thing: shallow questions. Shallow questions produce two things: noise and frustration.

Early pack delivery forces management to close the numbers properly, reconcile variances, align the narrative, clarify risks, prepare options. It makes the meeting about thinking, not catching up.

Sensitive topics get aligned 48 hours in advance. The board meeting is not where you want emotional surprises. The board meeting is where you want a good fight on the right issues, with shared context. Pre-alignment does not reduce debate. It reduces ambush.

The CEO and Coach rehearse questions, not slides. Most CEOs rehearse their narrative. They practice how to "say it." The better move is to rehearse the questions you will get and the decisions you want.

The Coach runs a "question rehearsal" that includes: the three most likely board concerns, the two questions that could trigger sponsor anxiety, the one metric that might be challenged, the one leadership topic that could become political.

You are not rehearsing defensiveness. You are rehearsing clarity.

The Board Agenda That Creates Value

A typical board agenda is built for reporting: finance update, sales update, operations update, people update, "other business."

That is a reporting meeting. Not a board meeting.

A value-creating agenda is built around decisions and risks.

Opening reality check, ten minutes. What changed since last meeting? Where are we ahead, behind, and why? What are the top three risks?

Decision block one, 30 to 45 minutes. One major decision that moves the plan. Presented with options, tradeoffs, and recommendation.

Decision block two, 30 to 45 minutes. Second major decision or deep dive on a constraint.

Risk block, 20 minutes. Covenant and cash risk, customer concentration, cyber, safety, or key talent. Not as fear, as discipline.

Talent block, 20 minutes. Key leadership seats, succession, upgrades, and culture signals. Not as gossip, as asset quality.

Close with commitments, ten minutes. What was decided? Who owns what? When is the next update?

This agenda does one thing very well. It makes the board meeting a mechanism for movement. Movement is value.

The Question Stack

A board does not need endless questions. It needs the right questions.

In PE, most valuable questions fall into three categories.

Truth questions. These establish reality and remove spin. "What do we know for sure?" "What is still uncertain?" "What evidence supports this claim?" "What is the leading indicator that will prove this within 30 days?"

Truth questions prevent optimism, defensiveness, and narrative drift.

Choice questions. These force decisions, not debates. "What are the real options?" "What is the tradeoff?" "What are we choosing not to do?" "What would we do if we had to improve EBITDA by two million within six months?"

Choice questions force prioritization.

Leverage questions. These focus on the few moves that create disproportionate impact. "What is the constraint?" "What is the one lever that changes the next quarter?" "Where is the hidden bottleneck?" "What decision, if made this month, would create a compounding effect over the next year?"

Leverage questions prevent the board from drowning in detail.

A Coach teaches the board and CEO to operate within these question categories. That is how you reduce noise and increase signal.

The 3-Second Dashboard Test

Does your CEO know the score? Prove it.

Open your current monthly board deck. Find the "Key Performance Indicators" slide. Now, apply the 3-Second Rule:

1. **Can you tell if we are winning or losing in 3 seconds?** If you have to read footnotes, you are losing.
2. **Is there a clear "Owner" for every red metric?** If "everyone" owns retention, no one owns retention.

3. **Is this a vanity metric or a value driver?** Tracking "social media likes" is vanity. Tracking "Customer Acquisition Cost" is value.

If your dashboard fails this test, stop reading and fix it. You cannot coach a team that does not know the score.

Function-Specific Questions

A PE board meeting gets much better when questions are prepared, not improvised. Prepared does not mean scripted. It means intentional.

CEO questions target coherence, momentum, and strategic truth.

What are the three most important truths about the business right now? Where are we ahead of plan, behind plan, and why? What is the one thing that changed since last meeting that matters most?

What is the current constraint, and what evidence proves it? What are we saying no to in order to say yes to the priority?

What decision are we delaying because we want more certainty? Which decisions are reversible and can be made faster?

Which leadership seat is strongest, and which is most fragile? What culture behavior is helping us, and what is hurting us?

What would a buyer challenge today?

A CEO who can answer these questions cleanly is usually in control. A CEO who answers vaguely is usually managing optics. Boards can feel the difference.

CFO questions target cash, quality, and credibility.

What does the 13-week cash forecast say, and what are the top three drivers? Where is cash diverging from EBITDA, and why? What is the most likely cash surprise, and what are we doing to prevent it?

What is happening to receivables, payables, and inventory, and which one is driving risk?

What is the bridge from EBITDA to cash, and what is nonrecurring? What adjustments should we stop relying on because a buyer will challenge them?

How accurate has forecast been over the last four quarters, and what are we doing to improve it?

CRO and commercial questions target pipeline reality and growth quality.

What is pipeline coverage, and how has it moved in the last 60 days? What is conversion rate by stage, and where is the bottleneck?

What is customer acquisition cost trending, and is it improving or deteriorating? What is churn by cohort, and what is the one driver that explains most of it?

Where are we winning against competitors, and where are we losing? What pricing power do we have, and how do we know?

COO and operations questions target execution discipline.

What is the capacity constraint, and when will it bind? What is on-time delivery, and what is driving misses?

What is the cost trend in our largest spend categories? What is the one process improvement that would unlock the most margin?

What is employee turnover in key functions, and what does it say about the operating environment?

Making Questions Safe

There is a paradox in board effectiveness. Hard questions produce the best answers, but only if the environment allows them.

If board questions are experienced as attacks, leaders will retreat into polish and performance. If board questions are experienced as genuine inquiry, leaders will open up and the room will learn.

The Coach influences this dynamic by how the CEO is prepared and by how questions are framed.

A question framed as blame sounds like: "Why did we miss again?" A question framed as learning sounds like: "Help me understand the miss. What did we learn?"

The content is the same. The climate is different.

A Coach also monitors the energy in the room. If the sponsor is getting sharp, the Coach may intervene with a clarifying frame: "Let us separate the diagnosis from the fix. First, do we agree on what happened?"

This is not about protecting the CEO from accountability. It is about keeping the meeting useful.

The Economics of Better Board Questions

Better questions translate directly into financial outcomes.

When questions surface truth faster, the company corrects faster. A two-month earlier course correction on pricing is real margin saved. A 30-day earlier identification of a churn driver is real revenue protected.

When questions force choices, resources move to their highest use. A board that asks "What is the one lever?" helps the CEO stop spreading resources thin. Focus creates velocity. Velocity creates returns.

When questions build confidence, the exit story strengthens. Buyers can sense whether a management team has been coached by a thoughtful board or battered by a chaotic one. Confidence shows up in how questions are answered in diligence. That confidence supports the multiple.

So the discipline of asking better questions is not governance hygiene. It is valuation engineering.

The Board That Stays in Its Lane

The best PE boards know what they are for and what they are not for.

They are for asking questions that clarify risk and accelerate decisions. They are not for debating tactics in real time.

They are for ensuring the CEO has the resources and authority to execute. They are not for directing functional leaders around the CEO.

They are for building a credible exit story over time. They are not for last-minute intervention when the story falls apart.

The Coach protects this lane. When a board member starts prescribing too specifically, the Coach may redirect: "That sounds like an execution detail. Can we get to the decision we need and let management work the how?"

When a sponsor is tempted to bypass the CEO for a side conversation with the CFO, the Coach flags it: "That needs to go through the triangle, not around it."

Lane discipline keeps the board useful and keeps the CEO empowered. Both outcomes serve value creation.

CHAPTER 6

The "Better Questions" Board Pack Page

Turn reporting into decision-making

The 3 Decisions Needed This Month	The 5 Signals We Are Watching	Risks + Mitigations with Owners
What requires board input or approval	Cash · Margin · Pipeline · Churn · Talent	What could derail us and who owns the response

☐ If it doesn't drive a decision, it's noise

Coach Cards Referenced

- **Board pack delivered 7 to 10 days in advance**
- **48-hour pre-alignment before sensitive topics**
- **13-week cash forecast as the CFO's credibility anchor**
- **Decision blocks on the board agenda (30 to 45 minutes per major decision)**
- **Question stack: truth, choice, leverage**
- **5 to 12 vital KPIs on the dashboard**

Field Drills

- **Redesign your next board agenda** around two decision blocks instead of functional updates. Measure whether the meeting produces clearer commitments.

- **Run a question rehearsal** with the CEO before the next board meeting. Identify the three hardest questions and prepare clear answers.
- **Set a 7-day board pack deadline** and enforce it. Track whether meeting quality improves.
- **Ask the CEO to identify one topic they are avoiding** raising with the board. Create a path to surface it at the next meeting.
- **After the next board meeting**, debrief with the CEO: what questions created value, what questions created noise?

Clinic Questions

- Are our board meetings producing decisions or just updates? How many real decisions were made in the last meeting?
- How much time do we spend reading in the room versus debating choices?
- What questions does the board ask that create defensiveness? What questions create learning?
- Is the CEO performing for the board or thinking with the board?
- What topic is the CEO avoiding, and what would it take to put it on the agenda?
- Does the board help the CEO prioritize, or does it add to the CEO's list without subtracting?
- If a buyer observed our last board meeting, would they see a disciplined system or a room trying to find control?

PART III

THE INNER GAME

Psychology, Pressure, and the Disciplines of Decision

Chapter 7

Coaching Under Pressure

The CEO's voice on the call was flat. Not angry. Not scared. Flat.

"We just lost the renewal. Fourteen percent of revenue. They told us Friday at five."

It was Sunday night. The board meeting was Thursday. The 13-week cash forecast, which had shown comfortable headroom, was now wrong. The covenant test at quarter end, which had looked routine, was now a question mark. The narrative about customer retention that anchored the value creation story was now a liability.

And the CEO, who had spent two decades building this company before the sponsor arrived, was sitting alone in his home office wondering if his career was about to end.

This is when coaching matters most. Not in the planning sessions. Not in the strategy offsites. In the moments when pressure compresses time, when options narrow, and when leaders feel the weight of consequences they cannot escape.

Pressure reveals what coaching has actually built. If the operating system is installed, the team will move. If it is not, the team will freeze, scatter, or perform.

The Coach's job under pressure is not to take over. It is to help the leader stay in the seat, see clearly, and act decisively. That sounds simple. It is not.

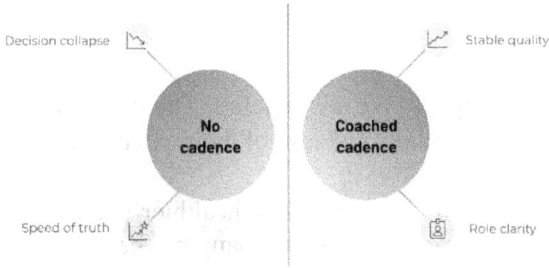

Coaching Under Pressure

Why the Inner Game Is a Performance Issue

This section addresses psychology. But let us be clear about why.

We do not manage the CEO's psychology for their personal well-being. That is a beneficial side effect. We manage psychology because psychological states directly impact execution.

The CEO who is overwhelmed makes worse decisions. The CEO who is isolated misses signals. The CEO who is defensive hides problems. The CEO who is exhausted cannot sustain the pace. The CEO who is afraid makes timid moves when bold moves are required.

Every psychological intervention in this chapter connects to a performance outcome:

Managing isolation enables better information flow and faster reality testing.

Managing ego enables feedback absorption and course correction.

Managing resilience enables sustained performance under extended pressure.

Managing fear enables appropriate risk-taking and decisive action.

We are not therapists. We are coaches. The difference is that we care about internal states because of their external consequences.

A well-coached CEO is not just a healthier person. They are a more effective operator. Their company performs better. Returns are higher. Value is created.

That is why the inner game matters. Not as a soft complement to hard business work, but as an essential component of it.

What Pressure Actually Does

Pressure does predictable things to human cognition. Understanding these patterns is the first step to coaching through them.

Pressure narrows attention. Under stress, leaders focus on the immediate threat and lose peripheral vision. They stop seeing the secondary effects of their decisions. They stop noticing what is happening in other parts of the business. They stop asking what they might be missing.

Pressure accelerates decision-making, often past the point of usefulness. The urge to "do something" becomes overwhelming. Leaders make moves before they understand the situation. They commit resources before they know what resources are needed. They announce decisions before they have thought through implementation.

Pressure triggers defensive behavior. Leaders start protecting themselves, consciously or not. They soften bad news. They shift blame. They distance themselves from problems they own. They stop asking for help because asking feels like weakness.

Pressure erodes trust. When everyone is stressed, small frictions become large conflicts. The CFO's cautious forecast feels like sabotage to the CEO. The sponsor's pointed question feels like an attack. The Coach's push for clarity feels like criticism. Relationships that worked fine in calm conditions start to fray.

Pressure rewards theater. The leader who looks calm and in control gets more rope, even if their plan is weak. The leader who looks rattled gets less support, even if their plan is sound. So leaders learn to perform confidence they do not feel, which disconnects them from the truth they need to face.

A Coach who understands these patterns can interrupt them. Not by lecturing about cognitive bias, but by creating conditions where the leader can think clearly despite the pressure.

The First Move: Slow Down to Speed Up

The most counterintuitive coaching move under pressure is to slow down.

Not to delay action. To create space for clear thinking before action.

When the CEO called about the lost renewal, the instinct was to start problem-solving immediately. What can we cut? Who do we call? How do we message the board?

Instead, the first question was: "Before we do anything, tell me exactly what happened. Not what it means. What happened."

This question does three things.

It interrupts the spiral. The CEO was already five moves ahead, catastrophizing. Coming back to facts creates a foundation.

It surfaces information. The full story often contains details that change the response. In this case, the customer had signaled dissatisfaction three months earlier, but the account team had not escalated. That mattered for understanding root cause.

It calibrates the actual severity. Pressure distorts perception. A 14 percent revenue loss sounds catastrophic. But if the customer was low-margin (they were, at 22 percent gross margin versus company average of 38 percent), if the loss was partially expected, if the contract was already being renegotiated, the situation may be serious but manageable. Or it may be worse than it sounds because the customer was a reference account that anchors three other relationships.

You cannot respond well until you understand well. The Coach's first job is to create the conditions for understanding.

What the Coach says: "Stop. Before we solve anything, tell me exactly what happened. Walk me through the facts."

Separating the Streams

Under pressure, everything feels like one undifferentiated crisis. The Coach helps the leader separate the streams.

There is the operational stream. What must happen in the next 48 hours to stabilize the situation? In the renewal loss case: update the cash forecast, assess covenant impact, brief the CFO, prepare a customer communication if needed.

There is the governance stream. What must the board know, when, and how? This is where the 24-hour surfacing norm applies. The sponsor should not discover this in the Thursday board meeting. They should know by Monday morning, with context and a preliminary response plan.

There is the strategic stream. What does this mean for the thesis? Is this a one-time event or a signal of a deeper problem? This question matters, but it does not need to be answered in the first 24 hours.

There is the personal stream. How is the leader holding up? What support do they need? This is often the stream that gets ignored, but it determines how well the leader handles the other three.

Separating the streams allows the leader to act on each one at the appropriate pace. The operational stream moves fast. The strategic stream moves deliberately. Conflating them creates either rushed strategy or paralyzed operations.

CHAPTER 7

The Coach's 3 Moves in a Crisis Week

Stabilize reality, stabilize people, stabilize decisions

Reality	People	Decisions
Cash/KPI truth · Stop narrative games	Tone · Expectations · Accountability without panic	What must be decided in 7 days · Who owns it

☐ The Coach reduces chaos by narrowing the field

The 48-Hour Focus

When pressure hits, the relevant time horizon shrinks. The Coach helps the leader focus on what must be true in 48 hours.

Not what must be solved. What must be true.

The cash forecast must be updated with the new reality. True or false in 48 hours.

The sponsor must be informed with the facts and a preliminary assessment. True or false in 48 hours.

The leadership team must be aligned on the immediate response. True or false in 48 hours.

The customer communication, if needed, must be drafted and reviewed. True or false in 48 hours.

This framing creates clarity. It converts a sprawling crisis into a short checklist. It gives the leader something to execute against instead of something to dread.

The 48-hour focus also prevents over-commitment. Under pressure, leaders often promise more than they can deliver. "We will have a full recovery plan by Thursday." That is unlikely and sets up a credibility failure. "We will have the facts, the cash impact, and initial options by Thursday." That is achievable and builds trust.

What the Coach says: "Forget Thursday for a moment. What must be true by Tuesday night? Give me four things, maximum."

Protecting Decision Quality

Pressure degrades decision quality. The Coach's job is to protect it.

One technique is the decision audit. Before the leader commits to a major move, the Coach asks: "Walk me through how you got to this decision. What options did you consider? What are you assuming? What could make this wrong?"

This is not second-guessing. It is quality control. Under pressure, leaders skip steps. They anchor on the first option that feels viable. They ignore information that complicates the picture. The decision audit surfaces these gaps before the decision is final.

Another technique is the reversal test. "If you were arguing against this decision, what would you say?" This forces the leader to confront the weaknesses in their own thinking. It often reveals concerns they were suppressing.

A third technique is the commitment check. "On a scale of one to ten, how confident are you in this decision? What would make it a ten?" This calibrates conviction. A leader who says "seven" is signaling that more work is needed. A leader who says "ten" too quickly may be performing confidence they do not feel.

These techniques slow decision-making slightly. That is the point. Under pressure, a small investment in decision quality prevents large costs from decision errors.

Managing the Sponsor Relationship

Pressure often strains the triangle. The Coach must actively manage the sponsor relationship during difficult periods.

Sponsors under pressure exhibit predictable behaviors. They ask more questions. They want more frequent updates. They start talking to people other than the CEO. They second-guess decisions they previously supported. They express frustration in ways that feel personal to management.

These behaviors are understandable. The sponsor has fiduciary duties and personal reputation at stake. But they can be destructive if they undermine the CEO's authority or slow decision-making.

The Coach serves as a buffer and a translator.

As a buffer, the Coach absorbs some of the sponsor's anxiety. A quick call to say "I just spoke with the CEO, here is where we are" can reduce the sponsor's urge to call the CEO directly with pointed questions. This is not about hiding information. It is about managing the flow so the CEO can focus on execution.

As a translator, the Coach helps each side understand the other. The sponsor's frustration often masks fear. The CEO's defensiveness often masks shame. Naming these dynamics, privately and with care, can prevent them from poisoning the relationship.

The weekly triangle touchpoint becomes even more important under pressure. It ensures that the sponsor feels informed, the CEO feels supported, and the narrative stays coherent.

What the Coach notices: The sponsor who starts calling the CFO directly. The CEO who stops returning the sponsor's calls promptly. The side conversation that creates a second channel.

What the Coach says: To the sponsor: "I hear your concern. Let me get you clarity by end of day. But let's keep this in the triangle so the CEO stays empowered." To the CEO: "The sponsor is anxious. That is not personal. Call them before they call you."

The Leader's Internal State

Coaching under pressure requires attention to the leader's internal state. This is not therapy. It is operational necessity.

A leader who is overwhelmed makes poor decisions. A leader who is ashamed hides information. A leader who is angry lashes out at the team. A leader who is exhausted misses signals.

The Coach monitors these states through direct observation and direct questions.

"How are you sleeping?" is not small talk. Sleep deprivation degrades judgment measurably. A CEO running on four hours of sleep for a week is not operating at full capacity, and they may not realize it.

"What is your biggest fear right now?" surfaces the catastrophic thinking that often runs in the background. Once named, catastrophic fears become more manageable. They can be examined for probability and prepared for if they materialize.

"Who is supporting you outside of work?" reminds the leader that they have resources beyond the professional context. A spouse, a friend, a mentor. Leaders under pressure often isolate themselves, which makes the pressure worse.

The Coach does not fix these internal states. The Coach notices them and creates space for the leader to address them. Sometimes that means encouraging the CEO to take an evening off. Sometimes it means connecting them with a professional who can help. Sometimes it means simply listening without judgment.

The Team Under Pressure

Pressure affects the entire leadership team, not just the CEO. The Coach pays attention to team dynamics during difficult periods.

Teams under pressure often fracture along predictable lines. The optimists and the pessimists separate. Those who want to act and those who want to analyze separate. Those who focus on the external problem and those who focus on internal blame separate.

These fractures are natural but destructive. They slow decision-making, create inconsistent messaging, and erode trust.

The Coach helps the CEO hold the team together. This means creating forums where disagreement is productive rather than divisive. It means ensuring that all perspectives are heard before decisions are made. It means shutting down blame dynamics quickly.

One practical technique is the "what we know, what we do not know, what we are doing" framework. In a team meeting, the CEO walks through each category explicitly. This creates shared reality and shared action, which reduces the anxiety that drives fracturing.

Another technique is assigning clear ownership for the response. Under pressure, everyone wants to help, which creates chaos. Designating one owner for each workstream, with explicit authority and clear deliverables, channels energy productively.

What the Coach shuts down: "If sales had escalated this three months ago, we would not be here." That is blame. It does not help. "What changes in our escalation process so this does not happen again?" That is learning. It helps.

When the Leader Is the Problem

Sometimes the pressure reveals that the leader is not capable of handling the situation. This is one of the hardest coaching moments.

The signs are recognizable. The leader keeps making the same errors. The leader cannot hold a coherent plan. The leader's relationship with the team has deteriorated beyond repair. The leader's relationship with the sponsor has lost trust.

In these cases, the Coach faces a choice. Continue coaching a leader who is unlikely to succeed, or surface the reality that a change may be needed.

The Coach's first obligation is to the outcome, not to the leader. If the business is at genuine risk because of leadership limitations, the Coach must say so. Not to the sponsor behind the CEO's back. To the CEO directly, and if necessary, to the triangle together.

This conversation is painful but sometimes essential. "I need to be honest with you. I am concerned that the current approach is not working, and I am not sure more coaching will change that. We need to talk about what options exist."

This is not abandonment. It is honesty. A Coach who protects a failing leader at the expense of the business is not serving anyone well.

The Recovery Phase

Pressure eventually subsides. The immediate crisis passes. The board meeting happens. The covenant test clears. The customer loss is absorbed.

The recovery phase is when the real learning happens. The Coach ensures it is not skipped.

A proper after-action review asks: What happened? Why did it happen? What did we do well? What would we do differently? What systemic changes should we make?

This review should happen within two weeks of the crisis passing, while memory is fresh. It should involve everyone who was part of the response. It should be conducted without blame, focused on learning rather than accountability.

The output should be specific. If the customer loss revealed a gap in account management escalation, what process change addresses that gap? If the cash forecast proved fragile, what additional stress testing gets added? If the team fractured under pressure, what norms need to be established?

Without this review, the organization learns nothing. The same crisis will happen again, and the response will be no better.

Building Pressure Tolerance

The best protection against pressure is preparation. The Coach helps leaders build pressure tolerance before crises arrive.

This starts with the operating system. A team that runs a disciplined 13-week cash forecast every week is not surprised by cash. A team that reviews pipeline coverage weekly is not surprised by revenue. A team that discusses risks openly is not blindsided when risks materialize.

It continues with scenario planning. What happens if we lose our largest customer? What happens if the market turns? What happens if a key leader leaves? These questions are uncomfortable, but asking them in calm conditions prepares the team to answer them under pressure.

It includes stress testing. Run the cash forecast with pessimistic assumptions. Model the covenant test with a 20 percent EBITDA miss. See what breaks. Fix the fragilities before they become crises.

And it requires practice. Some sponsors run "fire drills" with their portfolio companies, simulating a crisis to see how the team responds. This feels artificial, but it builds muscle. The team that has practiced crisis response performs better when a real crisis arrives.

The Coach's Own Pressure

Coaches are not immune to pressure. When the CEO is stressed, when the sponsor is worried, when the business is struggling, the Coach feels it too.

The Coach must manage their own state to be useful to others. This means recognizing when your own anxiety is affecting your judgment. It means having your own sources of support, whether a peer, a mentor, or a professional. It means taking care of your own resilience so you can sustain the work.

A Coach who is overwhelmed cannot help a leader who is overwhelmed. Self-care is not indulgence. It is professional responsibility.

Coach Cards Referenced

- **24-hour surfacing norm for material issues**

- **48-hour focus for immediate crisis response**
- **13-week cash forecast as the early warning system**
- **Weekly triangle touchpoint for sponsor relationship management**
- **70% decision rule to prevent paralysis under pressure**
- **After-action review within two weeks of crisis resolution**

Field Drills

- **Identify the last time you or your CEO faced significant pressure.** What worked in the response? What broke down?
- **Run a tabletop exercise with your leadership team:** Simulate losing your largest customer and walk through the 48-hour response.
- **Review your 13-week cash forecast.** Add a stress scenario with 20 percent lower collections. See what breaks.
- **Schedule a "how are you doing" conversation** with your CEO that is explicitly not about business updates.
- **After the next pressure event**, conduct an after-action review within two weeks. Document the systemic changes that result.

Clinic Questions

- When pressure hits, does our team move toward each other or away from each other?
- How quickly does bad news travel in a crisis? Is it faster or slower than in normal times?
- What is the CEO's typical response to pressure? Does it help or hurt decision quality?
- How does the sponsor behave under pressure, and does that behavior strengthen or weaken the CEO?
- What early warning systems do we have that would give us more lead time before the next crisis?

- When did we last conduct an after-action review, and what changed as a result?
- How resilient is the Coach? What support structures exist when the work becomes heavy?

Chapter 8

Decision Velocity

The CEO had been thinking about the pricing decision for six weeks.

The data was clear. The company was underpriced relative to competitors by 8 to 12 percent. Customers rarely pushed back on price. Win rates were high at 68 percent. Gross margin could expand by three to four points with a modest increase.

And yet, no decision.

Every week, the topic appeared on the leadership meeting agenda. Every week, someone raised a concern. What if customers leave? What if competitors respond? What if the sales team resists? What if we time it wrong?

The concerns were legitimate. They were also a form of avoidance dressed as rigor.

Six weeks of delay on a pricing decision that would add two million dollars to annual EBITDA. Six weeks of cash that did not materialize. Six weeks of signaling to the organization that decisions here are hard to make.

Decision velocity is the speed at which an organization converts information into action. In PE-backed companies, it is one of the most underleveraged sources of value. Faster decisions do not just feel better. They compound into real money.

Decision Velocity System

Speed is not recklessness; it's clarity + rules

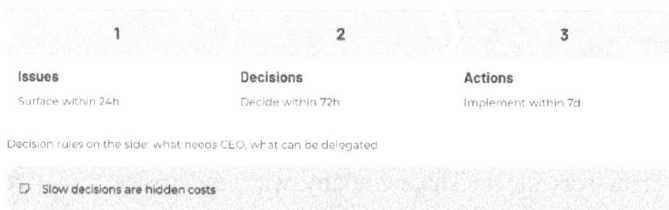

1	2	3
Issues	Decisions	Actions
Surface within 24h	Decide within 72h	Implement within 7d

Decision rules on the side: what needs CEO, what can be delegated

▢ Slow decisions are hidden costs

The Cost of Slow Decisions

Every delayed decision has a cost. Most organizations do not calculate it.

The pricing decision delayed six weeks cost roughly 230,000 dollars in foregone margin, assuming the increase would have been implemented immediately. That is real money that did not flow to EBITDA, did not pay down debt, did not fund the next initiative.

But the direct cost is only part of the story.

Slow decisions consume leadership attention. Every week the pricing topic sat on the agenda, the team spent energy discussing it, analyzing it, worrying about it. That energy could have gone elsewhere.

Slow decisions erode credibility. The organization watches. When leaders cannot decide, people notice. They start to wonder if leadership knows what it is doing. They become more cautious themselves, waiting for direction that does not come.

Slow decisions compound. The pricing decision delayed meant the sales team learned they could resist change. The next decision became harder because precedent had been set. Delay breeds delay.

And slow decisions miss windows. Markets move. Competitors act. Customers develop expectations. The right decision at the wrong time is often worse than a good decision at the right time.

A Coach tracks decision velocity explicitly. How long does it take for a decision to move from identified to made? Where do decisions stall? What patterns explain the stalls?

Why Decisions Stall

Decisions stall for predictable reasons. Understanding the pattern allows intervention.

Fear of being wrong. In PE-backed companies, leaders feel scrutinized. Every decision is a potential exhibit in a future post-mortem. So leaders delay, hoping for more information that will guarantee success. But guarantee never arrives. Perfect information is a myth. The fear of being wrong becomes a tax on the entire organization.

Unclear ownership. When nobody owns the decision, everybody waits. "We should discuss this as a team" sounds collaborative. It often means nobody has the authority or accountability to decide. The decision circles indefinitely, gathering opinions but never landing.

Misaligned incentives. Sometimes the person who should make the decision has reasons to delay. The sales leader delays the pricing decision because higher prices make their job harder. The operations leader delays the vendor change because the current vendor is a known quantity. The incentives favor waiting.

Insufficient forcing function. Decisions without deadlines expand to fill available time. If there is no consequence for delay, delay becomes the default. The topic stays "under discussion" until external pressure forces resolution.

Excessive consensus-seeking. Some cultures believe every decision requires broad agreement. This sounds democratic. It is often paralysis. The leader who waits for everyone to agree will wait forever, because someone will always have an objection.

The Coach diagnoses which pattern is operating and applies the appropriate intervention.

What the Coach notices: The decision that has appeared on three consecutive weekly agendas. The meeting where everyone shares an opinion but no one makes a call. The leader who asks for "one more analysis" on a topic that has already been analyzed twice.

What the Coach says: "This decision has been open for six weeks. What would it take to decide by Friday?"

The 70 Percent Rule

The 70 percent rule states that you should make decisions when you have about 70 percent of the information you wish you had. Waiting for 90 percent is too slow. The cost of delay exceeds the value of the additional information.

This rule is powerful but requires nuance.

It applies to reversible decisions. If you can undo the decision without catastrophic consequences, bias toward action. Try it, learn, adjust.

It does not apply to irreversible decisions. Selling a division, firing the CEO, signing a ten-year lease. These decisions warrant more diligence, because the cost of error is high and correction is difficult.

The key is correctly categorizing the decision. Many leaders treat reversible decisions as irreversible, which creates unnecessary delay. A pricing test in one region is reversible. A product feature can be rolled back. A new hire at the VP level can be exited if it does not work.

The Coach helps leaders see which category their decision falls into. "If this does not work, what happens? Can we reverse it? What would reversal cost?" These questions often reveal that the decision is more reversible than it feels.

For reversible decisions, the bias should be action. Decide, execute, learn, adjust. The 70 percent rule becomes a forcing function that moves the organization faster.

Two-Way Doors and One-Way Doors

A related framework distinguishes between two-way doors and one-way doors.

A two-way door is a decision you can walk back through. You try something. If it does not work, you return to where you started. Most operational decisions are two-way doors. Pricing changes, process adjustments, team reorganizations, pilot programs, vendor switches.

A one-way door is a decision that cannot be undone. Once you walk through, the door closes behind you. Acquisitions, divestitures, major capital commitments, strategic pivots that change the company's identity.

Two-way doors should be made quickly, often by the people closest to the information. Requiring senior approval for every two-way door creates bottlenecks that slow the entire organization.

One-way doors should be made carefully, with appropriate diligence and senior involvement. The cost of delay on a one-way door is often worth paying to ensure the decision is right.

The problem in most organizations is that two-way doors get treated like one-way doors. Every decision escalates. Every choice requires extensive analysis. The organization becomes slower than it needs to be, not because the decisions are hard, but because the decision process is broken.

The Coach helps the CEO install a clear framework. Which decisions are two-way doors that can be delegated? Which are one-way doors that require board involvement? Where is the organization slowing down unnecessarily?

Decision Rights

Velocity requires clarity about who decides what.

A decision rights framework specifies, for each category of decision, who has authority to make the call. It removes ambiguity and prevents the endless escalation that kills speed.

A simple framework has three levels.

Level one decisions are made by functional leaders without escalation. Hiring below director level. Vendor selection below a threshold (say, 50,000 dollars annually). Process changes within a function. Pricing within established guidelines. These decisions happen daily and should not require CEO involvement.

Level two decisions are made by the CEO, sometimes with input from the leadership team. Hiring at director level and above. Vendor commitments above the threshold. Cross-functional process changes. Pricing outside established guidelines. Strategic initiatives within the approved plan.

Level three decisions require board approval. CEO hiring and termination. Capital allocation above a threshold (say, 500,000 dollars). Acquisitions and divestitures. Debt restructuring. Changes to the strategic plan.

Clarity on decision rights eliminates the question "who decides this?" The answer should be known before the decision arises.

The Coach works with the CEO to define and communicate this framework. Then the Coach monitors whether the framework is being followed. If level one decisions keep escalating to the CEO, something is wrong. Either the framework is unclear, or the CEO is not letting go, or the functional leaders lack confidence.

What the Coach notices: The CEO who approves every hire, even entry-level. The leadership team that cannot order lunch without a committee. The functional leader who routes every decision through the CEO "just to be safe."

What the Coach says: "That is a level one decision. You do not need the CEO's approval. Make the call."

The Forcing Function

Decisions need deadlines. Without a forcing function, deliberation expands indefinitely.

The forcing function can be external. A customer deadline. A covenant test. A board meeting. A competitor move. These create urgency that the organization cannot ignore.

Or the forcing function can be internal. A decision deadline imposed by leadership. "We will decide on the pricing increase in our Tuesday meeting. Come with your recommendation."

The Coach helps the CEO install internal forcing functions for decisions that lack external pressure. This means identifying decisions that are stalling and assigning explicit deadlines.

"The pricing decision has been open for six weeks. We will decide by Friday. What information do you need before then?"

This framing does two things. It creates urgency. And it clarifies what additional work, if any, is genuinely necessary before deciding.

Some decisions do need more information. But the default should be a deadline, with delay requiring explicit justification.

CHAPTER 8

Decision Rights Matrix

One page that ends political ambiguity

Decision Type	CEO	CFO	COO	Sponsor	Board
Pricing	Decides	Consults	Informed	Informed	—
Hiring (exec)	Decides	—	—	Consults	Informed
Capex >$X	Recommends	Consults	Consults	Decides	Approves
Product bets	Decides	—	Executes	Informed	—
Acquisitions	Recommends	Consults	—	Decides	Approves

☑ If everyone owns it, nobody owns it

The Pre-Mortem

The pre-mortem is a decision quality tool that can be applied quickly and improves decision velocity.

Before making a significant decision, the leader asks the team: "Imagine it is one year from now and this decision has failed. What went wrong?"

This question surfaces risks that might otherwise go unspoken. It gives permission to express concerns. It often reveals the one or two issues that actually matter, as opposed to the long list of theoretical worries that can paralyze decision-making.

The pre-mortem takes 15 to 20 minutes. It does not slow the decision. It improves it.

Once the risks are surfaced, the leader can ask: "Given these risks, do we still want to proceed? If yes, what can we do to mitigate the most likely failure modes?"

This converts worry into action. The team moves forward with eyes open, rather than either ignoring risks or being paralyzed by them.

The Decision Log

High-performing organizations track their decisions explicitly. A decision log records what was decided, when, by whom, and the rationale.

This log serves multiple purposes.

It creates accountability. When the decision is recorded, the owner is clear. Follow-through can be tracked.

It enables learning. Reviewing decisions after outcomes are known reveals patterns. Which types of decisions are we getting right? Which are we getting wrong? What can we learn?

It reduces re-litigation. Once a decision is recorded, it is harder to pretend it was not made. Teams that lack decision logs often revisit the same topics repeatedly because there is no shared record of resolution.

The log does not need to be elaborate. A simple table: date, decision, owner, rationale, follow-up date. Updated weekly. Reviewed monthly.

The Coach encourages the CEO to implement a decision log and to use it as a management tool. Decisions that are logged get executed. Decisions that are not logged often drift.

The CEO as Decision Accelerator

The CEO sets the tempo for the entire organization. A CEO who decides slowly creates a slow organization. A CEO who decides quickly, with appropriate care, creates a fast organization.

The Coach helps the CEO see themselves as a decision accelerator, not just a decision maker.

This means being available when decisions need to be made. A CEO who is chronically unavailable creates bottlenecks. Important decisions wait in queue while the CEO attends to other things.

It means pushing decisions down whenever possible. The CEO should not be the decider on level one issues. Every decision the CEO makes that could have been made below them is a decision that slowed down unnecessarily.

It means modeling good decision behavior. Making decisions with 70 percent information. Distinguishing two-way doors from one-way doors. Using pre-mortems to surface risks. Committing clearly and following through.

The CEO's decision habits become the organization's decision habits. The Coach shapes those habits.

What the Coach reinforces: The CEO who decides in the meeting instead of "taking it offline." The leader who makes a call and owns the outcome. The team that executes a decision rather than re-debating it the following week.

What the Coach shuts down: "Let me think about it" as a default response. Decisions made in meetings that get revisited in hallways. The CEO who hoards decisions that should be delegated.

When Velocity Is Wrong

There are times when speed is not the right answer.

When the decision is irreversible and the stakes are high, slowing down is appropriate. A bad acquisition destroys value that cannot be recovered. A bad CEO hire sets the company back a year. These decisions warrant the extra time.

When the team is fractured on a fundamental issue, rushing to decision can create worse problems. Sometimes the work is alignment, not decision. Forcing a decision before alignment exists means the losing faction will undermine execution.

When new information is arriving rapidly, waiting may be correct. If a major customer is in flux, if a regulatory decision is pending, if a market is shifting, the right move may be patience.

The Coach helps the CEO distinguish between appropriate deliberation and avoidance. The question is always: "What is the cost of waiting, and what is the benefit?" If the cost exceeds the benefit, decide. If the benefit exceeds the cost, wait, but set a deadline.

Velocity as Culture

Decision velocity is not just a process. It is a culture.

In a high-velocity culture, people expect decisions to be made. They come to meetings with recommendations. They take ownership rather than waiting for direction. They move quickly when the decision is made, rather than re-litigating.

In a low-velocity culture, people expect delay. They bring options without recommendations. They defer to hierarchy rather than taking initiative. They slow-roll implementation, waiting to see if the decision will stick.

The Coach helps the CEO shift the culture toward velocity. This happens through repeated modeling, through celebrating fast decisions that worked, through addressing slow decisions explicitly, and through building systems that make speed the default.

Velocity begets velocity. Once the organization learns that decisions happen here, behavior changes. People prepare differently. They engage differently. They execute differently.

That cultural shift is one of the highest-leverage changes a Coach can enable.

Coach Cards Referenced

- **70% decision rule for reversible decisions**
- **Two-way door versus one-way door classification**
- **Decision rights framework (level one, two, three)**
- **Pre-mortem before significant decisions**
- **Decision log updated weekly**
- **48-hour deadline for decisions under pressure**

Field Drills

- **Identify three decisions currently stalled** in your organization. For each, determine: what is causing the stall, who should own the decision, and what is the deadline?
- **Create a decision rights framework** with your CEO. Define which decisions are level one, two, and three. Communicate it to the leadership team.
- **Implement a decision log.** Start simple: date, decision, owner, rationale. Review it at the end of each month.
- **Run a pre-mortem** on the next significant decision. Ask "what could make this fail in a year?" in a 20-minute session before deciding.

- **Measure your decision velocity:** Pick five recent decisions and calculate how long they took from identification to resolution. Set a target to improve.

Clinic Questions

- What is the average time from decision identified to decision made in our organization?
- Which decisions are we treating as one-way doors that are actually two-way doors?
- Where do decisions stall, and what pattern explains it?
- Does the CEO accelerate decisions or create bottlenecks?
- How clear is our organization on who decides what?
- When did we last revisit a decision that had already been made? What does that say about our decision process?
- If we made decisions 30 percent faster, what would change in our results?

Chapter 9

The First 30/60/90

The CEO started on a Monday. By Wednesday, she had already made three mistakes.

She announced a reorganization of the sales team without understanding the history. She questioned the CFO's forecast in a way that felt like accusation rather than curiosity. She scheduled a strategy offsite for week three, before she knew what questions the strategy should answer.

These were not character flaws. They were the predictable errors of a leader who moved before they understood.

The first 30, 60, and 90 days of any leadership transition are the most leveraged period of a tenure. What happens in these weeks establishes momentum, credibility, and relationships that either compound or constrain everything that follows.

The Coach's role in this period is not to hand the new leader a checklist. It is to help them navigate the tension between urgency and learning, between action and observation, between confidence and humility.

Move too fast, and you break things you do not understand. Move too slow, and the organization concludes you lack the drive to lead. The 30/60/90 framework provides structure for getting this balance right.

The First 30/60/90 Blueprint

Earn trust fast by showing disciplined execution

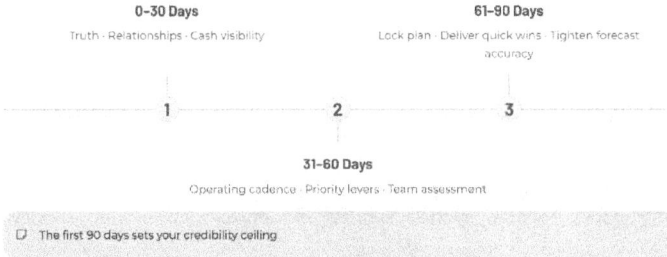

0–30 Days
Truth · Relationships · Cash visibility

61–90 Days
Lock plan · Deliver quick wins · Tighten forecast accuracy

1 —————— 2 —————— 3

31–60 Days
Operating cadence · Priority levers · Team assessment

☐ The first 90 days sets your credibility ceiling

The Stakes

New leadership transitions are high-risk moments for PE-backed companies.

The sponsor has expectations. They backed this leader because they believe this person can deliver the value creation plan. Patience exists, but it is not infinite. The clock started the moment the offer was accepted.

The organization is watching. Employees are uncertain. They want to know: will this leader understand us? Will they respect what we have built? Will they bring chaos or clarity? First impressions are sticky.

The incumbent leaders are evaluating. The CFO, COO, CRO, and other executives are assessing whether they can work with the new CEO, whether their positions are secure, whether this transition represents opportunity or threat.

And the new leader is vulnerable. They do not know what they do not know. They are pattern-matching from their previous experience, but this company is not their previous company. The playbook that worked before may not work here.

Mistakes in the first 90 days are costly because they are hard to reverse. A leader who alienates the CFO in week two has months of repair work ahead. A leader who announces the wrong strategy in week four has to either stick with it or admit error. A leader who fails to build trust with the sponsor early will face skepticism when things get hard.

The 30/60/90 framework is insurance against these mistakes.

The 30/60/90 Structure

The framework divides the first 90 days into three phases with distinct objectives.

Days 1 through 30: Learn and Listen. The primary objective is understanding. Who are the people? What are the real problems? What does the culture value? What has been tried before? Where is the truth that nobody says out loud?

The new leader should resist the urge to change things in this phase. The goal is to earn the right to lead by demonstrating that you understand before you act.

Days 31 through 60: Align and Prioritize. The primary objective is clarity. Based on what you learned, what are the three to five priorities that will drive value? What changes must happen? What must stay the same? What does the leadership team need to believe together?

The new leader begins shaping the agenda but does so collaboratively, testing ideas and building alignment before committing publicly.

Days 61 through 90: Execute and Communicate. The primary objective is momentum. The priorities are set. Now the organization needs to see action. The leader communicates a clear direction, makes visible decisions, and demonstrates that execution is underway.

By day 90, the organization should know where it is going and believe that the new leader can get it there.

Days 1 Through 30: The Listening Tour

The first 30 days should be dominated by listening.

This is harder than it sounds. Most leaders rose to their positions by being action-oriented. They want to solve problems. They see issues and feel compelled to address them. Sitting back and listening feels passive, even weak.

But listening is not passive. It is intelligence gathering. It is relationship building. It is humility made visible.

The listening tour includes multiple constituencies.

The leadership team. One-on-one conversations with each direct report. Not performance reviews. Not interrogations. Genuine curiosity. What do you do? What is working? What is frustrating? What should I know that is not in the board deck? What are you hoping I will do? What are you worried I will do?

The next level down. Conversations with the layer below the leadership team. These conversations often surface truth that executives filter. They also signal that the new leader values input from across the organization.

The frontline. Where possible, time with customers, with salespeople, with operators. The people who touch the work every day often see things that never reach the executive suite.

The sponsor. Understanding expectations. What does success look like? What are the concerns? How does the sponsor want to work together?

The board members. If there are independent directors or other board members, understanding their perspectives and priorities.

External stakeholders. Key customers, key suppliers, key partners. How do they see the company? What do they need?

The listening tour produces several outputs. A map of the organization's real dynamics, as opposed to the org chart dynamics. A sense of the culture and its strengths and weaknesses. Relationships that will be needed when hard decisions arrive. And a list of early hypotheses about what needs to change.

What the Coach says: "In month one, your job is to be curious, not clever. You will have plenty of time to be clever later. Right now, earn the right to lead by understanding first."

Days 31 Through 60: Shaping the Agenda

By day 30, the new leader should have enough input to start forming a point of view. Days 31 through 60 are about converting that input into priorities.

This is where the leader begins to lead, but does so with care.

The technique is hypothesis testing. The leader shares emerging conclusions with the leadership team and invites challenge. "Based on what I have learned, I believe our biggest constraint is X. Do you agree? What am I missing?"

This approach does several things. It demonstrates that the leader has listened and learned. It invites collaboration, which builds buy-in. It surfaces disagreement early, before the leader is publicly committed to a position.

By day 60, the leader should have a short list of priorities. Three to five major initiatives that will define the first year. Not a detailed plan, but a clear direction.

The priorities should pass several tests.

Thesis alignment. Do they connect to the investment thesis? If not, why not?

Leverage. Are these the highest-impact moves? A common mistake is pursuing many small improvements instead of the few big ones that matter.

Feasibility. Can we actually execute these with the team and resources we have?

Sequencing. What must come first? What depends on what?

The Coach helps the new leader pressure-test these priorities. Are you sure about number one? What if you are wrong? What would you have to see to change your mind?

Days 61 Through 90: Visible Action

By day 60, the preparation is complete. Days 61 through 90 are about execution and communication.

The leader communicates the direction clearly. A town hall. A leadership team session. Written communication to the organization. The message should be simple: here is where we are, here is where we are going, here is why, here is how.

Communication is not enough. The organization needs to see action.

Action might mean making a decision that had been deferred for months. Action might mean filling a role that had been vacant.

Action might mean launching an initiative, even if it is a pilot. Action might mean stopping something that was not working.

The visible action signals that things are different now. That decisions happen. That momentum exists.

By day 90, the organization should feel that the transition is complete. The new leader is in charge. The direction is set. Execution is underway. Uncertainty has been replaced by clarity.

This does not mean everything is solved. It means the foundation is laid for the solving that will follow.

CHAPTER 9

90-Day "Credibility Scorecard"

What sponsors actually interpret as competence

Cash Visibility	KPI Discipline
Evidence: 13-week forecast	Evidence: Weekly metrics
Signal: You know the truth	Signal: You manage proactively
Meeting Rhythm	Decision Speed
Evidence: Cadence installed	Evidence: Clear owners
Signal: You create structure	Signal: You execute fast
Talent Actions	Board Alignment
Evidence: Upgrades made	Evidence: Pre-wires work
Signal: You raise standards	Signal: You build trust

☐ Credibility buys time. Time buys transformation.

Common Mistakes

New leaders make predictable mistakes. The Coach watches for them.

Moving too fast. The reorganization announced in week one, before the leader understood why the structure existed. The strategy pivot declared in month one, before the leader understood what had been tried before. Speed feels decisive. It often creates problems that take months to repair.

Moving too slow. The opposite error. The leader who is still "learning" in month four. Who has not made any decisions. Who has not signaled direction. The organization starts to wonder if anyone is driving.

Ignoring the culture. The leader who imports their previous company's playbook without adaptation. Every company is different. What worked at the last place may not work here. Culture is not an obstacle to overcome. It is a reality to work with.

Alienating key people. The leader who threatens before they understand. The CFO who feels dismissed in week two becomes an enemy for the rest of the tenure. The COO who feels ignored becomes a passive resistor. Relationships damaged early are hard to repair.

Over-promising. The leader who tells the sponsor they will fix everything in six months. Who sets expectations that cannot be met. The gap between promise and delivery destroys credibility.

Failing to build a team. The leader who focuses entirely on external priorities and neglects the leadership team. By day 90, the team should be aligned and committed. If they are not, execution will suffer.

The Coach names these risks explicitly and watches for early signs. A course correction in week three is easy. A course correction in month three is hard.

What the Coach notices: The new CEO who has scheduled a strategy offsite for week three. The new leader who is already criticizing the CFO's work. The executive who is making promises to the board without checking feasibility.

What the Coach says: "Slow down. You are moving faster than your understanding. What do you know for certain, and what are you assuming?"

The Coach's Role in the First 90 Days

The Coach serves several functions during a leadership transition.

Sounding board. The new leader needs a safe space to think out loud. To test ideas before sharing them. To express doubts without appearing uncertain. The Coach provides this space.

Reality check. The new leader's perceptions may be skewed. They may be too optimistic about certain people or too pessimistic about others. They may be over-indexing on their previous experience. The Coach offers perspective.

Relationship navigator. The new leader is learning many new relationships simultaneously. The Coach can provide context on the sponsor's preferences, the board's dynamics, the leadership team's history.

Pace regulator. Helping the leader know when to speed up and when to slow down. When to push and when to pause. The right pace is not constant throughout the 90 days.

Accountability partner. Ensuring that the 30/60/90 plan is not just a document but a lived discipline. Checking in on progress. Adjusting as needed.

The Coach does not tell the new leader what to do. The Coach helps the new leader figure out what to do and then supports execution.

The 30/60/90 for Acquisitions

The 30/60/90 framework applies not only to new CEO transitions but also to acquisitions and integrations.

When a bolt-on acquisition closes, the first 90 days determine whether value will be captured or destroyed. The same principles apply.

Days 1 through 30: Learn and Listen. Understand the acquired company. Its people, its processes, its culture, its customers. What makes it valuable? What must be preserved? What can be changed?

Days 31 through 60: Align and Prioritize. Integrate where integration creates value. Preserve where preservation creates value. Identify the synergies that will be captured and the sequencing.

Days 61 through 90: Execute and Communicate. Implement the priority integrations. Communicate clearly to both organizations. Demonstrate momentum.

The failure rate of acquisitions is high. Much of that failure traces to poor first-90-days execution. Rushing integration before understanding. Destroying culture in pursuit of synergy. Failing to communicate. Losing key talent because they felt uncertain about their future.

The 30/60/90 framework, properly applied, reduces these risks.

The New Executive Below CEO

The same framework applies to new executives joining the leadership team.

A new CFO, CRO, COO, or other senior leader has their own first 90 days. They need to learn the company, build relationships, establish credibility, and deliver early value.

The Coach can work with the CEO to ensure that new executives have structured 30/60/90 plans. What should the new CFO learn in month one? What relationships must they build? What early wins should they target?

Structured onboarding for executives reduces time-to-productivity and increases success rates. Many companies leave this to chance. A Coach ensures it is deliberate.

After Day 90

Day 90 is not an endpoint. It is a foundation.

The work of leadership continues. The value creation plan extends for years. The 30/60/90 framework gives the leader the standing and the understanding to execute that plan.

But the habits established in the first 90 days persist. A leader who learned to listen will continue listening. A leader who built strong relationships will maintain them. A leader who demonstrated decisive action will be expected to continue.

The Coach remains engaged after day 90, but the nature of the coaching shifts. From onboarding support to ongoing development. From frequent check-ins to periodic strategic conversations. The intensity decreases as the leader finds their footing.

The best compliment for a 30/60/90 coaching engagement is when the leader says, at day 90: "I feel like I own this now. I know what I need to do."

That ownership is the goal.

The Coach's Scripts for Hard Conversations

Two conversations that often arise in the first 90 days:

The "Ceiling" Conversation (when a founder has been outgrown by the role): "Sarah, the company has grown faster than any of us expected. The skills that got us from zero to ten million are different from the skills we need to get to fifty million. I want to help you transition to a role where you can win, rather than struggling in a role that has outgrown you."

The "Missed Quarter" Conversation (with a defensive CEO): "David, I am not interested in the 'why' right now. I am interested in the 'now what.' Let us stop explaining the weather and start flying the plane. What is the one lever we pull tomorrow to get back on track?"

Coach Cards Referenced

- **30/60/90 plan for structured onboarding**
- **100-day plan for value creation momentum**
- **Weekly sponsor touchpoint during transition**
- **Listening tour in days 1 through 30**
- **5 Whys for understanding root causes during learning phase**
- **Decision rights clarity by day 60**

Field Drills

- **If you have a new leader starting soon**, build a structured 30/60/90 plan with them. Define the listening tour for month one, the priority-setting process for month two, and the visible actions for month three.
- **For an acquisition about to close**, apply the 30/60/90 framework to the integration. Who leads the listening? What priorities must be set by day 60? What visible actions signal momentum?
- **Review your last leadership transition.** Did it follow a structured approach? What would you do differently?

- **Schedule a day-90 review conversation** for any leader currently in their first quarter. Assess progress against the plan.
- **Identify one executive who joined in the past year without structured onboarding.** What did that cost in time-to-productivity?

Clinic Questions

- How structured is our approach to leadership transitions? Do we have a standard 30/60/90 framework, or does each leader figure it out alone?
- When we acquire companies, do we apply the same discipline to the first 90 days of integration?
- What mistakes have new leaders made in their first 90 days here? What patterns do we see?
- How well do we support new executives below the CEO level? Do they get structured onboarding?
- At day 90 of a new leader's tenure, how do we assess whether the transition was successful?
- What would happen if our next CEO started without a Coach supporting their first 90 days?
- How do we balance urgency for results with patience for learning during transitions?

PART IV
CADENCE AND CULTURE

The Rhythms That Sustain Performance

Chapter 10

The Meeting Architecture

The calendar told the whole story.

Monday had seven meetings. Tuesday had six. Wednesday was blocked for "strategic work" but had three meetings anyway. Thursday was the board call. Friday was supposed to be catch-up but filled with one-on-ones that had been rescheduled from earlier in the week.

The CEO was in meetings from 8 AM to 6 PM, most days. And yet, when asked what decisions had been made that week, she struggled to name three.

This is the meeting paradox. Organizations hold more meetings than ever and accomplish less. Calendars are full. Progress is slow. Leaders feel busy but not effective. The tyranny of the meeting has replaced the tyranny of the inbox as the primary productivity killer.

In PE-backed companies, this dysfunction is expensive. Every hour in a meeting that does not produce a decision, an insight, or an alignment is an hour not spent creating value. Multiply that across a leadership team and a year, and you have thousands of hours of potential value creation evaporating into conference room air.

Meeting architecture is the deliberate design of what meetings exist, who attends, what happens in them, and what decisions they produce. It is one of the highest-leverage interventions a Coach can make. Fix the meetings, and you fix a surprising amount of what ails the organization.

The Default Meeting Culture

Most organizations inherit their meeting culture. It accumulates over time, shaped by precedent, politics, and path dependency.

Someone started a weekly status meeting three years ago. It is still happening, even though half the attendees do not need to be there and the original purpose has been forgotten.

The leadership team meets every Monday for two hours. The agenda is a rotating tour of functional updates. Everyone presents. No one decides. The meeting ends with vague action items that may or may not be followed up.

One-on-ones happen sporadically, rescheduled when something "more urgent" arises. The CEO has not had a real conversation with the COO in three weeks.

The board meeting is a presentation marathon. Forty slides. Limited discussion. Decisions deferred to follow-up calls.

This default culture is not designed. It emerged. And because it emerged rather than being designed, it serves no one well.

The Coach helps the CEO see the meeting culture clearly and then redesign it with intention.

CHAPTER 10

The Meeting Architecture

Meetings are the operating system interface

Weekly
Exec KPI review · Cash status

Monthly
Operating review · Resourcing decisions

Quarterly
Strategy · Value creation lever review · Exit readiness

The wrong meeting system creates false confidence

The Principles of Meeting Architecture

Good meeting architecture follows several principles.

Every meeting must have a purpose. Not a topic. A purpose. "Discuss marketing" is a topic. "Decide on the Q3 campaign budget" is a purpose. "Review sales pipeline" is a topic. "Identify the three deals most at risk and assign owners for recovery" is a purpose.

Meetings without purposes become rituals. People attend because they always have. Nothing happens because nothing was supposed to happen. The calendar fills with motion that produces no movement.

Every meeting must have an owner. Someone who is accountable for the meeting achieving its purpose. Who sets the agenda. Who facilitates the discussion. Who ensures decisions are documented. Who follows up on commitments.

Meetings without owners drift. They start late. They wander. They end without clarity. Ownership creates discipline.

Every meeting must have the right people and only the right people. The decision makers. The people with essential information. Not the people who want to be included for political reasons. Not the people who attend out of habit.

Large meetings diffuse responsibility. Small meetings focus it. The bias should be toward fewer attendees, with information shared to others afterward.

Every meeting must produce an output. A decision. An alignment. An insight. A commitment. Something must be different after the meeting than before.

If you cannot articulate the output, the meeting should not happen. A status update can be an email. A document can be read asynchronously. Reserve meetings for the work that requires real-time human interaction.

The Meeting Hierarchy

An effective organization has a hierarchy of meetings that serve different purposes at different cadences.

Daily stand-ups serve operational coordination. Fifteen minutes. Same time each day. Same format. What did you accomplish yesterday? What will you accomplish today? What is blocking you?

The stand-up is not for problem-solving. It is for surfacing. If a blocker is identified, a separate conversation is scheduled. The stand-up keeps the team synchronized and makes problems visible before they grow.

Not every organization needs daily stand-ups. But organizations with significant operational interdependency benefit from them. The discipline of daily visibility compounds.

Weekly leadership meetings serve decision-making and alignment. Ninety minutes to two hours. Fixed agenda structure. The leadership team addresses the issues that require cross-functional coordination.

The weekly is the heartbeat of the operating cadence. If it is well-run, the organization moves. If it is poorly run, everything slows.

Monthly operations reviews serve performance assessment. Half-day sessions. Deep dives into one or two areas. Connecting actions to outcomes. Understanding what is working and what is not.

The monthly is where learning happens. Not blame. Learning. What did the numbers tell us? What did we try? What resulted? What will we do differently?

Quarterly strategic reviews serve thesis testing. Full-day or multi-day sessions. Stepping back from operations to assess strategy. Is the value creation plan on track? What assumptions have been validated or invalidated? What needs to change?

The quarterly is where the plan evolves. The organization should emerge with adjusted priorities, reallocated resources, and renewed alignment.

Annual planning serves priority setting for the year ahead. Multi-day session, often off-site. Reviewing the year behind. Setting targets for the year ahead. Aligning on the three to five priorities that will define the next twelve months.

Board meetings serve governance and major decisions. Typically quarterly. Focused on the topics that require board-level attention: strategy, risk, capital allocation, leadership, exit readiness.

The board meeting is not a reporting session. It is a decision forum. The architecture of the board meeting determines whether the board creates value or noise.

The Weekly Leadership Meeting

The weekly leadership meeting deserves special attention because it is the most frequent gathering of the senior team and therefore the most influential.

A poorly designed weekly creates cascading dysfunction. Leaders leave unclear about priorities. They make conflicting decisions. They schedule follow-up meetings to resolve what should have been resolved in the room. The organization receives mixed signals.

A well-designed weekly creates cascading clarity. Leaders leave aligned. They make consistent decisions. They communicate a coherent message to their teams. The organization moves as one.

The weekly should have a fixed structure that everyone knows.

Opening pulse check, ten minutes. What are the top three things that happened since last week that we all need to know? This is not a comprehensive update. It is signal detection. What changed? What surprised us? What risks emerged?

Metrics review, fifteen minutes. A glance at the dashboard. Not a deep dive on every number. A quick scan to identify what is on track, what is off track, and what needs attention. The numbers that warrant discussion go on the decision queue.

Decision queue, sixty to ninety minutes. The heart of the meeting. The topics that require leadership team discussion and resolution. Each topic has an owner who presents the issue, the options, and a recommendation. Discussion follows. A decision is made. The decision is documented.

The decision queue should be limited. Three to five topics maximum. If there are more topics than time allows, they are prioritized or deferred. The discipline of prioritization is itself valuable.

Commitments and communication, ten minutes. What did we decide? Who owns what? What are we communicating to the organization? This closing ensures that the meeting produces outputs that survive the meeting.

The CEO runs the weekly. The Coach may observe and provide feedback, especially in the early stages of establishing the rhythm. Over time, the weekly becomes self-sustaining.

What the Coach notices: The weekly meeting that runs over time every week. The leadership team that debates without deciding. The meeting where the same topic appears three weeks in a row.

What the Coach says: "This meeting has become a discussion forum, not a decision forum. Let us redesign the agenda around decisions."

Decision Hygiene in Meetings

Many meetings fail at the decision point. Discussion happens. Views are shared. But the decision does not land.

Decision hygiene requires explicit practices.

Name the decision before discussion begins. "The decision we are making today is whether to proceed with the pricing increase, and if so, what percentage and what timing."

Clarify who decides. In most cases, the CEO decides. But sometimes the decision belongs to a functional leader with the CEO's endorsement. Make it explicit.

Time-box the discussion. "We have thirty minutes on this topic." Without a time constraint, discussion expands to fill available time.

Call the question. When discussion has surfaced the key considerations, the decider calls the question. "I have heard the perspectives. Here is what I am deciding and why."

Document immediately. Before moving to the next topic, the decision is documented. What was decided. Who owns implementation. What is the timeline. This documentation becomes the record.

Follow up in the next meeting. The opening of the next weekly includes a review of commitments from the prior week. What was due? What was delivered? What slipped? This follow-up creates accountability.

Without decision hygiene, meetings feel productive but produce nothing. The same topics recur week after week. Leaders feel frustrated. The organization stalls.

The One-on-One

The one-on-one between a manager and direct report is the fundamental unit of management. It is also one of the most neglected meetings in most organizations.

One-on-ones should happen weekly. Thirty to sixty minutes. Fixed time. Not rescheduled unless absolutely necessary.

The purpose of the one-on-one is not status reporting. Status can be conveyed asynchronously. The purpose is development, problem-solving, and relationship maintenance.

The direct report owns the agenda. They come with the topics they need to discuss. What are they working on? Where are they stuck? What decisions do they need input on? What feedback do they need?

The manager's job is to listen, coach, unblock, and provide perspective. To ask good questions. To offer guidance without micromanaging. To ensure the direct report has what they need to succeed.

One-on-ones are also where issues surface early. A good one-on-one uncovers the concern that the direct report would not raise in a group setting. The frustration with a peer. The worry about a project. The personal issue affecting performance.

When one-on-ones are strong, everything else gets easier. Trust builds. Communication flows. Problems are caught early. Development happens continuously.

When one-on-ones are neglected, problems compound. The manager is surprised by issues that should have been visible. The direct report feels unsupported. Trust erodes.

The Coach encourages the CEO to model strong one-on-one practice and to expect the same from the leadership team. A quick audit: is everyone on the leadership team holding weekly one-on-ones with their direct reports? The answer is often revealing.

The Meeting Audit

Before redesigning the meeting architecture, the Coach helps the CEO understand the current state.

The meeting audit is a simple exercise. Take the CEO's calendar from the past month. Categorize every meeting by type and purpose. Estimate how much time was spent in each category. Assess how many meetings produced clear outputs.

The results are usually sobering.

Significant time in meetings that could have been emails. Status updates. Information sharing. Topics that did not require real-time discussion.

Multiple meetings on the same topic. The initial meeting did not produce a decision, so follow-up meetings were scheduled.

Key meetings being rescheduled or cancelled. The one-on-ones that keep getting bumped. The strategic thinking time that gets invaded.

Attendee bloat. Meetings with twelve people where four would suffice.

Missing meetings. No regular cadence for important topics. Ad hoc scheduling that creates unpredictability.

The audit makes the invisible visible. The CEO can see where time is going and make informed decisions about redesign.

The Redesign Process

Armed with the audit, the Coach guides the CEO through meeting redesign.

First, eliminate meetings that should not exist. The standing meeting that has lost its purpose. The recurring check-in that has become performative. The large gathering that produces nothing. Canceling unnecessary meetings is one of the fastest ways to reclaim leadership time.

Second, consolidate meetings that overlap. If three separate meetings address related topics, perhaps one meeting with a broader agenda would be more efficient.

Third, fix the meetings that remain. Clarify purpose. Assign ownership. Set agendas. Establish decision hygiene. Reduce attendee lists. Time-box discussions.

Fourth, add meetings that are missing. If the leadership team is not meeting weekly, establish that cadence. If one-on-ones have lapsed, restore them. If quarterly strategic reviews are not happening, schedule them.

Fifth, communicate the new architecture. The leadership team needs to understand what meetings exist, why they exist, and what is expected of participants. Clarity enables compliance.

The redesign is not a one-time event. Meeting architecture requires ongoing maintenance. Meetings drift back toward dysfunction unless leaders actively maintain the discipline.

CHAPTER 10

Pre-Wire Flow

How to prevent ambushes and wasted board time

01	02	03
Draft Board Memo	**CEO–CFO Alignment**	**Sponsor Pre-Wire**
Decisions + data + options	Numbers + narrative sync	Surface concerns early

04	05	
Board Member 1:1s	**Board Meeting**	
Only on decisions	Decisions + commitments	

> Board meetings are for decisions, not discovery

Selecting KPIs with Exit in Mind

When defining the 5 to 12 vital KPIs for your operating dashboard, apply the exit-back test:

Will buyers care about this metric? If not, why is it vital for operations?

Can we show a multi-year trend? Metrics without history have no story.

Does this connect to a multiple driver? Growth, predictability, quality, retention, efficiency. The metrics should link to what buyers pay for.

Can we explain variances? A metric you track but cannot explain is a liability in diligence.

The KPIs you select today are the proof points you present tomorrow. Choose accordingly.

The Board Meeting Architecture

The board meeting is a special case that warrants its own design attention.

Most board meetings are poorly designed. They are presentation heavy. They are discussion light. They produce few decisions. They leave both management and board members feeling that time was not well spent.

A well-designed board meeting has several characteristics.

The board pack goes out 7 to 10 days in advance and is genuinely read. This requires that the pack be readable. Concise. Clear. Not a data dump. A narrative with supporting evidence.

The meeting does not repeat the pack. If board members have read the materials, the meeting should build on that reading, not recapitulate it. The CEO can assume baseline knowledge and focus on what matters: discussion, decisions, and debate.

The agenda is structured around decisions. Not functional updates. Decisions. What does the board need to decide or advise on today? That should drive the time allocation.

Discussion time is protected. At least half of the board meeting should be discussion, not presentation. If the CEO is talking 80 percent of the time, the meeting is not leveraging the board.

Executive sessions happen. Time for the board to meet without management. Time for management to meet without the board. These sessions allow candid conversation that might not happen in the full room.

The meeting ends with clear commitments. What was decided? What follow-up is needed? When will it happen?

The Coach works with the CEO to design the board meeting architecture and to prepare the CEO to run it effectively.

Meetings as Culture

Meetings are not just operational tools. They are cultural artifacts.

The way meetings are run signals what the organization values. If meetings start on time, punctuality is valued. If meetings start late, punctuality is optional. If meetings produce decisions, decisiveness is valued. If meetings avoid hard topics, conflict avoidance is the norm.

The CEO's behavior in meetings is closely watched. If the CEO dominates discussion, others learn to defer. If the CEO invites dissent, others learn to speak up. If the CEO follows up on commitments, others learn that commitments matter.

Meeting culture cascades through the organization. The leadership team models what they experience with the CEO. Their teams model what they experience with leaders. The pattern replicates.

This makes meeting architecture a cultural lever. Change the meetings, and you change the culture. Not by declaring new values, but by embedding them in the daily practice of how people convene.

The Coach helps the CEO see meetings as a cultural tool and use them accordingly.

Coach Cards Referenced

- **Weekly leadership meeting (90 minutes, fixed structure, decision-focused)**
- **Weekly one-on-ones (30 to 60 minutes, direct report owns agenda)**
- **Monthly operations review (half-day, deep dive, learning orientation)**
- **Quarterly strategic review (full-day, thesis testing)**
- **Board pack 7 to 10 days in advance**
- **5 to 12 metrics on the dashboard for weekly review**

Field Drills

- **Conduct a meeting audit.** Review your calendar from the past month. Categorize meetings. Assess outputs. Identify what to eliminate, consolidate, or fix.
- **Redesign your weekly leadership meeting.** Write out the fixed structure. Define the decision queue process. Implement for four weeks and assess.
- **Audit one-on-one practice across the leadership team.** Is everyone holding weekly one-on-ones? What is the quality?
- **Redesign your next board meeting agenda** around decisions rather than updates. Measure whether discussion time increases.
- **Identify the three meetings that waste the most time** and eliminate or redesign them.

Clinic Questions

- How much of our leadership time is spent in meetings? What percentage of that time produces clear outputs?
- What meetings exist purely out of habit? When did we last assess whether they still serve a purpose?

- How strong is decision hygiene in our meetings? Are decisions documented and followed up?
- Are one-on-ones happening consistently at every level of leadership? What happens when they lapse?
- How do our meetings signal our culture? What values do they reinforce?
- If a new employee observed our meetings, what would they conclude about how we operate?
- What meeting practice, if changed, would have the biggest impact on our velocity?

Chapter 11

The Cash and Reality Engine

The CFO was proud of his reporting. Clean financial statements. Detailed variance analysis. Beautiful charts showing revenue, EBITDA, and gross margin trends. The board received a comprehensive package every month.

And yet, when the sponsor asked a simple question, the room went quiet.

"What does cash look like for the next 13 weeks?"

The CFO paused. "We forecast quarterly. I can give you the quarter-end projection."

"I do not want quarter-end. I want week by week. When does cash hit the floor? When do we need to draw on the revolver? What happens if the big customer payment is late?"

Another pause. "I would need to build that."

This is the gap between financial reporting and cash reality. Financial statements tell you where you have been. Cash forecasting tells you where you are going. In a PE-backed company with leverage, the second is more important than the first.

Cash is the ultimate reality check. Profit is an accounting opinion. Cash is a fact. You can argue about EBITDA adjustments, about revenue recognition, about accruals and deferrals. You cannot argue about whether the money is in the bank.

The 13-week cash forecast is the most important tool in the PE Coach's arsenal. It is not a finance exercise. It is a leadership discipline that forces truth, creates accountability, and enables proactive management of the most unforgiving resource in a leveraged business.

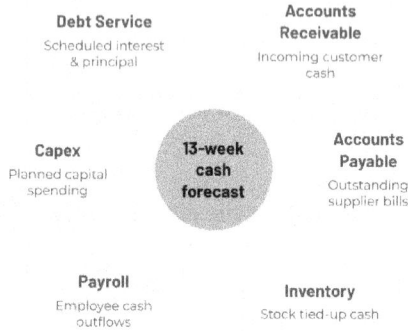

The Cash and Reality Engine

Debt Service
Scheduled interest & principal

Accounts Receivable
Incoming customer cash

Capex
Planned capital spending

13-week cash forecast

Accounts Payable
Outstanding supplier bills

Payroll
Employee cash outflows

Inventory
Stock tied-up cash

Why Cash Is Different

In PE-backed companies, cash operates under constraints that make it fundamentally different from other metrics.

Debt service is not negotiable. Principal and interest payments arrive on schedule. Miss them, and the consequences are severe. This is not like missing a revenue target, where you can explain the variance and promise to do better next quarter.

Covenants create trip wires. Leverage covenants, coverage covenants, liquidity covenants. Breach them, and the lender's disposition changes. Pricing may increase. Restrictions may tighten. In severe cases, control may shift.

Cash cannot be manufactured. You can accelerate revenue recognition through aggressive accounting. You can defer expenses to improve a quarter. But cash is cash. The bank balance does not lie.

Time compresses when cash is short. If you discover a cash problem in week one, you have options. If you discover it in week twelve, you have desperation. The earlier you see cash reality, the more degrees of freedom you have.

This is why the 13-week cash forecast matters. It provides early warning. It forces weekly discipline. It connects operating decisions to their cash consequences.

The Anatomy of the 13-Week Forecast

A 13-week cash forecast is a week-by-week projection of cash receipts and cash disbursements, rolling forward continuously.

The structure is straightforward.

Beginning cash balance. What is in the bank at the start of the week?

Plus: Cash receipts. Collections from customers. Other income. The money coming in.

Minus: Cash disbursements. Payroll. Vendor payments. Rent. Utilities. Interest. Principal. Taxes. Capital expenditures. The money going out.

Equals: Ending cash balance. What is in the bank at the end of the week?

The forecast extends 13 weeks, which is roughly one quarter. The near weeks are detailed and reliable. The outer weeks are more estimated but still useful for seeing trends and potential stress points.

The forecast rolls forward each week. Week one becomes actual. A new week 13 is added. The forecast is continuously updated based on what actually happened and what is newly known.

This rolling discipline is essential. A static forecast decays in accuracy immediately. A rolling forecast stays current.

Building the Forecast

Building a credible 13-week cash forecast requires inputs from across the organization.

Collections depend on sales. When did customers order? When were they invoiced? What are the payment terms? What is the historical payment pattern? Are any customers slow-paying or at risk of non-payment?

The sales and finance teams must collaborate on collections forecasting. Sales knows which customers are solid and which are shaky. Finance knows the invoicing and payment patterns.

Disbursements depend on operations. What is the payroll schedule? When are vendor payments due? What capital expenditures are planned? Are there any unusual or non-recurring payments coming?

Each function must contribute their disbursement schedule. Procurement knows vendor payment timing. HR knows payroll. Facilities knows rent and utilities. Treasury knows debt service.

The forecast is assembled centrally by finance but built collaboratively with the business. This collaboration is as important as the arithmetic. It forces cross-functional visibility into cash and creates shared ownership.

The Weekly Discipline

The 13-week cash forecast is not a document. It is a discipline.

Every week, the forecast is updated. Every week, actuals are compared to projections. Every week, variances are explained.

The weekly rhythm creates several benefits.

Accuracy improves. When you forecast weekly and compare to actuals weekly, you learn where your assumptions are wrong. The collections forecast that consistently underestimates actual collections gets recalibrated. The payroll forecast that misses bonus cycles gets corrected. Over time, the forecast becomes more reliable.

Accountability increases. When the sales leader knows that their collections forecast will be compared to reality every Friday, they pay more attention to it. When the procurement leader knows that their vendor payment schedule is visible to leadership, they manage it more carefully.

Early warning emerges. The forecast shows where stress is coming. If week eight shows cash dropping below the minimum threshold, you have seven weeks to act. You can accelerate collections. Delay discretionary spending. Adjust capital expenditures. Draw on the revolver proactively rather than reactively.

Surprises decrease. The sponsor who receives a weekly cash update is not surprised. The board that sees the 13-week trend is not ambushed. The discipline of weekly visibility prevents the "we did not know" moment that destroys trust.

The Cash Huddle

Many PE-backed companies formalize the weekly discipline through a cash huddle.

The cash huddle is a short meeting, 30 to 45 minutes, focused exclusively on cash. The CFO presents the updated 13-week forecast. Key variances from the prior week are explained. Risks and opportunities are surfaced. Decisions are made.

The huddle includes the CEO, CFO, and the functional leaders most relevant to cash: typically sales (collections), operations (disbursements), and any function with significant cash impact.

The agenda is simple.

Last week versus forecast. What did we project for cash receipts and disbursements? What actually happened? Why the variance?

Updated 13-week forecast. What does the new forecast show? Where is cash headed? Any stress points emerging?

Risks and opportunities. What could make cash worse than forecast? What could make it better? What actions are we taking?

Decisions. Are there cash-related decisions to make? Accelerate a collection effort? Defer a vendor payment? Adjust the capital expenditure timing?

The cash huddle keeps cash visible at the leadership level. It prevents the slow drift into trouble that happens when cash is monitored quarterly rather than weekly.

What the Coach notices: The cash huddle that gets cancelled when things are busy. The forecast that is presented without variance explanation. The risks section that is always empty.

What the Coach says: "Walk me through the cash forecast. Not the summary. The drivers. What changed from last week, and who owns the fix?"

Cash and Operating Decisions

The 13-week forecast is not just about monitoring. It is about connecting operating decisions to cash impact.

Every significant operating decision has a cash consequence. Hiring affects payroll disbursements. Inventory purchases affect vendor payments. Pricing changes affect collections timing. Capital investments affect outflows.

A cash-aware organization asks the cash question before making these decisions. "What does this mean for cash in the next 13 weeks?"

The Coach encourages this cash awareness by making the 13-week forecast a standard reference in decision discussions. When the COO proposes an inventory build, the CFO shows the cash impact. When the CRO proposes extended payment terms to win a deal, the forecast shows when that decision affects collections.

This integration is powerful. It prevents decisions that look good on a P&L basis but create cash stress. It forces trade-off thinking. It makes cash a first-class consideration, not an afterthought.

CHAPTER 13

Cash War Room Dashboard

The 8 signals that matter every week

Runway Weeks	Collections vs Plan
One owner per metric	Weekly tracking

DSO	Payables Timing
Days sales outstanding	Strategic sequencing

Inventory Turns	Gross Margin Leakage
Working capital efficiency	Pricing + mix discipline

Capex Variance	Covenant Headroom
Spend control	Debt compliance buffer

If cash is tight, everything is strategy

Working Capital as a Cash Lever

Working capital is the biggest controllable driver of cash in most operating businesses.

Working capital consists of accounts receivable, inventory, and accounts payable. Changes in working capital flow directly to cash.

If receivables increase, cash decreases. The company has delivered goods or services but has not collected payment. The cash is tied up in customer balances.

If inventory increases, cash decreases. The company has purchased or manufactured goods but has not sold them. The cash is tied up in warehouses.

If payables increase, cash increases. The company has received goods or services but has not paid for them. The cash is preserved.

The working capital equation is straightforward: Receivables + Inventory - Payables = Working Capital. A decrease in working capital releases cash. An increase in working capital consumes cash.

Many PE-backed companies underestimate the cash locked in working capital. A manufacturing company with 60 days of receivables, 90 days of inventory, and 30 days of payables has a cash conversion cycle of 120 days. Every million dollars of revenue requires substantial working capital funding.

Improving working capital is often the fastest path to cash release. Accelerating collections by five days on a company with 50 million in annual revenue releases roughly 685,000 dollars. Reducing inventory days from 90 to 75 releases meaningful cash. Extending payment terms with suppliers by ten days preserves cash that would otherwise flow out.

The 13-week forecast makes working capital visible. It shows the cash tied up in receivables. It shows the cash tied up in inventory. It creates the pressure to manage these drivers actively.

The Receivables Discipline

Receivables deserve particular attention because they represent cash you have earned but not collected.

Many companies treat receivables passively. They invoice and hope for payment. They follow up when payments are overdue. They tolerate slow-paying customers because they do not want to damage relationships.

A cash-disciplined organization treats receivables actively.

Invoice promptly. Every day between delivery and invoice is a day of unnecessary delay. Same-day invoicing should be the standard where feasible.

Invoice accurately. Errors create disputes. Disputes delay payment. A clean invoice gets paid faster than a contested one.

Monitor payment patterns. Know which customers pay on time and which pay late. The customer who consistently pays in 45 days will not suddenly start paying in 30. Plan accordingly.

Escalate appropriately. Overdue accounts should be escalated quickly. Not with hostility, but with clarity. "Your account is past due. When can we expect payment?"

Negotiate terms thoughtfully. Payment terms are negotiated, not dictated. Understand the cash cost of extended terms before agreeing to them. Net 60 instead of Net 30 costs real money.

Consider incentives. Early payment discounts can accelerate collections. A two-percent discount for payment in ten days may be worth it if your cost of capital is high enough.

The 13-week forecast makes receivables discipline visible. It shows which collections are expected when. It shows when slippage occurs. It creates accountability.

The Cash Conversion Cycle

The cash conversion cycle brings together receivables, inventory, and payables into a single metric.

Cash Conversion Cycle = Days Sales Outstanding + Days Inventory Outstanding - Days Payables Outstanding.

DSO is how long it takes to collect receivables. DIO is how long inventory sits before being sold. DPO is how long you take to pay suppliers.

A shorter cash conversion cycle means cash flows through the business faster. Every day you shorten the cycle releases cash.

The 13-week forecast is a tool for improving the cash conversion cycle. It creates visibility into each component. It enables targeted improvement efforts. It tracks progress.

A Coach helps the CEO understand the cash conversion cycle and set improvement targets. Reduce DSO by five days. Reduce DIO by ten days. Extend DPO by five days. Each improvement releases cash that can be used to pay down debt, fund growth, or provide a buffer against uncertainty.

What the Coach notices: The cash conversion cycle that has drifted from 65 days to 85 days over 18 months without anyone noticing. The DSO that is 15 days longer than industry benchmark. The DPO that could be extended but has never been negotiated.

What the Coach says: "Our cash conversion cycle is 85 days. Industry benchmark is 60. That is 25 days of cash sitting idle. What would it take to close half that gap?"

Cash and Covenant Management

In leveraged companies, cash is intimately connected to covenant compliance.

Most loan agreements include covenants. Leverage covenants limit debt relative to EBITDA. Coverage covenants require EBITDA to exceed interest expense by a minimum ratio. Liquidity covenants require minimum cash or availability.

Covenant breaches have consequences. At minimum, they trigger conversations with lenders that no one wants to have. At worst, they trigger acceleration, pricing increases, or loss of control.

The 13-week forecast is the first line of defense against covenant surprises.

Integrate covenant testing into the forecast. At each forecast period, calculate the covenant ratios implied by the forecast. If the forecast shows a potential breach, you have early warning.

Model scenarios. Run the forecast with pessimistic assumptions. What if collections slip by 10 percent? What if a major customer delays payment? What if sales come in below plan? See where the covenants are at risk under stress.

Build headroom. Do not operate at the edge of covenants. Build a buffer. If the leverage covenant is 5.0x, manage to 4.5x. The buffer provides cushion for the unexpected.

Communicate proactively. If covenant stress is emerging, communicate with lenders early. Lenders hate surprises more than they hate problems. A borrower who surfaces issues proactively and with a plan maintains trust. A borrower who surprises lenders loses it.

The Coach ensures that covenant awareness is embedded in cash management. The 13-week forecast is not just about cash flow. It is about covenant protection.

The CFO as Cash Guardian

The CFO has a special role in cash management. They are the guardian of cash reality.

This means building the 13-week forecast infrastructure. The systems, processes, and skills to produce a reliable rolling forecast.

This means leading the cash huddle. Presenting the forecast, explaining variances, driving accountability.

This means challenging the organization. Asking hard questions about collections. Pushing back on inventory builds. Holding disbursements to commitments.

This means communicating to the sponsor. Providing the weekly cash update. Flagging risks early. Building credibility through transparency.

A CFO who is strong on cash management is invaluable in a PE-backed company. A CFO who is weak on cash management is a liability, regardless of their other skills.

The Coach assesses CFO capability in this area and helps the CEO address gaps if they exist.

Cash as Leadership Signal

How leadership talks about cash signals what the organization values.

If the CEO asks about cash weekly, the organization learns that cash matters. If the CEO only asks about revenue and EBITDA, cash becomes an afterthought.

If collections accountability is real, the sales organization treats receivables seriously. If collections accountability is nominal, customers pay late because no one is pushing.

If cash impact is part of operating decisions, managers think about cash. If cash impact is someone else's problem, managers optimize their functions without regard to cash consequences.

The 13-week forecast is a cultural tool as much as a financial tool. It signals that cash is a priority. It creates a vocabulary for discussing cash. It makes cash visible in a way that profit-focused reporting does not.

The Coach helps the CEO use cash management as a leadership signal. The way the CEO talks about cash shapes how the organization thinks about cash.

Coach Cards Referenced

- **13-week cash forecast updated weekly**
- **Weekly cash huddle (30 to 45 minutes)**
- **Days Sales Outstanding as a receivables discipline metric**
- **Days Inventory Outstanding as an inventory discipline metric**
- **Days Payables Outstanding as a payables strategy metric**
- **Cash Conversion Cycle as the integrated working capital metric**
- **Covenant headroom management**

Field Drills

- **If you do not have a 13-week cash forecast, build one this week.** If you have one, audit its accuracy by comparing the last four weeks of forecast to actuals.
- **Implement a weekly cash huddle.** Define the attendees, agenda, and decision rights. Run it for four weeks and assess.
- **Calculate your current cash conversion cycle.** Set targets for improvement in each component: DSO, DIO, DPO.
- **Review your top ten receivable accounts by balance.** Identify which are at risk and assign recovery actions.
- **Model a stress scenario in your 13-week forecast.** What happens if collections slip 15 percent for four weeks? Where do covenants become at risk?

Clinic Questions

- How accurate is our cash forecast? What is the average variance between projection and actuals?
- How frequently does leadership discuss cash? Is it weekly, monthly, or only when there is a problem?
- What is our cash conversion cycle, and how has it changed over the past year?
- Who owns collections, and how strong is that ownership?
- Do we have covenant headroom, and do we monitor it weekly?
- When was the last time we were surprised by cash? What would have prevented that surprise?
- Does the organization understand the connection between operating decisions and cash impact?

Chapter 12

Translate the PE Equation for Humans

The CFO presented the value creation bridge with obvious pride. Entry multiple of 7x. Exit multiple of 9x. EBITDA growth from 12 million to 22 million. Debt paydown of 18 million. The math produced a 3.2x return and a 28 percent IRR.

The CEO nodded. The sponsor partner smiled. The operating partner took notes.

Then the CFO turned to the COO and asked: "Any questions?"

The COO stared at the slide for a moment. "I understand the numbers. But what does this mean I should do differently on Monday morning?"

Silence.

This is the translation gap. PE economics are expressed in a language that makes sense to financial professionals but means nothing to the operators who must execute the plan. Multiples, IRR, MOIC, leverage ratios, equity value waterfalls. These concepts drive investment decisions at the sponsor level but create glazed eyes in the operating room.

The Coach's job is to translate PE economics into human terms. To convert the financial equation into behaviors, decisions, and priorities that operators can act on. Without this translation, the value creation plan remains an abstraction, something that exists in board decks but does not shape daily work.

Translate the PE Equation for Humans

Make the math actionable for the leadership team

EBITDA	Multiple	Net Debt
Pricing · Mix · Productivity	Risk · Growth quality	Cash conversion

Equity Value = (EBITDA × Multiple) – Net Debt

> ☐ The point is not the formula. It's the behaviors behind it.

The Language Barrier

PE professionals speak a dialect that feels native to them but foreign to most operating executives.

They talk about multiples. "We bought at 7x and need to exit at 9x." But what does a multiple actually mean? It is a shorthand for how much buyers will pay for a dollar of earnings. A higher multiple means more confidence in the future. But what creates that confidence? Growth? Margins? Predictability? Market position? The multiple is an output of many inputs, most of which are operational.

They talk about returns. "We need a 25 percent IRR to meet fund targets." But IRR is an abstraction that combines amount, timing, and duration in ways that are not intuitive. A CEO cannot manage to an IRR directly. They can manage the drivers that produce the IRR.

They talk about leverage. "We are at 4.5x and need to get to 3x." But leverage is a ratio that moves when either the numerator or denominator changes. Paying down debt reduces leverage. Growing EBITDA reduces leverage. The operator needs to know which path they are on and what actions move the ratio.

They talk about waterfalls. "The management equity pool participates above an 8 percent preferred return." But waterfalls are complex structures that determine who gets paid and when. The operator cares about outcomes, not mechanics. Will I make money if we succeed? What do I need to do to succeed?

The financial language is precise but opaque. The Coach translates it into operational language that is actionable.

Every Number Tells an Exit Story

The numbers you review weekly are not just operating metrics. They are the chapters of your exit narrative.

When a buyer conducts diligence, they are not just checking current performance. They are reading the history of how this company was managed. They are assessing whether the story of improvement is real.

Consider what your numbers will say:

The 13-week cash forecast. A history of accurate forecasting says: this team knows their business. Variance analysis that shows learning says: this team improves. A pattern of surprises says: this team does not control their cash.

The covenant tracking. Consistent headroom says: this is a stable credit. Near-misses that required amendments say: this is a risk. The history is visible in lender documentation.

The EBITDA bridge. A clear walk from entry to exit, with quantified contribution from each lever, says: this team understands value creation. An inability to explain the bridge says: success was accidental.

The working capital trends. Improving DSO and inventory turns say: this team manages cash, not just profits. Static or worsening metrics say: cash management is not a priority.

Every month you run the cadence, you are writing history that will be read at exit. Write a story you want buyers to pay for.

The Five Drivers of PE Value

PE value creation, stripped to its essence, comes from five drivers. The Coach helps operating teams understand each one in practical terms.

Revenue growth is the top line. More customers, higher prices, new products, new markets. Revenue growth shows up in the P&L and, eventually, in cash. It also influences the exit multiple because buyers pay more for growing businesses.

The operating translation: What are we doing to acquire new customers? What are we doing to retain existing customers? What are we doing to sell more to current customers? What are we doing to raise prices? These are the actions that drive revenue.

Margin expansion is the efficiency of converting revenue to profit. Better procurement, leaner operations, smarter pricing, favorable product mix. Margin expansion flows directly to EBITDA.

The operating translation: Where are we spending money that does not contribute to value? What can we buy more cheaply? What processes are inefficient? Where is labor productivity below benchmark? These are the actions that expand margins.

Debt paydown is the reduction of leverage over time. Cash generated by the business pays down principal, reducing the debt burden and increasing equity value.

The operating translation: How much cash are we generating? Where is cash being consumed unnecessarily? What working capital improvements release cash for debt service? The actions that generate cash enable debt paydown.

Multiple expansion is the increase in what buyers will pay for a dollar of earnings. Multiples expand when risk decreases, when growth accelerates, when quality improves, when the story becomes more compelling.

The operating translation: What would make a buyer more confident in our future? What risks are we carrying that we could reduce? What proof points demonstrate our trajectory? What story will we tell at exit? These are the actions that support multiple expansion.

Capital efficiency is the return on invested capital. How much value are we creating relative to the capital employed? This matters for bolt-on acquisitions, for capital expenditure decisions, for working capital management.

The operating translation: Is this investment worth it? What return will we get? How does this compare to alternatives? Every dollar of capital has an opportunity cost.

When operating teams understand these five drivers, they can connect their daily work to PE outcomes. The salesperson closing a deal contributes to revenue growth. The procurement manager negotiating a better contract contributes to margin expansion. The controller accelerating collections contributes to debt paydown. The product leader reducing defects contributes to multiple expansion.

The Value Creation Bridge

The value creation bridge is a visual representation of how entry equity becomes exit equity. It shows the contribution of each driver: EBITDA growth, multiple expansion, debt paydown, and sometimes additional capital invested.

The bridge is a powerful communication tool when properly translated.

The Coach helps the CEO present the bridge to the operating team in terms they understand.

"We started with 30 million dollars of equity value. Here is how we get to 100 million."

"First, we grow EBITDA from 12 million to 22 million. That is 10 million of additional profit, coming from a combination of revenue growth and margin improvement. This contributes 70 million to our value at exit, assuming we maintain our current multiple."

"Second, we improve our multiple from 7x to 9x. This reflects the market's increased confidence in our business, driven by our growth rate, our predictability, and the quality of our earnings. This multiple improvement adds 44 million to our exit value."

"Third, we pay down 18 million of debt over the hold period. Every dollar of debt paid down is a dollar that goes to equity holders instead of lenders."

"Add it up, and we go from 30 million to roughly 100 million. That is a 3.3x return."

This narrative connects the financial math to operational reality. The team can see that EBITDA growth is the biggest lever. They can see that multiple improvement matters. They can see that cash generation funds debt paydown.

The bridge becomes a touchstone that the CEO can return to throughout the hold period. "Remember the bridge. This initiative contributes to margin expansion, which is the second bar on our chart. This is how we get to 22 million of EBITDA."

Translating Multiples

Multiples deserve particular translation attention because they are so central to PE value creation and so poorly understood.

A multiple is a ratio: Enterprise Value divided by EBITDA. If a company has 15 million of EBITDA and sells for 120 million of enterprise value, the multiple is 8x.

But what determines the multiple? Why do some companies trade at 6x and others at 12x?

The answer involves several factors, each of which connects to operating reality.

Growth rate. Faster-growing companies command higher multiples because buyers are paying for future earnings, not just current earnings. A company growing EBITDA at 15 percent per year is worth more than one growing at 5 percent.

The operating translation: Our growth rate affects what someone will pay for us. Initiatives that accelerate sustainable growth improve our multiple.

Predictability. Companies with predictable, recurring revenue command higher multiples than those with volatile, project-based revenue. Predictability reduces buyer risk.

The operating translation: Recurring revenue is more valuable than one-time revenue. Subscription models, long-term contracts, and sticky customer relationships support our multiple.

Quality of earnings. Adjusted EBITDA is scrutinized during diligence. If adjustments are aggressive or non-recurring items are frequent, buyers discount the multiple. Clean earnings command a premium.

The operating translation: The way we run the business affects how our earnings are perceived. Reducing one-time items, eliminating related-party transactions, and building clean financial records protects our multiple.

Market position. Companies with strong competitive moats, market leadership, or differentiated offerings command higher multiples than commoditized businesses.

The operating translation: Strengthening our market position supports our multiple. Investments in brand, product differentiation, and customer loyalty have multiple implications beyond their P&L impact.

Risk profile. Companies with concentrated customers, key-person dependencies, regulatory exposure, or operational fragility trade at lower multiples.

The operating translation: Reducing concentration, building bench strength, and improving operational resilience supports our multiple. Risk reduction is value creation.

When operating teams understand what drives multiples, they can make decisions that protect and enhance them. The product investment that increases recurring revenue percentage. The customer diversification that reduces concentration. The process improvement that makes earnings more predictable. These are multiple-expanding actions.

Translating IRR and MOIC

IRR and MOIC are the two primary return metrics in PE. Both deserve translation.

MOIC, multiple on invested capital, is the simpler concept. It answers: for every dollar we invested, how many dollars did we get back? A 3x MOIC means three dollars returned for every dollar invested.

The operating translation: MOIC is about magnitude. How big is the win? Bigger EBITDA at exit, higher multiple at exit, and more debt paydown all increase MOIC.

IRR, internal rate of return, is more complex. It measures the annualized return, accounting for the timing of cash flows. A 25 percent IRR means the investment is growing at 25 percent per year, compounded.

The subtlety of IRR is that timing matters enormously. A 3x return in three years has a much higher IRR than a 3x return in seven years. Getting to exit faster, all else equal, improves IRR.

The operating translation: IRR is about speed. Time is money, literally. Accelerating value creation, hitting milestones sooner, and shortening the path to exit all improve IRR. Delay destroys IRR even if the eventual outcome is good.

This translation has practical implications. When the sponsor pushes for quick wins in the first year, they are not being impatient for impatience's sake. Early EBITDA improvement has a disproportionate impact on IRR because the value is created sooner. The Coach helps operating teams understand why speed matters, not just that it matters.

The Incentive Translation

Management equity participation is a powerful alignment tool, but only if managers understand how it works.

Most PE-backed companies have management equity pools. Executives receive options, profits interests, or co-investment opportunities that give them a share of the upside if the investment succeeds.

The mechanics are often complex. Vesting schedules. Participation thresholds. Waterfall priorities. Dilution from follow-on investments. Many executives hold equity they do not fully understand.

The Coach encourages transparency about how incentives work.

"You hold options that vest over four years. They have an exercise price of X. If we exit at our target value, your options will be worth Y after taxes. If we exit above target, they will be worth more. If we exit below the preferred return threshold, they may be worth less or nothing."

This translation is not about promising riches. It is about creating clarity. When executives understand the connection between company performance and personal outcome, they are more motivated and more aligned.

The Coach also helps executives understand the behaviors that drive their outcomes.

"Your equity value depends on exit equity value. Exit equity value depends on EBITDA at exit, the multiple we achieve, and how much debt we have paid down. Every initiative you lead that grows EBITDA, improves our story, or generates cash is increasing your personal outcome."

This is alignment in action. The executive who understands the equation makes decisions that support it.

The Monthly Translation Rhythm

Translation is not a one-time event. It is an ongoing discipline.

The Coach helps the CEO build translation into the regular operating rhythm.

Monthly financial reviews should include a value creation lens. Not just "here is revenue and EBITDA," but "here is how we are tracking against the value creation bridge."

A simple monthly update might include:

EBITDA year-to-date versus plan. Are we on track for the EBITDA growth that drives value?

Cash generated and debt paid down. Are we on track for the debt reduction that increases equity value?

Leading indicators of multiple. How are we performing on the metrics that support our exit story? Revenue growth rate, customer retention, earnings quality.

Key initiative status. What progress are we making on the specific initiatives that drive the plan?

This monthly translation keeps the operating team connected to PE economics. It prevents the drift where operators focus on their functions and lose sight of the overall value creation equation.

Value Creation "Translation Table"

From initiative language → to value language

Initiative Language	Value Language
New CRM	Pipeline conversion + forecast accuracy
Lean program	Throughput + margin + cash
Hiring sales leaders	Revenue per rep + churn reduction
Digital transformation	Decision speed + cost reduction
Product innovation	Mix improvement + pricing power

☐ If you can't translate it to value, don't fund it

The "Buy-Side" Litmus Test

Do not build for yourself. Build for the buyer. Before you approve any major initiative, ask these three questions:

1. **Will the next buyer pay for this?** If you invest one million dollars in a new ERP, will a buyer credit you one million in value? Or will they view it as "maintenance"?
2. **Is this "pro forma" or "proven"?** Buyers pay for proven cash flow. They discount "projected" synergies.

3. **Does this simplify or complicate the story?** A complex business trades at a discount. A focused business trades at a premium.

Rule: If you cannot explain how an initiative increases the exit multiple, kill it.

The Danger of Mistranslation

Bad translation is worse than no translation.

Mistranslation creates false confidence. The operating team believes they understand the economics but actually does not. They make decisions based on wrong mental models. They optimize for the wrong outcomes.

Common mistranslations include:

Revenue at all costs. The team believes revenue growth is the primary driver and pursues growth that is unprofitable or unsustainable. They win customers at negative margin. They discount to hit targets. Revenue goes up, but value goes down.

The correct translation: profitable revenue growth matters. Unprofitable revenue can actually destroy value by consuming resources and masking underlying problems.

EBITDA manipulation. The team believes EBITDA is the target and manages to the number through accounting games. Aggressive capitalization of expenses. Deferred maintenance. Channel stuffing. EBITDA looks good, but the underlying business is weaker.

The correct translation: sustainable EBITDA matters. Buyers see through manipulation during diligence. Earnings quality affects multiple. Short-term EBITDA gains that create long-term problems destroy value.

Exit myopia. The team believes only the exit matters and neglects the business fundamentals. They defer investments that would pay off after exit. They optimize for the sale rather than for the business.

The correct translation: a strong business creates exit value. The best exit preparation is building a business that the next owner will be excited to own.

The Coach guards against mistranslation by testing understanding regularly. "Tell me why this initiative matters for value creation." If the answer reveals a flawed mental model, correction is needed.

Translation as Leadership

The CEO who can translate PE economics into operational terms is a more effective leader.

They can explain why certain initiatives are prioritized. Not because the board said so, but because of the value creation logic.

They can motivate the team around a shared objective. Not an abstract financial target, but a concrete vision of building a more valuable company.

They can make trade-offs when resources are scarce. Not based on politics, but based on value creation impact.

They can communicate to all levels of the organization. The senior leader gets the full bridge. The frontline manager gets the piece that matters to their role.

Translation is a leadership skill. The Coach develops it.

Coach Cards Referenced

- Value creation bridge (entry to exit equity walk)
- The five drivers: revenue, margin, debt paydown, multiple, capital efficiency
- MOIC as magnitude of return
- IRR as speed of return
- Rule of 40 as a growth-margin balance indicator
- Multiple drivers: growth, predictability, quality, market position, risk

Field Drills

- **Present the value creation bridge to your leadership team.** Ask each person to explain how their function contributes to the bridge.
- **Translate your three largest initiatives into value creation terms.** Which driver does each affect? By how much?
- **Review how management equity works with your key executives.** Ensure they understand the connection between company performance and personal outcome.
- **Add a value creation lens to your monthly financial review.** Track EBITDA versus plan, debt paydown, and leading indicators of multiple.
- **Identify one mistranslation risk in your organization.** Where might the team be optimizing for the wrong outcome?

Clinic Questions

- Can our operating leaders explain the value creation bridge in their own words?
- Do our frontline managers understand how their work connects to PE outcomes?
- Are we making trade-offs based on value creation logic or based on politics and habit?
- Have we clearly communicated how management equity works and what drives its value?

- Where might our team be pursuing revenue or EBITDA in ways that actually destroy value?
- Does our board understand the operational complexity behind our financial targets?
- How often do we explicitly connect operating decisions to the PE equation?

Chapter 13

The mVMS and the Execution Backbone

The value creation plan was comprehensive. Twelve initiatives across five workstreams. Revenue growth through new market expansion. Margin improvement through procurement optimization. Working capital release through receivables acceleration. Organizational effectiveness through spans and layers redesign. Technology enablement through ERP upgrade.

Each initiative had a business case, a timeline, and an expected EBITDA impact. The plan totaled 14 million dollars of improvement over three years. The investment committee loved it.

Eighteen months later, the results were different. Two initiatives had delivered. Three were behind schedule. Four had stalled entirely. Three had been quietly abandoned. Realized value was 4 million dollars, less than a third of the plan.

The CEO was frustrated. "We had the right plan. We had the right people. What happened?"

What happened was execution. Or rather, the lack of a system to ensure execution. The plan existed. The execution backbone did not.

This is where the mVMS comes in. The Merit-driven Value Management System is an execution infrastructure that converts strategy into action and action into results. It is not a methodology that sits on a shelf. It is a living operating system that keeps the value creation plan on track.

The Execution Gap

The gap between plan and results is universal in business. It is especially pronounced in PE-backed companies because the plans are ambitious and the timelines are compressed.

Why does execution fail?

Initiatives lack ownership. The plan says "improve procurement," but no one person owns the outcome. Responsibility is diffused across functions. When everyone owns it, no one owns it.

Progress is not tracked rigorously. The plan launches with energy. Then daily operations take over. Months pass without formal review. The initiative drifts. By the time someone notices, the window for correction has closed.

Dependencies are not managed. Initiative A requires output from Initiative B. But no one is coordinating. B falls behind, and A cannot proceed. The delay cascades.

Resources are not allocated. The plan assumes people will work on initiatives alongside their day jobs. But day jobs consume all available time. The initiative becomes "extra work" that never gets done.

Obstacles are not escalated. The team hits a problem. They try to solve it locally. They fail. They try again. Meanwhile, time passes. If the problem had been escalated, leadership could have intervened. But the escalation path is unclear.

Accountability is weak. The initiative misses its milestone. Nothing happens. The miss is explained, rationalized, forgiven. The pattern repeats. The organization learns that milestones are suggestions, not commitments.

The mVMS addresses each of these failure modes systematically.

The mVMS Architecture

The mVMS consists of five integrated components that together create an execution backbone.

Initiative Ownership assigns a single accountable leader to each value creation initiative. Not a committee. Not a steering group. One person who is responsible for delivering the outcome.

The owner has authority to marshal resources, make decisions within defined boundaries, and remove obstacles. They have accountability for results. Their performance evaluation and compensation are connected to initiative success.

Ownership creates clarity. When you ask "who owns procurement optimization?" there is one name. That person can explain status, risks, and next steps at any moment.

Milestone Mapping breaks each initiative into discrete milestones with specific deliverables and deadlines. Not vague phases, but concrete outputs. "Complete supplier analysis and identify top 20 negotiation targets by March 15." "Achieve signed contracts with 10 of 20 targets by June 30." "Realize first 500K of savings in Q3 actuals."

Milestones create checkpoints. You know whether you are on track because you can see whether milestones are being hit. Missing a milestone is a signal that requires attention.

Cadenced Review establishes a regular rhythm for tracking progress and addressing issues. Weekly status updates from initiative owners. Bi-weekly steering reviews with the CEO. Monthly integration into the leadership team agenda. Quarterly deep dives with the board.

Cadence creates visibility. Problems surface quickly because there is a regular forum for surfacing them. Drift is caught early because someone is always watching.

Escalation Protocol defines how obstacles are raised and resolved. If an initiative owner encounters a blocker they cannot resolve, there is a clear path to escalate. The escalation reaches someone with authority to act. Resolution timelines are defined.

Escalation creates speed. Problems do not fester. They move up the chain until they reach someone who can solve them. The organization learns that escalation is expected, not a sign of failure.

Value Tracking quantifies the impact of each initiative in financial terms. Not activity metrics, but outcome metrics. EBITDA contribution. Cash released. Revenue generated. Each initiative has a target, and actuals are tracked against target.

Value tracking creates accountability. You cannot hide behind activity. Either the value materialized or it did not. The numbers do not lie.

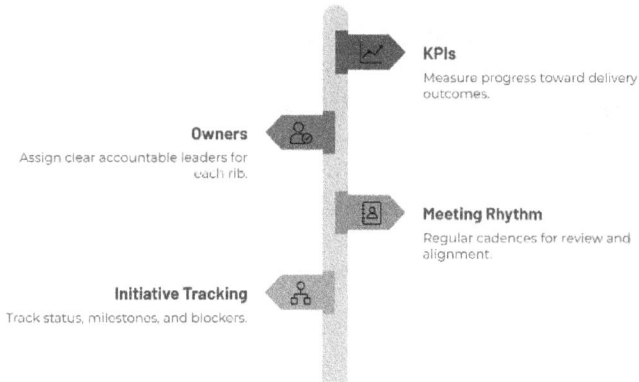

mVMS and the Execution Backbone

KPIs
Measure progress toward delivery outcomes.

Owners
Assign clear accountable leaders for each rib.

Meeting Rhythm
Regular cadences for review and alignment.

Initiative Tracking
Track status, milestones, and blockers.

Installing the mVMS

Installing the mVMS is a deliberate process that requires leadership commitment and organizational discipline.

Step one: Define the initiatives. Starting from the value creation plan, identify the discrete initiatives that will be tracked. Typically five to fifteen initiatives, depending on the complexity of the plan. Each initiative should be large enough to matter but specific enough to manage.

Step two: Assign owners. For each initiative, identify the accountable leader. This should be a senior person with the authority to drive the work. Not a project manager coordinating activities, but a business leader who owns the outcome.

The owner assignment conversation should be explicit. "You own this initiative. You are responsible for delivering the outcome. Your success will be measured by whether this initiative delivers its target value. What support do you need to succeed?"

Step three: Map milestones. Work with each owner to define the milestones for their initiative. What are the key deliverables? What are the deadlines? What does success look like at each checkpoint?

Milestones should be specific and verifiable. "Complete analysis" is not a good milestone because completion is subjective. "Deliver analysis document with recommendations to steering committee" is better because it is verifiable.

Step four: Establish cadence. Define the review rhythm. When does the CEO review initiative status? When does the leadership team review? When does the board review? What information is expected at each review?

The cadence should be documented and published. Everyone knows when reviews happen and what is expected.

Step five: Define escalation. Create the escalation protocol. What types of issues should be escalated? To whom? Within what timeframe? What response is expected?

Escalation should be normalized. The message should be: "Escalation is how we solve problems. If you are stuck, escalate. We would rather know early and help than discover late and scramble."

Step six: Build tracking. Create the tracking infrastructure. A dashboard that shows initiative status, milestone completion, and value realization. Updated regularly. Visible to leadership.

The tracking should be simple and honest. Green, yellow, red status indicators. Milestone completion percentages. Value delivered versus target. No spin.

The Weekly Rhythm

The mVMS runs on a weekly rhythm that keeps initiatives moving.

Each initiative owner updates their status weekly. A brief summary: What was accomplished last week? What is planned for this week? What is the current status (green, yellow, red)? Are there any escalations needed?

These updates feed into a consolidated view that the CEO reviews. The CEO can see at a glance which initiatives are on track and which need attention.

Weekly steering meetings address the initiatives that are not on track. If an initiative is yellow or red, the owner presents the situation and the recovery plan. The steering group provides guidance, removes obstacles, or makes decisions.

The weekly rhythm creates pressure. Initiative owners know they will be asked about progress every week. Milestones that slip cannot be hidden because they are visible in the tracking system.

The weekly rhythm also creates support. Problems surface quickly and get attention. Owners are not left alone to struggle. The organization mobilizes to help when help is needed.

What the Coach notices: The initiative that has been yellow for six consecutive weeks without a recovery plan. The owner who always has explanations but never has results. The steering meeting that reviews status but never makes decisions.

What the Coach says: "This initiative has been yellow for six weeks. That is not yellow. That is red. What needs to change for this to get back on track, and what decision do we need to make today?"

The Monthly Integration

Beyond the weekly rhythm, the mVMS integrates into the monthly leadership team meeting.

Once a month, the leadership team reviews the full portfolio of initiatives. Not just the ones that are struggling, but all of them. This creates a holistic view of value creation progress.

The monthly review asks several questions.

Are we on track overall? Looking at the portfolio, are we delivering the value we planned? If not, why not, and what is the recovery plan?

Are resources allocated correctly? Are the initiatives with the highest value potential receiving adequate attention? Are there initiatives that should be deprioritized to focus resources on higher-impact work?

Are there interdependencies to manage? Are initiatives blocking each other? Are there coordination issues that require leadership attention?

Are there new risks or opportunities? Has anything changed that affects the plan? Should we add initiatives, remove initiatives, or reprioritize?

The monthly review keeps the value creation plan dynamic. It is not a static document but a living portfolio that evolves based on what is learned.

The Quarterly Deep Dive

Quarterly, the board reviews value creation progress in detail.

The quarterly deep dive covers each major initiative. Status, milestones achieved, value delivered, risks, and outlook. The board can see whether the investment thesis is being executed.

The quarterly review also includes a financial reconciliation. The value delivered by initiatives should show up in the actual financial results. If the initiatives are delivering but the financials are not improving, something is wrong. If the financials are improving but the initiatives are behind, the improvement is coming from somewhere else.

This reconciliation creates integrity. It prevents the scenario where everyone reports green but the numbers are red. It forces honesty about what is actually creating value.

The Owner's Accountability

The initiative owner is the linchpin of the mVMS. Their accountability makes the system work.

Accountability means the owner is responsible for the outcome, not just the activity. They cannot delegate blame. If the initiative fails, the owner failed. This concentrated accountability creates urgency.

Accountability also means the owner has authority. They can make decisions within their scope without seeking approval for every move. They can marshal resources from across the organization. They can escalate when needed and expect response.

The owner's accountability should be visible in their performance evaluation and compensation. If the initiative succeeds, the owner is recognized and rewarded. If it fails, there are consequences. This connection between outcome and reward aligns incentives.

Selecting the right owners is critical. Not every leader can carry initiative accountability effectively. The best owners are driven, organized, willing to escalate, comfortable with ambiguity, and focused on outcomes rather than activity.

The Coach helps the CEO select owners thoughtfully and supports them in their accountability.

Common Pitfalls

The mVMS can fail if certain pitfalls are not avoided.

Too many initiatives. If the portfolio has 30 initiatives, none will receive adequate attention. Focus is power. A smaller number of well-resourced initiatives will deliver more value than a large number of under-resourced ones.

The guidance is typically five to fifteen initiatives, depending on organizational capacity. If the value creation plan has more than that, prioritize ruthlessly.

Owners without authority. If the initiative owner cannot make decisions or access resources, accountability is hollow. They become project managers who track activities rather than leaders who drive outcomes.

Ensure owners have genuine authority commensurate with their accountability.

Tracking without consequences. If milestones are missed and nothing happens, the organization learns that milestones do not matter. The tracking becomes theater.

Consequences for missed milestones should be proportionate but real. Investigation into root cause. Recovery plans. In persistent cases, owner changes.

Escalation that is punished. If leaders who escalate are viewed as weak or incompetent, escalation stops. Problems fester in silence.

The culture should celebrate escalation as responsible behavior. Leaders who surface problems early are helping, not failing.

Value tracking disconnected from financials. If the initiative dashboard shows 10 million of value delivered but the P&L shows no improvement, credibility collapses. Value tracking must reconcile to actual financial results.

Quarterly reconciliation prevents this disconnect.

The mVMS and the Coach

The Coach plays a specific role in making the mVMS effective.

The Coach helps install the system. Working with the CEO to define initiatives, select owners, map milestones, and establish cadence. The initial setup requires rigor that the Coach can provide.

The Coach monitors system health. Is the weekly rhythm actually happening? Are escalations being resolved? Is value tracking honest? The Coach provides an independent view of whether the system is working.

The Coach supports initiative owners. Coaching calls with owners who are struggling. Helping them think through problems, plan recovery, and navigate organizational obstacles.

The Coach connects to the sponsor. Ensuring the board has visibility into value creation progress. Translating initiative status into the language of investment returns.

The Coach holds the CEO accountable. Is the CEO giving the mVMS adequate attention? Are they participating in steering reviews? Are they responding to escalations? The CEO's engagement determines whether the system is taken seriously.

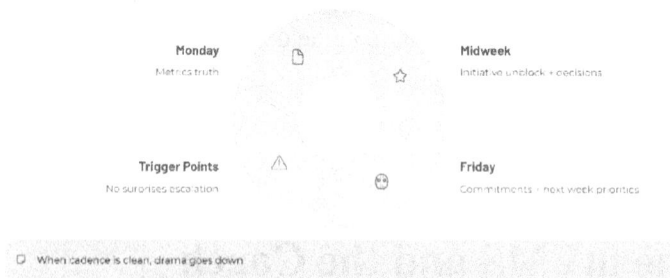

The Weekly Execution Loop

A simple loop that compounds performance

Monday — Metrics truth

Midweek — Initiative unblock + decisions

Trigger Points — No surprises escalation

Friday — Commitments / next week priorities

When cadence is clean, drama goes down

Beyond Initiatives: The Execution Culture

The mVMS is a system, but its ultimate goal is to create an execution culture.

An execution culture is one where commitments are taken seriously. Where milestones are met. Where obstacles are surfaced and resolved. Where accountability is real. Where value creation is not a plan but a practice.

In an execution culture, the mVMS becomes almost invisible. The behaviors it enforces become habits. Owners naturally track their initiatives. Teams naturally escalate problems. Leaders naturally review progress. The system is internalized.

Building this culture takes time. The first year of mVMS implementation is often mechanical. The rhythms feel imposed. The tracking feels like overhead. Resistance appears.

By the second year, if the system is maintained, behaviors shift. People start to see the benefit. Progress accelerates. The system becomes "how we do things here."

The Coach helps the organization move from mechanical compliance to cultural embedding. This is a multi-year journey, but it produces an organization that executes reliably, one of the most valuable assets in PE.

The Integration with Other Systems

The mVMS does not stand alone. It integrates with the other elements of the PE Coach Operating System.

The 13-week cash forecast connects to initiatives that have cash impact. Working capital initiatives should show up in the cash forecast. The reconciliation between initiative tracking and cash reality keeps both honest.

The weekly leadership meeting incorporates mVMS review. The meeting agenda includes a check on initiative status. The two systems reinforce each other.

The board meeting draws on mVMS data. The value creation update at the board level uses the same tracking as the operating level. Consistency builds credibility.

The value creation bridge connects to mVMS initiatives. Each bar on the bridge should trace to specific initiatives. The bridge is not a conceptual aspiration but a sum of concrete efforts.

This integration creates a coherent operating system. The pieces connect. Information flows. The whole is greater than the sum of the parts.

Coach Cards Referenced

- **mVMS: Merit-driven Value Management System**
- **Initiative ownership: one accountable leader per initiative**
- **Milestone mapping: specific deliverables with deadlines**
- **Weekly steering rhythm for initiative review**
- **Escalation protocol: clear path for surfacing and resolving blockers**
- **5 to 15 initiatives as the typical portfolio size**
- **Value tracking reconciled to financial actuals quarterly**

Field Drills

- **List all current value creation initiatives.** For each, identify the owner. If ownership is unclear or diffused, clarify it this week.
- **For your top three initiatives, map milestones for the next 90 days.** Make them specific and verifiable.
- **Establish a weekly initiative review rhythm.** Define when it happens, who attends, and what information is expected.

- **Document your escalation protocol.** What should be escalated? To whom? Within what timeframe?
- **Reconcile initiative value tracking to actual financial results.** Do the two match? If not, investigate.

Clinic Questions

- Do we have clear ownership for each value creation initiative? Can we name one person accountable for each?
- Are milestones specific and verifiable, or vague and subjective?
- How often do we formally review initiative progress? Is the cadence sufficient to catch problems early?
- What happens when milestones are missed? Are there real consequences?
- Is escalation normalized, or is it seen as a sign of weakness?
- Does our value tracking reconcile to actual financial results?
- How would we describe our execution culture? Is it strong, developing, or weak?

PART V

STRATEGY AND ADAPTATION

Learning Faster Than Your Constraints

Chapter 14

The Value Creation Plan Is a Hypothesis

The value creation plan was beautiful. Sixty pages of analysis. Market sizing. Competitive positioning. Operational benchmarking. Financial modeling. Initiative prioritization. Implementation roadmaps.

The investment committee approved it with enthusiasm. The CEO presented it to the leadership team with conviction. The board received quarterly updates tracking progress against it.

Eighteen months later, the plan was fiction.

Not because the team had failed to execute. They had executed diligently. But the market had moved. A competitor had launched a disruptive product. A key customer had changed procurement strategy. A technology shift had altered unit economics. The carefully constructed plan was built on assumptions that no longer held.

The team was executing a plan designed for a world that no longer existed.

This is the central problem with value creation plans. They are built at a moment in time, based on information available at that moment. But the world does not stop moving. Assumptions decay. Conditions change. The plan that was right in month one may be wrong by month twelve.

The Coach's job is to help the organization treat the value creation plan as what it actually is: a hypothesis. Not a commitment to be fulfilled regardless of reality. Not a contract that cannot be renegotiated. A hypothesis to be tested, learned from, and revised as evidence accumulates.

CHAPTER 14

The Value Creation Plan Is a Hypothesis

Treat the plan like a testable model, not scripture

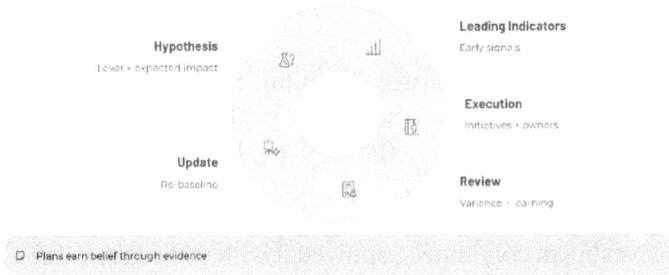

Hypothesis
Lever + expected impact

Leading Indicators
Early signals

Execution
Initiatives + owners

Update
Re-baseline

Review
Variance + learning

Plans earn belief through evidence

The Hypothesis Mindset

A hypothesis is a proposed explanation that can be tested. It is not a guess, which implies no basis. It is not a fact, which implies certainty. It is a reasoned belief that awaits confirmation or refutation.

The value creation plan contains dozens of hypotheses, most of them implicit.

We hypothesize that the market will grow at 8 percent annually.

We hypothesize that we can take share from competitors through superior service.

We hypothesize that pricing increases will not materially affect volume.

We hypothesize that procurement savings of 3 million are achievable.

We hypothesize that the ERP implementation will be complete by Q3.

We hypothesize that the sales team can increase productivity by 20 percent.

Each of these hypotheses could be wrong. Some will be wrong. The question is not whether the plan will prove perfectly accurate. It will not. The question is how quickly the organization recognizes which hypotheses are failing and adapts accordingly.

The hypothesis mindset transforms how the organization relates to its plan. Instead of defending the plan against contradictory evidence, the team seeks out that evidence. Instead of explaining away variances, they investigate them. Instead of waiting until the annual review to update the plan, they adjust continuously.

The Danger of Plan Attachment

Organizations become attached to their plans in ways that impede performance.

Plan attachment manifests in several recognizable patterns.

Variance rationalization. The results come in different from plan. Instead of investigating why, the team explains the variance in ways that preserve the plan. "It is timing." "It is a one-time factor." "We will catch up next quarter." The variance is rationalized rather than understood.

Selective attention. Information that confirms the plan is emphasized. Information that contradicts it is minimized or ignored. The market research that supports the growth assumption gets cited. The customer feedback that challenges it gets filed away.

Sunk cost escalation. Resources have been committed to an initiative. Evidence suggests the initiative is not working. Instead of stopping, the team doubles down. "We have come this far. We cannot stop now." The sunk cost drives continued investment in a failing approach.

Performance theater. The plan becomes the script for board presentations. Management presents progress against plan, selecting metrics that look favorable and contextualizing those that do not. The board receives a curated narrative rather than unvarnished truth.

Plan attachment is understandable. People worked hard on the plan. They made commitments based on it. Their credibility is tied to it. Admitting the plan is wrong feels like admitting failure.

But plan attachment is expensive. It delays necessary pivots. It wastes resources on initiatives that are not working. It erodes trust when the gap between narrative and reality eventually becomes undeniable.

The Coach helps the organization release plan attachment and embrace adaptive execution.

Building Testable Hypotheses

The first step toward hypothesis-driven execution is making the hypotheses explicit and testable.

Many value creation plans contain assumptions that are implicit. The model assumes 8 percent market growth, but nobody explicitly states "we believe the market will grow at 8 percent, and here is why." The assumption is buried in the spreadsheet.

Implicit assumptions cannot be tested because no one is watching them. They become visible only when results diverge from expectations, and by then the damage is done.

The Coach helps the CEO surface the key assumptions underlying the value creation plan and convert them into explicit, testable hypotheses.

An explicit hypothesis has three components.

The belief. A clear statement of what we think is true. "We believe we can increase prices by 5 percent without material volume loss."

The evidence we expect. What should we observe if the belief is true? "If this hypothesis is correct, we should see volume decline of less than 2 percent within 90 days of the price increase."

The timeline for testing. When will we know? "We will evaluate this hypothesis based on Q2 volumes, with a preliminary read after six weeks."

Converting assumptions to explicit hypotheses creates accountability. Someone owns watching each hypothesis. There is a defined moment when the hypothesis is evaluated. The organization cannot drift in ignorance.

The Assumption Register

A practical tool for hypothesis management is the assumption register.

The assumption register is a document that lists the key assumptions underlying the value creation plan. For each assumption, it records:

The assumption itself. Stated clearly and specifically.

The owner. Who is responsible for monitoring this assumption?

The indicators. What metrics or signals will tell us if the assumption is holding?

The review cadence. How often do we evaluate this assumption?

The contingency. If the assumption proves wrong, what is our alternative approach?

A typical value creation plan might have 15 to 25 key assumptions on the register. Revenue assumptions about market growth, win rates, pricing, and churn. Cost assumptions about procurement savings, labor productivity, and overhead efficiency. Timing assumptions about initiative completion and ramp-up curves. Capital assumptions about working capital and investment requirements.

The assumption register is reviewed monthly. The owner of each assumption reports whether it is holding, weakening, or failing. Assumptions that are weakening get additional attention. Assumptions that are failing trigger contingency planning.

This discipline prevents the scenario where assumptions quietly erode until the gap between plan and reality becomes a crisis.

Early Warning Indicators

For each hypothesis, the organization should identify early warning indicators that signal whether the hypothesis is on track.

Lagging indicators tell you what happened. Revenue, EBITDA, cash flow. By the time lagging indicators reveal a problem, the problem has already materialized.

Leading indicators tell you what will happen. They provide advance warning that allows intervention before the lagging indicators turn negative.

For a revenue growth hypothesis, leading indicators might include pipeline coverage, website traffic, quote activity, win rates at each sales stage. If these leading indicators weaken, revenue will follow, but you have time to respond.

For a margin improvement hypothesis, leading indicators might include purchase order commitments, supplier negotiation progress, process efficiency metrics. If these leading indicators stall, margin improvement will stall, but you have time to intervene.

For a customer retention hypothesis, leading indicators might include usage patterns, support ticket trends, NPS scores, renewal conversation outcomes. If these leading indicators decline, churn will increase, but you have time to act.

The Coach helps the CEO identify the leading indicators for each major hypothesis and build them into the regular operating review. Watching leading indicators creates reaction time.

Lever Prioritization Grid

The 90-Day Hypothesis Cycle

Hypotheses should be tested on a defined cycle. Ninety days is a useful default.

Every 90 days, the organization conducts a formal hypothesis review. For each key assumption:

What did we believe? Restate the hypothesis as it was defined.

What did we observe? Summarize the evidence from the past 90 days.

Was the hypothesis confirmed, challenged, or refuted? Based on the evidence, what is our assessment?

What do we do now? If confirmed, continue. If challenged, investigate further and possibly adjust. If refuted, pivot.

The 90-day cycle creates rhythm without excessive overhead. It is frequent enough to catch failing hypotheses before they cause major damage. It is infrequent enough to allow meaningful evidence to accumulate.

The quarterly board meeting is a natural anchor for the hypothesis review. The board receives an update not just on results but on assumption health. Which assumptions are holding? Which are under pressure? What pivots are being considered?

This transparency builds trust. The board sees that management is not rigidly defending a plan but actively managing a portfolio of hypotheses.

Pivoting Without Panic

When a hypothesis fails, the organization must pivot. But pivoting in a PE context requires care.

A pivot is not an admission of failure. It is a recognition that conditions have changed or that initial beliefs were incorrect. The alternative to pivoting is continuing down a path that does not lead to value creation. That is the real failure.

A pivot should be data-driven. The decision to change course should be based on evidence, not frustration or political pressure. "The evidence from Q1 and Q2 indicates that our pricing hypothesis is not holding. Volume decline is 7 percent, not the 2 percent we expected. We need to reconsider our approach."

A pivot should be communicated clearly. The leadership team and the board should understand what changed, why the original hypothesis did not hold, and what the new approach entails. Ambiguity creates confusion and erodes confidence.

A pivot should be committed. Once the decision is made to change course, the organization must commit to the new direction. Half-pivots, where the organization partially shifts but retains elements of the old approach, often produce the worst of both worlds.

The Coach helps the CEO navigate pivots with discipline. Recognizing when a pivot is needed. Building the case with evidence. Communicating the change clearly. Committing the organization to the new path.

What the Coach notices: The initiative that keeps missing milestones but never gets killed. The assumption that everyone knows is wrong but no one addresses. The leadership team that debates endlessly instead of deciding to pivot.

What the Coach says: "The evidence is clear. This hypothesis is not holding. What is our Plan B, and when do we trigger it?"

The Living Plan

The value creation plan should be a living document, not a historical artifact.

A living plan is updated continuously as hypotheses are tested and evidence accumulates. The plan that exists in month 18 looks different from the plan that existed at close because it has evolved based on what was learned.

Updating the plan is not moving the goalposts. It is incorporating reality. The goalposts are the outcomes: EBITDA target, cash generation target, exit value target. The plan is the path to reach those goalposts. If the path proves blocked, you find another path. The destination remains.

A practical approach is to maintain two versions of the plan.

The baseline plan is the original plan as approved at close. It serves as a reference point. Performance can be measured against it to understand how reality diverged from expectations.

The current plan is the updated plan reflecting current hypotheses and current evidence. It is the plan the organization is actually executing. It incorporates all pivots and adjustments made since close.

Comparing the two reveals the story of the investment. Where did we outperform our original expectations? Where did we fall short? What did we learn? This comparison is valuable for the current deal and for improving planning on future deals.

The Sponsor Relationship

Treating the plan as a hypothesis has implications for the sponsor relationship.

Sponsors invest based on a thesis and a plan. They expect management to execute that plan. When management says "the plan is a hypothesis," some sponsors hear "we are not committed."

The Coach helps the CEO frame hypothesis-driven execution in terms the sponsor can embrace.

The frame is: commitment to outcomes, flexibility on path.

"We are fully committed to the EBITDA and cash targets we agreed upon. We are also committed to continuously learning and adapting our approach based on what we discover. The market is not static. Our competitors are not static. Our customers are not static. A rigid plan that ignores changing conditions will underperform a dynamic plan that adapts to them."

"We will be transparent about which assumptions are holding and which are under pressure. We will bring you evidence, not excuses. When we need to pivot, we will tell you why and what we are doing instead. We would rather adjust course early than defend a plan that is not working."

Most sponsors, when presented this way, appreciate the approach. They have seen too many management teams defend failing plans until the gap became undeniable. A team that surfaces issues early and adapts proactively is a team they can trust.

The Cultural Dimension

Hypothesis-driven execution requires a specific culture. The Coach helps build it.

Intellectual honesty. The willingness to acknowledge when evidence contradicts belief. To say "I was wrong" without shame. To value truth over ego.

Curiosity. The interest in understanding why results differ from expectations. Not to assign blame, but to learn. The variance investigation that produces insight.

Adaptability. The willingness to change course when evidence warrants. To release attachment to prior plans. To embrace new approaches.

Speed. The urgency to test hypotheses quickly, interpret evidence rapidly, and pivot without delay. In PE, time is the scarcest resource. Slow learning is expensive learning.

Psychological safety. The environment where people can surface disconfirming evidence without fear. Where the messenger of bad news is thanked rather than punished. Where challenge is welcomed.

Building this culture is a leadership task. The CEO must model the behaviors. The Coach must reinforce them. Over time, hypothesis-driven execution becomes not a methodology but a mindset.

The Learning Organization

The ultimate goal is to build an organization that learns faster than the market changes.

Such an organization treats every initiative as an experiment. It defines what it expects to happen, observes what actually happens, and extracts lessons from the difference.

Such an organization treats every variance as information. Not noise to be explained away, but signal to be investigated. The variance that seems anomalous today may reveal a pattern that matters tomorrow.

Such an organization treats every pivot as progress. Not a failure to be hidden, but an adaptation to be celebrated. The pivot represents learning applied.

In PE, where the timeline is compressed and the margin for error is thin, this learning capability is a competitive advantage. The portfolio company that learns faster will outperform the one that clings to outdated plans.

The Coach builds learning capability by installing the disciplines described in this chapter: explicit hypotheses, assumption registers, early warning indicators, 90-day review cycles, disciplined pivots, living plans. These are the mechanics of organizational learning applied to value creation.

Coach Cards Referenced

- **Assumption register for tracking key hypotheses**
- **90-day hypothesis review cycle**
- **Leading indicators versus lagging indicators**
- **Living plan: baseline versus current**
- **5 Whys for investigating variances**
- **70% decision rule for pivot decisions**
- **Commitment to outcomes, flexibility on path**

Field Drills

- **Identify the ten most important assumptions in your value creation plan.** Write each as an explicit, testable hypothesis.
- **Create an assumption register.** Assign an owner to each assumption. Define the indicators that will tell you if it is holding.
- **Review your last three significant variances from plan.** Did you investigate the root cause, or did you rationalize and move on?
- **Identify the leading indicators for your three largest initiatives.** Are you tracking them? What are they telling you?
- **Schedule a 90-day hypothesis review.** Make it a standing item on the quarterly calendar.

Clinic Questions

- Are the key assumptions in our value creation plan explicit, or are they buried in spreadsheets?
- How quickly do we recognize when a hypothesis is failing? Do we have early warning indicators?
- When results diverge from plan, do we investigate or rationalize?

- When was the last time we made a significant pivot? How did we handle it?
- Does our culture support intellectual honesty, or do people tell leadership what they want to hear?
- Is our plan a living document that evolves, or a historical artifact we defend?
- How does our sponsor react when we surface assumption challenges? Is there trust?

Chapter 15

Digital, AI, and Modern Signals

The board meeting had gone smoothly until the sponsor partner asked a question that changed the room's temperature.

"What is your AI strategy?"

The CEO paused. The company had invested in a new ERP system. They had dashboards. They had automated some manual processes. But an AI strategy? That felt like something for technology companies, not a regional services business.

"We are using technology to improve efficiency," the CEO offered. "Our new ERP gives us better visibility. We have automated invoicing. We are exploring some analytics for forecasting."

The sponsor pressed. "But what about AI specifically? Machine learning? What is the competitive moat this business is building in the digital era?"

The CEO had no good answer. The meeting moved on, but the question lingered.

This exchange captures a tension that exists in many PE-backed companies. Digital transformation and artificial intelligence have moved from buzzwords to board-level expectations. Sponsors increasingly view technology capability as a driver of value and a component of exit multiple. Yet many portfolio companies, particularly in traditional industries, are uncertain about what this means for them practically.

The Coach's role is to help leadership navigate this terrain without falling into two traps: dismissing technology as irrelevant to their business, or chasing technology for its own sake without connection to value creation.

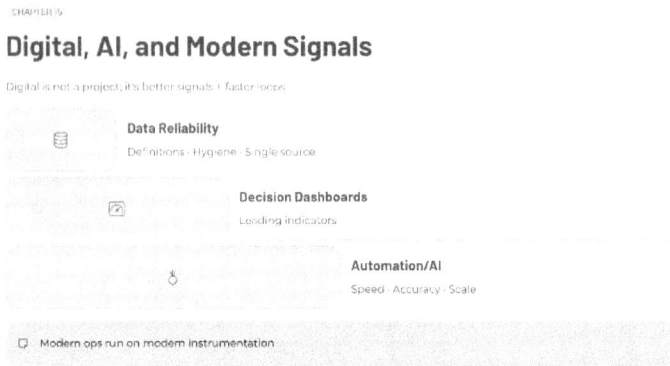

CHAPTER 15

Digital, AI, and Modern Signals

Digital is not a project; it's better signals + faster loops.

Data Reliability
Definitions · Hygiene · Single source

Decision Dashboards
Leading indicators

Automation/AI
Speed · Accuracy · Scale

Modern ops run on modern instrumentation

The Technology Question in PE

Technology has always mattered in business. What has changed is the speed of change and the stakes involved.

Digital capabilities that were differentiators five years ago are now table stakes. Customers expect digital interfaces. Employees expect modern tools. Competitors who embrace technology gain efficiency advantages that compound over time.

Artificial intelligence has added another dimension. AI is not just automation of existing processes. It is the capability to make predictions, identify patterns, and optimize decisions in ways that were previously impossible. Companies that harness AI effectively can achieve step-function improvements in efficiency, customer experience, and strategic insight.

For PE, these dynamics create both opportunity and risk.

The opportunity is value creation through technology. Digital transformation can drive margin improvement, revenue growth, and multiple expansion. A company that demonstrates technology sophistication commands a premium from buyers who see scalability and defensibility.

The risk is technology obsolescence. A company that falls behind technologically may find its competitive position eroding. Buyers discount businesses that require significant technology investment to remain competitive.

The sponsor question, "What is your AI strategy?" is really asking: Is this business positioned for the future, or is it a legacy asset that will require rescue investment?

Cutting Through the Hype

Technology discussions are plagued by hype. Vendors promise transformation. Consultants propose initiatives. The business press breathlessly covers the latest advances.

The Coach helps the CEO cut through the hype with practical questions.

What specific problem are we solving? Technology is a tool. Tools are valuable when they solve problems. A technology initiative without a clear problem statement is likely to waste resources.

What is the expected impact? In financial terms, what will this technology investment deliver? Cost reduction? Revenue increase? Risk mitigation? The business case should be quantified.

What is the implementation reality? How long will it take? What resources are required? What organizational change is needed? What could go wrong?

What is the alternative? If we do not make this investment, what happens? Is the risk of inaction greater than the risk of action?

These questions apply whether the technology in question is basic automation or advanced AI. The evaluation framework is the same: problem, impact, implementation, alternative.

The Technology Audit

Before developing a technology strategy, the organization needs an honest assessment of its current state.

The technology audit examines several dimensions.

Core systems. What are the foundational systems that run the business? ERP, CRM, HR systems, operational technology. Are they modern and integrated, or legacy and fragmented? Do they provide accurate, timely data?

Data quality. How good is the data? Is it complete, accurate, and accessible? Or is it scattered across systems, inconsistent in format, and difficult to extract?

Digital capabilities. What can the organization do digitally? E-commerce, digital marketing, online customer service, mobile access. How do these capabilities compare to competitors?

Automation level. What processes have been automated? What remains manual? Where is manual effort creating cost or error?

Analytics maturity. What decisions are informed by data and analytics? What remains intuition-based? Is there capability to do predictive analytics, or only descriptive?

Technology talent. Does the organization have people who understand technology? Can they evaluate options, manage implementations, and maintain systems?

Technology culture. Is the organization open to technology change, or resistant? Have past technology initiatives succeeded or failed?

The audit produces a baseline understanding. From here, the organization can prioritize where technology investment will create the most value.

CHAPTER 15

Signal Map

Stop steering with lagging metrics

Lagging	Leading
Important, but late	Early warning signals
• Revenue	• Pipeline velocity
• EBITDA	• Retention drivers
• Cash balance	• Unit economics
	• Cycle time
	• Price realization
	• Forecast accuracy

If you only look backward, you will only manage regret

The Value-Driven Technology Agenda

Technology strategy should be driven by value creation, not by technology for its own sake.

The value-driven approach starts with the value creation plan. What are the initiatives that will drive EBITDA growth, margin expansion, and multiple improvement? Which of these initiatives have technology implications?

Revenue growth initiatives might require CRM enhancement, e-commerce capability, marketing automation, or customer analytics.

Margin improvement initiatives might require process automation, procurement systems, workforce management tools, or operational optimization.

Working capital initiatives might require better forecasting, automated invoicing and collections, or inventory optimization systems.

Risk reduction initiatives might require cybersecurity hardening, compliance systems, or business continuity infrastructure.

For each value creation initiative, the technology question is: What technology enablement is required? The technology agenda becomes the set of technology investments needed to execute the value creation plan.

This approach prevents technology sprawl. The technology investments are justified by their connection to specific value creation outcomes. Projects that do not connect to value creation do not make the agenda.

AI for EBITDA: Five Applications That Move the P&L

For most PE-backed companies, AI should not be a science project. It should be a profit lever.

The question is not "What is our AI strategy?" in the abstract. The question is: "Where can AI directly impact EBITDA within twelve months?"

Application 1: Automating Accounts Payable and Accounts Receivable

The Opportunity: AP/AR departments are labor-intensive. Invoice processing, matching, coding, exception handling, collection follow-up. Much of this work is repetitive and rule-based, which is exactly where AI excels.

The Implementation: Modern AI-powered AP/AR platforms can automate 70 to 80 percent of invoice processing. They read invoices (even paper ones via OCR), match to purchase orders, code to the correct GL accounts, flag exceptions, and route approvals. On the AR side, they automate collection workflows, predict payment timing, and prioritize follow-up.

The EBITDA Impact: A company processing 50,000 invoices annually with a five-person AP team can typically reduce to two people, saving 200,000 to 300,000 dollars in direct labor. Faster processing also improves working capital: accelerating collections by three days on 50 million in receivables releases over 400,000 dollars in cash.

Time to Value: Three to six months for full implementation.

What the Coach asks: "How many FTEs are touching invoices? What would happen if that number dropped by 60 percent?"

Application 2: Predictive Customer Churn Reduction

The Opportunity: Churn is a silent killer in recurring revenue businesses. By the time a customer cancels, it is too late. The signals of dissatisfaction existed months earlier, buried in data.

The Implementation: AI models analyze customer behavior patterns: usage frequency, support ticket volume, payment delays, engagement with communications, feature adoption. The model identifies customers with high churn probability 60 to 90 days before they leave, enabling proactive intervention.

The EBITDA Impact: In a SaaS business with 20 million ARR and 15 percent annual churn, reducing churn by 3 percentage points saves 600,000 dollars annually. More importantly, retained customers expand over time. The lifetime value impact often exceeds the direct retention savings by 2 to 3x.

Time to Value: Four to eight months, depending on data readiness.

What the Coach asks: "Do we know which customers are at risk before they tell us? If not, we are playing defense."

Application 3: Dynamic Pricing Optimization

The Opportunity: Most companies price based on cost-plus, competitor matching, or historical precedent. None of these approaches capture the full value customers are willing to pay. Money is left on the table daily.

The Implementation: AI-powered pricing tools analyze transaction data, customer characteristics, competitive positioning, and market conditions to recommend optimal prices. For B2B, this means deal-specific guidance for the sales team. For B2C or e-commerce, this means automated price adjustments.

The EBITDA Impact: Pricing is the most powerful margin lever. A 2 percent improvement in realized price flows directly to EBITDA. On 100 million in revenue, that is 2 million of incremental profit with zero additional cost.

Time to Value: Two to four months for initial deployment, with continuous improvement.

What the Coach asks: "When did we last systematically analyze whether our prices are optimized? What data are we using?"

Application 4: Demand Forecasting and Inventory Optimization

The Opportunity: Inventory is cash sitting on shelves. Too much inventory ties up working capital and creates obsolescence risk. Too little creates stockouts and lost sales. The balance is difficult to maintain with traditional forecasting.

The Implementation: AI-powered demand forecasting analyzes historical sales, seasonality, promotions, market trends, and external factors to predict demand with greater accuracy. The improved forecast enables leaner inventory with better service levels.

The EBITDA Impact: A distribution company with 15 million in inventory can typically reduce inventory by 15 to 20 percent while maintaining or improving fill rates. That is 2.5 to 3 million of cash released. Additionally, reduced obsolescence and warehousing costs contribute 100,000 to 200,000 dollars to EBITDA annually.

Time to Value: Four to six months.

What the Coach asks: "What are our inventory turns? How much cash is trapped in slow-moving stock?"

Application 5: Intelligent Document Processing for G&A Reduction

The Opportunity: Back-office functions spend enormous time processing documents: contracts, compliance forms, HR paperwork, customer applications, regulatory filings. Much of this is manual review and data entry.

The Implementation: AI document processing extracts information from unstructured documents, classifies and routes them, checks for completeness, and flags exceptions. Applications include contract analysis, loan processing, insurance claims, compliance documentation, and employee onboarding.

The EBITDA Impact: Varies by process, but 50 to 70 percent reduction in processing time is typical. A financial services company processing 10,000 applications annually might save 300,000 to 500,000 dollars in labor while improving processing speed and accuracy.

Time to Value: Three to six months.

What the Coach asks: "Where are our people doing work that a machine could do? What would they do instead if that work disappeared?"

The AI Implementation Discipline

AI initiatives fail when they are treated as technology projects rather than business transformations.

Start with the P&L impact. Quantify the expected benefit before investing. If the benefit is not clear, the initiative should not start.

Ensure data readiness. AI requires data. If the data does not exist, is not clean, or is not accessible, the AI will fail. Assess data readiness before committing.

Plan for change management. AI changes how people work. The AP clerk whose job changes, the salesperson who must use pricing guidance, the operations planner who must trust the forecast. Without adoption, the technology delivers nothing.

Measure rigorously. Track actual P&L impact against the business case. Did the savings materialize? Did the churn reduction occur? Measurement creates accountability.

Start small, then scale. Pilot in one function or one region. Prove the impact. Then expand. This reduces risk and builds organizational confidence.

The Coach ensures AI initiatives are grounded in EBITDA reality, not technology fascination. Every AI investment should answer: "How does this improve profit or cash within the next twelve months?"

The Data Foundation

AI and advanced analytics require data. Without quality data, AI initiatives fail.

The data foundation includes several elements.

Data availability. The data needed for analysis must exist and be accessible. If customer behavior data is not captured, customer analytics is impossible.

Data quality. The data must be accurate, complete, and consistent. AI trained on bad data produces bad results. The phrase "garbage in, garbage out" applies directly.

Data integration. Data often resides in multiple systems. For analysis, it must be integrated into a coherent view. A customer 360 view, for example, requires integrating CRM, transaction, service, and marketing data.

Data infrastructure. There must be systems capable of storing, processing, and analyzing data at scale. Cloud data platforms have made this more accessible, but capability must be built.

Data governance. There must be clarity about who owns data, who can access it, how it should be protected, and how quality is maintained.

For many PE-backed companies, the data foundation is the first investment. Before advanced analytics or AI, the basics must be in place. Clean, integrated, accessible data is a prerequisite.

The Coach helps the CEO assess data readiness and prioritize data foundation work when needed.

Cybersecurity: The Downside Risk

Technology creates upside opportunity but also downside risk. Cybersecurity is the most significant risk for most businesses.

Cyber attacks are increasingly common and increasingly damaging. Ransomware can halt operations. Data breaches can expose customer information and trigger regulatory penalties. Business email compromise can result in fraudulent payments.

For PE-backed companies, cybersecurity matters for several reasons.

Business continuity. A successful cyber attack can disrupt operations for days or weeks. The operational and financial impact can be severe.

Regulatory compliance. Depending on the industry, there may be regulatory requirements for data protection. Non-compliance creates legal and financial risk.

Due diligence exposure. Buyers conduct cybersecurity due diligence. Weaknesses identified during exit due diligence can reduce price or kill deals.

Insurance implications. Cyber insurance is increasingly important, and insurers are increasingly demanding. Poor cybersecurity posture can increase premiums or limit coverage.

The Coach ensures that cybersecurity is on the CEO's agenda. This does not mean the CEO becomes a cybersecurity expert. It means they ensure that someone competent is managing cybersecurity, that basic protections are in place, that the organization is prepared for incidents, and that the board is informed about cyber risk.

A practical starting point is a cybersecurity assessment by a qualified third party. This identifies gaps and provides a roadmap for remediation.

Speed to Insight and Cost Takeout

For PE-backed companies, technology investments must connect to two outcomes: faster information and lower costs. Everything else is optional.

Speed to insight means getting the data you need to make decisions before the window closes. Cost takeout means using technology to reduce the human effort required to run the business.

Both drive EBITDA. Both support exit multiples. Both should dominate your technology agenda.

The Monthly Close. How many days after month-end do you have reliable financials? If the answer is ten or more, you are flying blind for a third of every month.

Modern financial systems enable a Day 3 or Day 5 close. This requires automated reconciliations, integrated subledgers, and elimination of manual spreadsheet work. The investment is modest. The payoff is visibility.

A company that closes in three days can identify problems in week one and intervene. A company that closes in fifteen days discovers problems when it is too late to affect the month.

Real-Time Dashboards. The weekly KPI review should not require an analyst to pull data. The dashboard should refresh automatically. Leadership should see current performance, not last week's snapshot.

Cloud-based BI tools enable this. The barrier is not technology. It is data integration. Invest in connecting your systems so the dashboard reflects reality.

Customer Health Visibility. Do you know which customers are at risk today? Or do you discover churn after it happens?

AI-powered customer health scoring integrates usage data, support interactions, payment patterns, and engagement signals to predict risk. The output is a prioritized list for intervention, updated daily.

The Build Versus Buy Decision

Technology capability can be built internally, purchased from vendors, or acquired through technology-enabled services.

The build option provides maximum customization and control but requires internal capability and takes time.

The buy option provides faster implementation and external expertise but may not perfectly fit requirements and creates vendor dependency.

The services option outsources entire functions to providers who bring technology capability. Payroll, IT support, marketing automation, and many other functions can be delivered as services.

For most PE-backed companies, the bias should be toward buy and services rather than build. The timeline is too short to build custom technology. The scale may not justify the investment. The risk of failed internal development is high.

Cloud-based software has made the buy option much more accessible. Modern SaaS applications provide sophisticated capability with minimal implementation burden. The CFO can implement a new forecasting tool in weeks rather than months.

The CRO can deploy marketing automation without a technology team.

The Coach helps the CEO evaluate build versus buy decisions by asking: What is the core competency we must own? For most companies, the answer is not technology development. Technology is an enabler, not the core business.

Technology and Exit Multiple

Technology capability increasingly affects exit multiple.

Buyers evaluate technology as part of due diligence. They assess:

Systems modernity. Are core systems modern and scalable, or legacy and constrained?

Data capability. Is data available, integrated, and actionable?

Digital presence. Does the business have appropriate digital capabilities for its market?

Automation level. Are processes efficiently automated, or is there manual overhead that creates cost and risk?

Cybersecurity posture. Are basic protections in place? Is the business managing cyber risk appropriately?

Technology talent. Are there people who can maintain and advance technology capability?

Weaknesses in any of these areas create concern. The buyer must factor in the investment required to remediate.

Strengths in these areas support premium valuation. The buyer sees a business that is positioned for the future and does not require rescue investment.

The Coach helps the CEO understand how technology will be perceived at exit and prioritize investments that address gaps.

Avoiding Technology Theater

Technology theater is investment that looks impressive but does not create value.

The dashboard no one uses. Expensive BI implementation, beautiful visualizations, no change in decisions.

The AI pilot that never scales. Proof of concept succeeds, production implementation never happens, value never materializes.

The ERP upgrade that takes three years. By the time it is complete, the hold period is over and the buyer inherits the disruption.

The digital transformation with no transformation. New technology layered on old processes. Cost increases. Benefit does not.

The Coach ensures technology investments are grounded in reality. Clear problem statement. Quantified benefit. Realistic implementation timeline. Accountability for results.

Technology should accelerate value creation. It should not become a distraction from it.

Coach Cards Referenced

- **Technology audit across core systems, data, digital, automation, analytics**

- **Value-driven technology agenda connected to value creation initiatives**
- **Build versus buy decision framework**
- **Cybersecurity as board-level risk**
- **Technology roadmap over the hold period**
- **Data foundation as prerequisite for advanced analytics**

Field Drills

- **Conduct a technology audit.** Assess core systems, data quality, digital capabilities, automation, analytics maturity, and cybersecurity. Identify the three biggest gaps.
- **Map technology requirements to your value creation initiatives.** What technology enablement does each initiative require?
- **Commission a cybersecurity assessment.** Understand your current posture and prioritize remediation.
- **Evaluate one AI use case for your business.** Define the problem, the expected impact, and the implementation requirements.
- **Build a technology roadmap for the hold period.** What investments are needed in year one, year two, and year three?

Clinic Questions

- How would a buyer evaluate our technology capability? What would they see as strengths and weaknesses?
- Do we have a data foundation that supports analytics and AI, or is our data fragmented and unreliable?
- What is our cybersecurity posture, and when did we last assess it?
- Are we investing in technology based on value creation logic, or based on vendor pressure and buzzwords?

- Do we have the internal capability to evaluate, implement, and maintain technology, or are we dependent on external help?
- How would our leadership team answer the question "What is your AI strategy?"
- What technology investment, if made now, would have the biggest impact on our exit multiple?

PART VI

THE EXIT AND THE STORY

Building Credibility Before the Process Begins

Chapter 16

Exit Readiness Starts Now

The CEO was surprised by the question.

"We just closed six months ago. Why are we talking about exit?"

The operating partner smiled. "Because exit readiness is not something you do at the end. It is something you build from the beginning. Every decision we make, every system we install, every story we tell should make this company more valuable to the next owner."

This reframe changed how the CEO thought about the work ahead. Not as a holding pattern until exit, but as a deliberate construction of value that would be recognized and rewarded when the time came.

Exit readiness is not exit preparation. Exit preparation is the frantic work that happens in the final months: cleaning up financials, preparing management presentations, rehearsing for buyer meetings. By then, most of the value has already been determined. You are packaging what exists, not creating what should exist.

Exit readiness is the continuous discipline of building a company that a buyer will want to own. It starts on day one and continues throughout the hold period. It shapes operating decisions, organizational investments, and narrative development. It ensures that when exit preparation begins, there is something excellent to prepare.

CHAPTER 15

Exit Readiness Starts Now

Build for the buyer's diligence questions from Day 1

Today ---- 1
Initial proof point establishes

2 ---- Quarterly Proof Points
Revenue quality · Margin · Cash · Leadership · Systems

QoE-Ready ---- 3
Clean data room

4 ---- Buyer Confidence
Durability · growth story

Exit ---- 5
Premium multiple

ⓘ Exit readiness is operational hygiene, not a last-minute sprint

The Buyer's Perspective

Exit readiness requires thinking like a buyer.

A buyer considering your company asks a series of questions. The answers to these questions determine both whether they will buy and what they will pay.

Is the business growing? Buyers pay for growth because growth means the business will be larger and more profitable in the future. Sustainable growth commands higher multiples than one-time spikes.

Are the economics attractive? Gross margins, EBITDA margins, capital efficiency, cash conversion. Buyers want businesses that generate returns on invested capital.

Is the growth sustainable? What is the moat? Why will this business continue to win? Is growth coming from market expansion, share gains, pricing, or new products? How durable is each source?

Is the business predictable? Can management forecast accurately? Are there recurring revenue streams? Is customer retention strong? Predictability reduces risk, and reduced risk supports higher multiples.

Is the management team capable? Will the team stay and perform under new ownership? Is there depth beyond the CEO? Are key roles filled with strong performers?

Are there risks to understand? Customer concentration, regulatory exposure, technology obsolescence, key person dependencies. What could go wrong?

Is the story compelling? Does the investment thesis make sense? Is there a credible path to continued value creation?

Every decision during the hold period either strengthens or weakens the answers to these questions. Exit readiness is the discipline of consistently strengthening them.

The Exit Readiness Framework

Exit readiness can be organized around six dimensions. The Coach helps the CEO assess and improve each dimension throughout the hold period.

Financial quality. The cleanliness, accuracy, and credibility of financial reporting. Adjusted EBITDA that can withstand scrutiny. Clear bridge from EBITDA to cash. Minimal related-party transactions. Consistent accounting policies. Auditable records.

Operational excellence. The efficiency and scalability of operations. Documented processes. Performance metrics. Quality systems. Operational resilience. A business that runs smoothly, not one that depends on heroic effort.

Strategic position. The market position and competitive advantage. Growing markets. Defensible differentiation.

Customer diversity. Supplier relationships. A clear answer to "why will this business continue to win?"

Organizational capability. The strength and depth of the team. A capable CEO. A complete leadership team. Succession for key roles. Culture that attracts and retains talent. An organization that will perform under new ownership.

Risk profile. The identification and mitigation of key risks. Customer concentration reduced. Regulatory compliance ensured. Cybersecurity addressed. Legal matters resolved. Insurance adequate. Contingencies planned.

Growth story. The credible narrative for continued value creation. Clear growth levers. Evidence of execution. A roadmap that the next owner can believe and extend.

Each dimension requires attention throughout the hold period. Weaknesses identified early can be addressed. Weaknesses discovered during due diligence become discounts.

CHAPTER 16

Buyer Lens Scorecard

What increases multiple, what compresses it

Multiple Expanders
- Durable growth
- Low customer concentration
- Strong management bench
- Clean data
- Scalable systems

Multiple Compressors
- Surprises
- Heroics
- Single points of failure
- Weak reporting
- Messy cash
- Churn risk

You don't 'argue' for a multiple. You earn it.

The KPI-to-Exit Connection

The metrics you track today must be the proof points for the exit narrative you sell in three years.

This is not a coincidence to hope for. It is a discipline to install.

When you select your Vital Few KPIs, you are making a bet about what will matter at exit. The metrics that earn weekly attention from the leadership team will be the metrics with historical trend lines, improvement stories, and credible trajectories when buyers conduct diligence.

Consider the inverse. If customer retention is critical to your exit multiple, but you only start tracking NRR in year three, you have no story. No trend line. No proof of improvement. Buyers will discount what you cannot demonstrate.

The exit-back discipline requires asking a specific question when establishing your operating dashboard:

"If a buyer asked for the historical trend on this metric, would we be proud of what we show them?"

For each Vital Few KPI, project forward to the exit conversation:

Revenue growth rate. Buyers will want to see consistent, accelerating growth. If you are tracking quarterly revenue but not the underlying drivers (pipeline, win rate, average deal size, expansion revenue), you will not be able to explain the trend or project it forward credibly.

Customer retention and NRR. Buyers pay premium multiples for businesses where customers stay and grow. If you start tracking retention in year one, you have three years of proof. If you start in year three, you have a single data point.

Gross margin by product and customer. Buyers will dissect your margin structure. If you cannot show margin trend by segment, you cannot demonstrate mix improvement or pricing discipline.

Cash conversion cycle. Buyers, especially PE buyers, care intensely about working capital efficiency. A three-year trend showing DSO improvement from 55 to 42 days is a compelling story. No historical data means no story.

EBITDA bridge. The ability to walk from prior year EBITDA to current year EBITDA, showing the contribution of each driver (volume, price, cost, mix), demonstrates management sophistication. Build this bridge monthly so you have it quarterly and annually.

Initiative ROI. For each major value creation initiative, track the investment and the return. At exit, you want to show: "We invested X in commercial transformation and generated Y in incremental EBITDA." This is a proof point of execution capability.

The practical discipline is this: when you build your operating dashboard in month one, ask your banker or M&A advisor what metrics buyers will want to see. Then track those metrics from the beginning.

You cannot manufacture history. You can only create it as you go.

The Proof Point Accumulation System

Exit readiness is not a phase. It is an accumulation.

Every month, you should be adding to your evidence base. Customer wins. Margin improvements. Retention gains. Initiative completions. Each is a proof point that strengthens the exit narrative.

Create a simple proof point log. Update it monthly. Capture:

What happened. The specific win or improvement.

When it happened. The date.

The metric impact. Revenue, margin, retention, efficiency.

The narrative value. How this supports the exit story.

By month 36, you should have 30 to 50 meaningful proof points. These become the raw material for the management presentation, the CIM, and the buyer conversations.

The CEO who tracks proof points monthly arrives at exit preparation with a compelling portfolio of evidence. The CEO who does not arrives with a scramble to remember what happened and a thin story to tell.

Linking the Cadence to the Exit

The weekly leadership meeting is not just an operating forum. It is an exit preparation engine.

Every week, the team reviews the Vital Few KPIs. Every variance is investigated. Every initiative is tracked. Every decision is documented.

Over three years, this produces:

Trend lines. The visual demonstration of improvement over time.

Variance explanations. The understanding of what drives performance.

Decision records. The evidence of disciplined management.

Initiative outcomes. The proof that the team can execute.

When the buyer's diligence team arrives, you hand them a binder (or data room) that tells a coherent story. Not reconstructed history. Real-time documentation of a well-run company.

The leadership team that operates with cadence creates exit readiness as a byproduct. The leadership team that operates ad hoc creates exit preparation as a scramble.

Financial Quality

Financial quality is foundational. Buyers will scrutinize financials in detail. Weaknesses create concern, delay deals, and reduce price.

Quality of earnings is a specific focus. Buyers will conduct QofE analysis, often with a third-party accounting firm. They will examine every adjustment to EBITDA. They will challenge revenue recognition, expense timing, and one-time items.

The exit-ready company has clean adjustments. Every add-back to EBITDA can be supported with documentation. Non-recurring items are genuinely non-recurring. Run-rate assumptions are defensible.

The exit-ready company has consistent policies. Accounting treatment is consistent year over year. Changes in policy are disclosed and explained. There are no surprises in how revenue is recognized or expenses are categorized.

The exit-ready company has strong controls. Financial processes are documented. Segregation of duties exists. Reconciliations are performed. Auditors provide clean opinions.

The exit-ready company can explain the bridge from EBITDA to cash. Working capital changes are understood. Capital expenditure is categorized between maintenance and growth. Cash conversion is predictable.

The Coach encourages the CEO to commission a sell-side QofE analysis midway through the hold period. This identifies issues that can be addressed before buyers discover them. It is far better to fix problems proactively than to negotiate from weakness during a sale process.

Organizational Capability

Organizational capability determines whether the business can execute its strategy after the transaction.

Buyers need confidence that the team will stay and perform. They are not buying a business that depends on the seller's continued involvement, at least not without a significant earnout.

The exit-ready company has a capable CEO. Someone who can lead under new ownership, manage the board relationship, and drive continued value creation. If the current CEO is departing at exit, a successor should be identified or a transition plan in place.

The exit-ready company has a complete leadership team. All key roles are filled. Performance is strong. There is alignment around strategy and culture.

The exit-ready company has succession depth. For each key role, there is a potential successor identified and developing. The business is not dependent on any single individual.

The exit-ready company has a culture that attracts and retains talent. Employee engagement is strong. Turnover is manageable. The employer brand supports recruiting.

The exit-ready company has employment matters in order. Compensation structures are documented. Key employees have appropriate agreements. There are no lurking employment disputes.

The Coach helps the CEO build organizational capability throughout the hold period. This includes upgrading underperformers, developing successors, and ensuring that the team is ready for transition.

Risk Profile

Every business has risks. Exit readiness requires that risks are identified, understood, and mitigated where possible.

Buyers will conduct extensive due diligence on risks. Unknown risks that surface during diligence create concern and often reduce price. Known risks that are managed demonstrate competence.

Customer concentration is a common risk. If a single customer represents 20 percent or more of revenue, buyers worry about what happens if that customer leaves. The exit-ready company has diversified its customer base or, where concentration exists, has long-term contracts and strong relationships that mitigate the risk.

Regulatory compliance is often scrutinized. The exit-ready company is compliant with applicable regulations. Where there have been compliance issues, they have been remediated and documented.

Legal matters should be resolved. Pending litigation, unresolved disputes, and potential claims create uncertainty. The exit-ready company has resolved what can be resolved and has clear documentation on what remains.

Cybersecurity is increasingly examined. The exit-ready company has appropriate protections in place and can demonstrate its security posture.

The Coach encourages a risk audit midway through the hold period. Identify what a buyer would find concerning and address it before the sale process.

The Timing Paradox

There is a paradox in exit readiness. You must always be ready for exit, but you should not manage to a specific exit date.

The reason you must always be ready is that exit timing is uncertain. Market conditions change. Strategic opportunities emerge. Sponsor needs evolve. You may be asked to exit earlier than planned. You should not be caught unprepared.

The reason you should not manage to a specific exit date is that doing so creates perverse incentives. Decisions get optimized for the exit rather than for the business. Short-term results get prioritized over long-term health. The business is dressed up rather than built up.

The resolution of the paradox is to focus on building a genuinely excellent business. A genuinely excellent business is always exit-ready because it has the qualities that buyers value. Financial quality, operational excellence, strategic position, organizational capability, managed risk, and credible growth story are the attributes of an excellent business, whether or not an exit is imminent.

The Coach helps the CEO hold this perspective. Build the business as if you will own it forever. Build it so that someone else would be thrilled to own it tomorrow.

Coach Cards Referenced

- **Exit readiness framework: financial quality, operational excellence, strategic position, organizational capability, risk profile, growth story**
- **Quality of earnings as a sell-side discipline**
- **Customer concentration as a multiple risk**
- **Proof points as evidence of value creation**
- **Midpoint exit readiness audit**
- **Gap list with remediation plans**

Field Drills

- **Assess your company against the six exit readiness dimensions.** Rate each on a scale of one to five. Identify the two weakest areas.
- **Commission a sell-side quality of earnings analysis.** Identify adjustments that will be challenged and address them.
- **List your top three customer concentration risks.** Develop a plan to diversify or mitigate.
- **Identify five proof points you have built in the past year.** Identify five proof points you want to build in the next year.
- **Conduct an exit readiness audit at the next appropriate interval.** Engage an external perspective for objectivity.

Clinic Questions

- If a buyer approached tomorrow, what would be our biggest vulnerabilities?
- How clean are our financials? Would a quality of earnings analysis produce surprises?
- What risks exist that we have not fully addressed? What would a buyer find concerning in due diligence?
- Do we have a complete, capable leadership team that would give a buyer confidence?
- What is our growth story, and what evidence supports it?

- Are we building a genuinely excellent business, or are we managing to an exit?
- How would our sponsor rate our exit readiness today?

Chapter 17

Coaching the Narrative

The management presentation was technically accurate. Revenue up 12 percent. EBITDA up 18 percent. New product launched. Customer count increased. The slides had all the numbers, all the charts, all the facts.

And yet, the buyers in the room seemed unmoved.

After the presentation, the lead banker pulled the CEO aside. "The numbers are good. But I did not hear a story. I heard a list. What is the narrative? Why should a buyer be excited about this business?"

The CEO was puzzled. "The numbers are the story. We grew. We improved. We executed."

"Numbers are evidence," the banker replied. "The story is what the evidence proves. What makes this business special? What will it become? Why is it worth a premium?"

This exchange captures a truth that many operators miss. Numbers matter, but narrative matters more. In a competitive process, multiple companies will have good numbers. The company that commands a premium is the one whose numbers are embedded in a compelling story.

The Coach's job is to help the CEO understand and craft that narrative, not just for exit, but as an ongoing discipline that shapes how the company is perceived by boards, lenders, employees, and eventually buyers.

Coaching the Narrative

A credible narrative is evidence, not adjectives

1	2	3
Act 1: Starting Truth	**Act 2: Moves**	**Act 3: Proof**
Baseline Constraints	Cadence Levers Team upgrades	Metrics Systems Repeatability

▢ Narrative = strategy + execution + proof

Why Narrative Matters

Narrative matters because humans are storytelling creatures. We make sense of the world through stories. We remember stories better than facts. We are persuaded by stories more than data.

In business, narrative is the structure that gives meaning to data. The same numbers can tell different stories depending on how they are framed.

A company with flat revenue and expanding margins could be positioned as "struggling to grow" or as "successfully pivoting to profitability." A company with high customer acquisition cost could be "burning cash inefficiently" or "investing in growth that will pay off as customers mature." The facts do not change. The narrative determines how the facts are interpreted.

For PE-backed companies, narrative matters at several moments.

Board meetings. The narrative shapes how the board perceives management. A coherent narrative builds confidence. An incoherent narrative creates concern.

Lender relationships. The narrative affects lender appetite and terms. A compelling story of value creation supports access to capital.

Employee communication. The narrative affects engagement and retention. A clear, compelling vision attracts and retains talent.

Exit process. The narrative directly affects valuation. Buyers pay for confidence in the future. The narrative creates that confidence.

The Coach helps the CEO recognize that narrative is a leadership tool, not a marketing exercise.

The Elements of a Strong Narrative

A strong narrative has several essential elements.

The premise establishes the context. What is the market? What is the opportunity? Why does this business exist? The premise sets the stage.

The thesis is the central claim. What is the unique value this business creates? Why does it win? What is the source of competitive advantage? The thesis is the heart of the story.

The evidence supports the thesis. What proof demonstrates that the thesis is true? Financial results, customer wins, market data, operational metrics. Evidence makes the thesis credible.

The trajectory shows where the business is going. What will the future look like? How will the thesis play out over time? What will the business become? The trajectory creates excitement about the future.

The proof of execution demonstrates that management can deliver. What has the team accomplished? What challenges have they overcome? What does their track record say about their ability to execute the trajectory? Proof of execution builds confidence in the team.

Together, these elements create a coherent story: Here is the opportunity. Here is why we win. Here is the evidence. Here is where we are going. Here is why you can trust us to get there.

Crafting the Thesis

The thesis is the most important element. It answers the question: why is this business special?

A weak thesis is generic. "We provide quality products and excellent service." That could describe any business. It does not differentiate. It does not compel.

A strong thesis is specific and defensible. "We are the only provider in our region with both the technical capability and the service infrastructure to handle complex industrial applications. Our customers have no comparable alternative, which gives us pricing power and retention rates above 95 percent."

The thesis should pass several tests.

Is it true? The thesis must be grounded in reality. A thesis that sounds good but cannot be supported by evidence will collapse under scrutiny.

Is it differentiated? The thesis should describe something distinctive about this business. What is different from competitors? What is the source of competitive advantage?

Is it durable? The thesis should describe an advantage that will persist. A temporary advantage does not justify a premium multiple.

Is it relevant to buyers? The thesis should address what buyers care about: growth, margin, predictability, risk. A thesis that is interesting but does not connect to value is not useful.

The Coach helps the CEO develop and refine the thesis. This often requires several iterations. The first version is usually too generic. Subsequent versions become sharper and more compelling.

Building the Evidence Base

A thesis without evidence is an assertion. A thesis with evidence is a case.

The evidence base includes multiple types of support.

Financial evidence. Revenue growth, margin improvement, cash generation. The numbers that demonstrate performance.

Customer evidence. Customer wins, retention rates, Net Promoter Scores, reference accounts. The signals that customers value what the business provides.

Market evidence. Market size, growth rates, competitive positioning. The data that demonstrates the opportunity.

Operational evidence. Efficiency metrics, quality scores, delivery performance. The indicators that the business executes well.

Strategic evidence. Competitive wins, market share gains, successful product launches. The proof that the strategy is working.

Team evidence. Leadership tenure, talent upgrades, succession depth. The indicators that the organization is strong.

The evidence should be curated and organized. Not every fact is relevant. The evidence base should support the thesis and the trajectory. Irrelevant evidence is noise.

The Coach helps the CEO identify the most compelling evidence and organize it into a coherent presentation of proof.

The Trajectory: The Forward Story

Buyers are buying the future, not the past. The trajectory is the forward story that justifies the investment.

The trajectory should be specific. Not "we will continue to grow" but "we will grow revenue 15 percent annually through three specific levers: geographic expansion into the Southeast, product line extension into adjacent applications, and pricing optimization in our core business."

The trajectory should be credible. Each element should be supported by evidence or logic. Why do we believe geographic expansion will work? Because we have already proven the model in our initial market, and the Southeast has similar dynamics.

The trajectory should show upside. The trajectory should create excitement. There should be meaningful value creation potential that a new owner can participate in.

The trajectory should be achievable. Overly aggressive projections undermine credibility. A trajectory that management cannot deliver destroys trust. The right balance shows ambition without fantasy.

The Coach helps the CEO develop a trajectory that is compelling and credible. This requires pressure-testing each element: why do we believe this? What is the evidence? What could go wrong?

The Management Presentation

The management presentation is where the narrative comes to life. It is the CEO's opportunity to tell the story directly to buyers.

The presentation should be CEO-led. While other team members may present portions, the CEO should own the narrative. The CEO's confidence and conviction are part of what buyers are evaluating.

The presentation should follow narrative structure. Premise, thesis, evidence, trajectory, proof of execution. Not a tour of functions or a recitation of slides.

The presentation should anticipate questions. Sophisticated buyers will probe weaknesses. The presentation should address likely concerns proactively, not wait to be caught.

The presentation should be rehearsed. Not scripted to the point of being mechanical, but practiced enough that the CEO is comfortable, confident, and able to handle interruptions gracefully.

The Coach works with the CEO on management presentation skills. This includes message development, slide design, delivery practice, and Q&A preparation. The presentation is a performance, and like any performance, it benefits from rehearsal.

What the Coach notices: The CEO who reads slides instead of telling a story. The presentation that buries the thesis in slide twelve. The Q&A where the CEO becomes defensive rather than curious.

What the Coach says: "You are presenting facts. I need you to tell me a story. Why should I be excited to own this business?"

Narrative Consistency

The narrative must be consistent across audiences and over time.

Consistency across audiences means the story told to the board is the same story told to employees is the same story told to buyers. The facts may be tailored to the audience, but the core narrative is the same. Inconsistency creates confusion and, if discovered, destroys trust.

Consistency over time means the narrative evolves rather than lurches. If the thesis changes dramatically from quarter to quarter, it suggests management does not understand its own business. The narrative should develop as the business develops, with changes explained and connected to prior versions.

The Coach monitors narrative consistency. Are we telling the same story to everyone? Has the story changed, and if so, why and how? Inconsistency is a warning sign that requires attention.

Narrative and Reality

There is a tension between narrative and reality. The narrative is a curated presentation of the business. Reality is messier.

The tension becomes dangerous when narrative departs from reality. When the story management tells is materially different from what is actually happening, credibility is at risk.

The Coach helps the CEO maintain alignment between narrative and reality.

The narrative should be aspirational but grounded. It is appropriate to present the best version of the business. It is not appropriate to present a version that contradicts the facts.

The narrative should acknowledge weaknesses. A narrative that ignores obvious weaknesses is not credible. Sophisticated audiences will see through it. Better to acknowledge weaknesses and explain how they are being addressed.

The narrative should evolve as reality evolves. If performance diverges from the story, the story must be updated. Clinging to an outdated narrative destroys credibility.

The right frame is that narrative is an honest presentation of the business at its best. Not fiction. Not fantasy. The truth, compellingly told.

CHAPTER 17

Proof Point Library

What to document quarterly — make diligence easy by building the file as you go

Commercial	Operational
Pipeline · Retention · Pricing · Segmentation	Throughput · Quality · Cycle times

Financial	Talent
Cash conversion · Working capital · Forecast accuracy	Org design · Bench strength · Attrition

Digital	Risk
Dashboards · Systems maturity	Controls · Compliance · Concentration

☐ The best story is the one your data can defend

Narrative and Multiple

Narrative directly affects exit multiple.

Two companies with identical financial performance can command different multiples based on narrative. The company with a compelling growth story and credible trajectory will trade at a premium to the company that is just a collection of numbers.

The multiple reflects buyer confidence. Confidence that the business will perform. Confidence that growth will materialize. Confidence that risks are manageable. Confidence that the investment will pay off.

Narrative creates confidence. It provides the framework for understanding the numbers. It addresses concerns before they become objections. It paints a picture of the future that buyers want to own.

The Coach helps the CEO understand the multiple implications of narrative. What story would support a 9x multiple versus a 7x multiple? What evidence and trajectory would justify the premium? Working backward from the desired multiple clarifies what the narrative must achieve.

When the Story Is Weak

Sometimes the story is weak. The business has challenges that cannot be narratively erased. The thesis is not compelling. The evidence is thin. The trajectory is uncertain.

In these cases, the Coach helps the CEO face reality. A weak story cannot be fixed with better slides. It can only be fixed with better performance.

If the thesis is not compelling, the strategic work is to build a better competitive position.

If the evidence is thin, the operational work is to generate proof points.

If the trajectory is uncertain, the planning work is to develop credible growth paths.

The narrative reflects the business. To improve the narrative, improve the business.

The Coach helps the CEO see the narrative as a diagnostic. Where is the narrative weak? That is where operational focus is needed. The work to improve the narrative is the work to improve the business.

Coach Cards Referenced

- **Narrative elements: premise, thesis, evidence, trajectory, proof of execution**
- **Thesis as the central differentiating claim**
- **Evidence base curated and organized**
- **Management presentation as CEO-led narrative delivery**
- **Narrative consistency across audiences and over time**
- **Multiple expansion through narrative confidence**

Field Drills

- **Write your thesis in two sentences.** What makes this business special? Test it with someone outside the company. Does it resonate?
- **Catalog your evidence base.** List the financial, customer, market, operational, strategic, and team evidence that supports your thesis.
- **Develop your trajectory narrative.** What are the specific growth levers? What evidence supports each? What could challenge them?
- **Conduct a management presentation practice session** with the Coach or advisor. Get feedback on message, delivery, and Q&A handling.
- **Audit narrative consistency.** Compare the story told to the board, employees, and lenders. Are they aligned?

Clinic Questions

- What is our thesis? Can our CEO articulate it clearly in two sentences?
- What evidence supports our thesis? Is the evidence compelling and documented?
- What is our trajectory narrative? Is it specific, credible, and exciting?
- How consistent is our narrative across audiences? Are there gaps or contradictions?

- How well does our narrative align with reality? Where might we be stretching?
- What questions will sophisticated buyers ask, and how prepared are we to answer them?
- If we improved our narrative, what multiple premium might we achieve?

PART VII

THE TOOLKIT

Numbers, Cards, and Clinics for the Working Coach

Chapter 18

The Canon 50 Coach Cards

Throughout this book, numbers have appeared as coaching tools. The 13-week cash forecast. The Rule of 40. The 70 percent decision rule. The 100-day plan. These are not arbitrary metrics. They are guardrails that shape behavior, force discipline, and translate PE economics into operating reality.

This chapter presents the Canon 50: fifty numbers, rules, and heuristics that every PE Coach should know. Each card contains the concept, its context, when it applies, when it breaks, and the coaching lesson it carries.

These cards are not decorations. They are instruments. Use them in coaching conversations, in board discussions, in leadership meetings, in moments of decision. They create a common language between sponsor, CEO, and Coach. They anchor abstract strategy in concrete discipline.

The cards are organized into eight categories: Cash and Liquidity, Growth and Revenue, Margins and Efficiency, Decision Making, Time and Urgency, Governance and Alignment, People and Organization, and Exit and Value.

Using the Canon as a Coaching Tool

The Canon 50 is not a reference to read once and shelve. It is an active instrument in the coaching practice.

Each card has three uses:

As a standard. The number defines what good looks like. A 13-week cash forecast is the standard. DSO below 45 days is the standard. Covenant headroom above 15 percent is the standard. The standard creates a target.

As a diagnostic. Each card includes a diagnostic question. The question reveals whether the organization is meeting the standard. If the CEO cannot state the cash conversion cycle, that is a finding. If the leadership team has no succession plan, that is a finding. The diagnostic creates insight.

As a conversation starter. The card provides a framework for coaching conversations. "Let us talk about your 13-week forecast. How confident are you in the accuracy? What would it take to improve it?" The conversation creates change.

In practice, the Coach carries a handful of cards into every engagement. The cards shift based on context. A turnaround focuses on Cards 1-5 (cash and liquidity). A growth company focuses on Cards 6-12 (revenue and retention). An exit-ready company focuses on Cards 38-45 (value and readiness).

The Canon is a toolkit. Reach for the right tool at the right moment.

How to Use the Canon 50 Coach Cards

A toolkit for speed, clarity, and repeatable coaching outcomes

Diagnose

Name the **real problem fast**

Align

Create shared language with **CEO + board**

Pick **1 card** per meeting. **No card-stacking.**

Act

Convert discussion into **commitments**

When to Pull a Card

- **Pre-board:** tighten the narrative
- **Post-board:** convert feedback to actions
- **When drift starts:** reset cadence + standards
- **When trust cracks:** restore "no surprises"
- **When exit nears:** proof points over promises

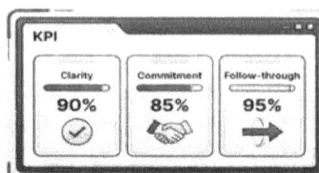

KPI

Clarity	Commitment	Follow-through
90%	85%	95%

Cash and Liquidity

Card 1: The 13-Week Cash Forecast

The Number: 13 weeks of rolling cash projection, updated weekly.

Context: Thirteen weeks is roughly one quarter, long enough to see patterns and short enough to forecast with reasonable accuracy. The rolling nature ensures the forecast stays current.

When It Applies: Every PE-backed company with leverage. Non-negotiable. The 13-week forecast is the heartbeat of cash management.

When It Breaks: In businesses with very long cash cycles (major capital projects, long-term contracts), supplemental longer-range forecasting may be needed. The 13-week remains the operational core.

When to Use This Card: Use when assessing cash discipline and leadership ownership of liquidity. Essential during onboarding, turnarounds, or when covenant headroom is tightening.

Diagnostic Question: Does your CEO review this personally every week? If not, do they truly own the cash?

Coaching Lesson: The 13-week forecast is not a finance exercise. It is a leadership discipline. It forces weekly truth about liquidity. It connects operating decisions to cash consequences. It prevents the "we did not know" moment that destroys trust. If the forecast is consistently inaccurate, that is not a spreadsheet problem. It is an ownership problem.

Card 2: The 12-Month Runway

The Number: Minimum 12 months of cash runway before requiring external financing.

Context: Runway is the time until cash runs out at the current burn rate. Twelve months provides cushion to react to problems and to raise capital from a position of strength rather than desperation.

When It Applies: Growth-stage companies, turnarounds, any situation where cash burn is significant.

When It Breaks: Stable, cash-generative businesses do not think in runway terms. But even profitable businesses should maintain liquidity buffers.

When to Use This Card: Use when evaluating burn rate sustainability, fundraising urgency, or assessing whether leadership has adequate breathing room to execute strategic initiatives.

Diagnostic Question: If revenue stopped tomorrow, how many months could the company survive? Does the leadership team know this number?

Coaching Lesson: Runway creates options. Short runway creates panic. When runway drops below 12 months, everything else becomes secondary. The CEO cannot focus on strategy when they are worried about making payroll in 90 days.

Card 3: Cash Conversion Cycle

The Number: Days Sales Outstanding + Days Inventory Outstanding - Days Payables Outstanding.

Context: The cash conversion cycle measures how long cash is tied up in operations. A shorter cycle means cash flows faster. Each day reduced releases cash.

When It Applies: Any business with meaningful working capital. Particularly important in distribution, manufacturing, and businesses with physical inventory.

When It Breaks: Service businesses with minimal inventory may focus primarily on DSO and DPO.

When to Use This Card: Use when diagnosing working capital inefficiency or when seeking quick wins to release trapped cash. Critical for businesses with inventory or extended receivables.

Diagnostic Question: Can your CFO state the current cash conversion cycle without looking it up? If not, is working capital being managed or just measured?

Coaching Lesson: Working capital is often the largest controllable cash lever. A five-day improvement in the cash conversion cycle can release millions in cash. Yet many leadership teams cannot state their current cycle or their improvement targets.

Card 4: Covenant Headroom

The Number: Minimum 15-20% headroom on leverage and coverage covenants.

Context: Covenants are trip wires. Breaching them triggers lender intervention. Headroom provides buffer against unexpected performance shortfalls.

When It Applies: Any leveraged business with financial covenants.

When It Breaks: If headroom is abundant (40%+), it may not need weekly monitoring. But most PE-backed companies operate with tighter margins.

When to Use This Card: Use when evaluating CEO financial fluency, assessing risk of covenant breach, or determining whether performance volatility creates unacceptable covenant risk.

Diagnostic Question: What is the current headroom to the nearest covenant? If no one can answer immediately, you are flying blind.

Coaching Lesson: Covenant management is not a finance task. It is a leadership responsibility. The CEO should know covenant headroom at all times. Surprises on covenants are among the most damaging events in a sponsor relationship.

Card 5: The 1% Price Rule

The Number: A 1% price increase, with volume held constant, flows directly to EBITDA.

Context: Pricing is the most powerful margin lever. Unlike cost cuts, which require operational change, pricing flows straight to the bottom line.

When It Applies: Any business with pricing discretion. The impact varies by gross margin structure, but the principle holds.

When It Breaks: In commoditized markets with zero pricing power, the lever does not exist. But many businesses have more pricing power than they use.

When to Use This Card: Use when margin improvement is needed quickly or when evaluating whether leadership has pricing discipline. Particularly relevant when costs are rising.

Diagnostic Question: When did the company last raise prices? What prevented it from happening sooner?

Coaching Lesson: Pricing is often under-managed. CEOs fear customer pushback and leave money on the table. A disciplined pricing review often reveals opportunities that have been ignored for years.

Growth and Revenue

Card 6: Rule of 40

The Number: Revenue growth rate + EBITDA margin should equal or exceed 40.

Context: The Rule of 40 balances growth and profitability. A company growing 30% with 10% margins passes. A company growing 10% with 30% margins passes. The rule acknowledges the trade-off between investing in growth and generating current profit.

When It Applies: SaaS and technology businesses primarily. Increasingly applied to other recurring revenue models.

When It Breaks: Early-stage companies may deliberately operate below 40 to capture market share. Mature businesses may exceed 40 comfortably. The rule is a checkpoint, not a mandate.

When to Use This Card: Use when debating growth versus profitability trade-offs, benchmarking SaaS performance, or assessing whether current performance is balanced or lopsided.

Diagnostic Question: What is your current Rule of 40 score? Is the leadership team aligned on whether to prioritize growth or margin?

Coaching Lesson: The Rule of 40 forces a conversation about balance. Should we lean into growth or improve margins? The answer depends on market conditions, competitive dynamics, and investor expectations. The rule frames the trade-off.

Card 7: LTV/CAC Ratio 3:1

The Number: Customer lifetime value should be at least 3x customer acquisition cost.

Context: LTV/CAC measures the efficiency of customer acquisition. A ratio of 3:1 means you get three dollars of value for every dollar spent acquiring a customer. This provides margin for error and funds continued investment.

When It Applies: Subscription businesses, recurring revenue models, any business with measurable acquisition costs and customer lifetimes.

When It Breaks: New products or markets may have unfavorable ratios initially while the model is refined. The ratio should improve as the business matures.

When to Use This Card: Use when evaluating unit economics health, determining whether to scale customer acquisition, or diagnosing whether retention or acquisition efficiency needs improvement.

Diagnostic Question: Do you know this ratio by customer segment? Are you investing in the segments with the best economics?

Coaching Lesson: LTV/CAC is a health indicator. Below 3:1 suggests either acquisition is too expensive or retention is too weak. The ratio points to where the problem is: fix acquisition efficiency or improve retention.

Card 8: CAC Payback Under 12 Months

The Number: The time to recover customer acquisition cost should be under 12 months.

Context: CAC payback measures how quickly a new customer becomes profitable. Under 12 months means cash invested in acquisition is recovered within a year.

When It Applies: Subscription businesses, SaaS, recurring revenue models.

When It Breaks: Enterprise sales with long cycles may have longer payback that is still acceptable if LTV is high. The key is that payback occurs well before the customer relationship ends.

When to Use This Card: Use when assessing whether growth is self-funding or cash-consumptive, or when determining acceptable acquisition spend levels given cash constraints.

Diagnostic Question: Is your go-to-market self-funding, or is growth consuming cash? What would change if payback extended to 18 months?

Coaching Lesson: CAC payback is a cash flow discipline. Long payback means growth consumes cash. Short payback means growth is self-funding. In PE, where cash matters, shorter payback is better.

Card 9: Net Revenue Retention Over 100%

The Number: Revenue from existing customers this year divided by revenue from those same customers last year should exceed 100%.

Context: NRR above 100% means existing customers are spending more over time, even accounting for churn. This is the hallmark of a healthy recurring revenue business.

When It Applies: Subscription and recurring revenue businesses.

When It Breaks: Transactional businesses measure differently. But the principle of growing wallet share applies broadly.

When to Use This Card: Use when evaluating customer success effectiveness, product stickiness, or whether upsell and cross-sell motions are working.

Diagnostic Question: Are your existing customers growing or shrinking? If NRR is below 100%, you are running uphill.

Coaching Lesson: NRR above 100% means you can grow even without acquiring new customers. It is the most efficient form of growth. NRR below 100% means you are running uphill: acquiring new customers just to replace lost revenue from existing ones.

Card 10: Pipeline Coverage 3x

The Number: Sales pipeline should be at least 3x the revenue target for the period.

Context: Not all pipeline converts. A 3x coverage ratio provides buffer for deals that slip or are lost. If historical conversion is 33%, 3x coverage means you should hit target.

When It Applies: B2B sales organizations with defined pipelines.

When It Breaks: If conversion rates are higher, less coverage is needed. If conversion rates are lower or volatile, more coverage is required. The ratio should calibrate to historical performance.

When to Use This Card: Use when forecasting revenue reliability, identifying early warning signs of revenue shortfalls, or assessing sales leadership capability.

Diagnostic Question: What is coverage for next quarter? If it is below 3x, what is being done this week to fix it?

Coaching Lesson: Pipeline coverage is a leading indicator. If coverage falls below 3x, revenue will be at risk in 60-90 days. Watching pipeline coverage weekly provides early warning that allows intervention.

Decision Making

Card 17: The 70% Decision Rule

The Number: Make decisions when you have about 70% of the information you wish you had.

Context: Waiting for perfect information is too slow. The marginal value of additional information rarely exceeds the cost of delay. At 70%, you have enough to make a well-informed bet.

When It Applies: Reversible decisions. The bias should be action.

When It Breaks: Irreversible decisions with high stakes warrant more diligence. Acquisitions, CEO changes, strategic pivots deserve more than 70% certainty.

When to Use This Card: Use when coaching leaders prone to analysis paralysis or when decision velocity is lagging. Essential for creating bias toward action.

Diagnostic Question: What decision is currently stalled waiting for more information? Is that information actually coming?

Coaching Lesson: The 70% rule combats analysis paralysis. It creates a forcing function for decision velocity. In PE, where time is the scarcest resource, faster decisions create more value.

Card 18: Two-Way Door vs. One-Way Door

The Number: Classify decisions as reversible (two-way door) or irreversible (one-way door).

Context: Two-way doors can be walked back. If wrong, reverse course. One-way doors close behind you. If wrong, you live with consequences.

When It Applies: Every decision benefits from this classification.

When It Breaks: Some decisions seem reversible but have hidden switching costs. Be honest about true reversibility.

When to Use This Card: Use when leaders are treating reversible decisions as if they are permanent, or when appropriate caution is needed for irreversible commitments.

Diagnostic Question: What decision are you treating as irreversible that is actually reversible? What would happen if you just tried it?

Coaching Lesson: Most decisions are two-way doors that get treated as one-way doors. The classification reveals where speed is appropriate and where caution is warranted. Speed up two-way doors. Slow down one-way doors.

Card 21: The 5 Whys

The Number: Ask "why" five times to find root cause.

Context: The 5 Whys is a root cause analysis technique from Toyota. Surface explanations are usually symptoms. Repeated "why" questions drive to underlying cause.

When It Applies: Problem-solving, variance analysis, failure investigation.

When It Breaks: Five is not magical. Sometimes root cause emerges in three whys. Sometimes it takes seven. The discipline is relentless pursuit of cause.

When to Use This Card: Use when investigating failures, diagnosing recurring problems, or when surface explanations are preventing real solutions.

Diagnostic Question: When something goes wrong, do you stop at the first explanation, or do you dig until you find the root cause?

Coaching Lesson: Most organizations stop at symptom. The customer churned because they were unhappy. Why were they unhappy? The product underperformed. Why did it underperform? And so on. Root cause analysis reveals what must actually change.

Time and Urgency

Card 23: The 100-Day Plan

The Number: 100 days of focused action with specific deliverables.

Context: The 100-day plan creates urgency and focus at the beginning of a leadership tenure or investment. It forces prioritization and demonstrates early execution.

When It Applies: New CEO onboarding, post-close integration, turnarounds, major transformations.

When It Breaks: If 100 days is already past, create a 100-day plan from now. The number is a forcing function, not a specific calendar requirement.

When to Use This Card: Use when establishing early momentum post-close or post-leadership transition, or when creating accountability for new leaders to deliver quick wins.

Diagnostic Question: Does your current leadership have a 100-day plan, or did urgency disappear after onboarding?

Coaching Lesson: The 100-day plan prevents drift. It transforms vague commitment into specific action. By day 100, everyone knows whether the new leader or new owner is delivering.

Card 25: The 48-Hour Rule

The Number: Align on sensitive topics 48 hours before board meetings.

Context: Surprises in board meetings damage trust. The 48-hour rule ensures the sponsor and CEO are aligned before walking into the room.

When It Applies: Any sensitive board topic: misses, risks, leadership changes, covenant concerns.

When It Breaks: Truly emergent issues may not allow 48 hours. But most sensitive topics are known in advance and should be pre-aligned.

When to Use This Card: Use when preventing board meeting surprises, maintaining triangle trust, or coaching CEOs on sponsor relationship management.

Diagnostic Question: When was the last time a sensitive topic surprised the board? What would have prevented it?

Coaching Lesson: Board meetings should be decision forums, not discovery forums. Pre-alignment enables productive debate without emotional surprise.

Card 26: The 24-Hour Surfacing Norm

The Number: Material issues surface within 24 hours.

Context: In leveraged businesses, slow truth is expensive. The 24-hour norm ensures leadership knows about material issues before they become crises.

When It Applies: Covenant risk, major customer events, safety incidents, cyber events, leadership failures.

When It Breaks: Not everything is material. The organization must define thresholds clearly.

When to Use This Card: Use when establishing transparency norms, diagnosing information flow problems, or building culture where bad news travels fast.

Diagnostic Question: How long does it take for bad news to reach the CEO? The sponsor? Is that fast enough?

Coaching Lesson: The 24-hour norm is a values statement. It says: truth matters more than comfort. How leadership responds to surfaced issues determines whether the norm becomes real.

Governance and Alignment

Card 28: One Voice Outward

The Number: One coherent narrative across all audiences.

Context: Inconsistent messaging creates confusion and erodes trust. The sponsor, CEO, and leadership team must align on what is communicated to board, lenders, employees, and market.

When It Applies: Any multi-stakeholder environment. All PE-backed companies.

When It Breaks: Tailoring detail to audience is appropriate. Contradicting core messages is not.

When to Use This Card: Use when diagnosing messaging consistency, preventing mixed signals to stakeholders, or aligning leadership on communication discipline.

Diagnostic Question: If I asked three executives to describe the company's situation, would I get one story or three?

Coaching Lesson: One voice outward requires discipline. Weekly triangle alignment prevents drift. Pre-alignment before major communications ensures consistency.

Card 29: Weekly Triangle Touchpoint

The Number: 15-30 minutes weekly between sponsor, CEO, and Coach.

Context: The weekly touchpoint maintains alignment, surfaces issues, and prevents side channels. It is the backbone of triangle health.

When It Applies: Throughout the hold period. More frequent in early stages or during stress.

When It Breaks: If the business is running smoothly and trust is high, the cadence might extend. But weekly is the default.

When to Use This Card: Use when establishing triangle cadence, preventing sponsor-CEO drift, or maintaining shared reality across the triangle.

Diagnostic Question: When did the sponsor, CEO, and Coach last speak? What is preventing a weekly rhythm?

Coaching Lesson: The touchpoint prevents surprises. It reduces sponsor anxiety and CEO defensiveness. It keeps one shared reality across the triangle.

People and Organization

Card 32: Level 5 Leadership

The Number: Humility + will. Personal humility combined with professional will.

Context: From Jim Collins, Level 5 leaders channel ego toward organizational success, not personal glory. They take blame and give credit.

When It Applies: CEO selection and development.

When It Breaks: Level 5 is an ideal. Few leaders fully embody it. But aspiration toward Level 5 behaviors is valuable.

When to Use This Card: Use when assessing CEO candidates, coaching leaders on accountability and credit-sharing, or diagnosing whether ego is limiting organizational performance.

Diagnostic Question: Does your CEO take blame and give credit? Or the reverse?

Coaching Lesson: Level 5 leaders build enduring organizations. They are coachable, which enables development. They build teams, which creates depth. They own failures, which enables learning.

Card 33: A-Players Attract A-Players

The Number: Talent begets talent.

Context: Strong performers want to work with other strong performers. Tolerating mediocrity drives away excellence.

When It Applies: Recruiting and performance management.

When It Breaks: Not every role requires an A-player. Some roles require solid B-players who execute reliably.

When to Use This Card: Use when setting talent standards, addressing performance management avoidance, or building organizational talent density.

Diagnostic Question: Who was the last truly exceptional hire? Who brought them in? Are your A-Players recruiting more A-Players?

Coaching Lesson: The first few hires set the talent trajectory. Getting strong people early creates a magnet for more strong people. Settling early creates a ceiling.

Card 34: The 9-Box Talent Grid

The Number: Performance x Potential matrix for talent assessment.

Context: The 9-box plots employees on two dimensions: current performance and future potential. It enables differentiated development and investment. High performers with high potential are your future leaders. High performers with lower potential are your reliable operators. Low performers in any box need action.

When It Applies: Leadership talent management, succession planning, development investment decisions.

When It Breaks: The 9-box can become bureaucratic if over-applied. It is a tool for calibration and conversation, not a rigid classification system. Do not confuse the exercise with actual development.

When to Use This Card: Use when calibrating talent assessments across the leadership team, planning succession, or deciding where to invest development resources. Critical during exit preparation when buyers assess bench strength.

Diagnostic Question: Have you formally assessed your leadership team on performance and potential in the last six months? Can you name who sits in each box?

Coaching Lesson: The 9-box forces uncomfortable conversations. The CFO who performs well but has topped out. The VP who has potential but is not delivering. The grid structures the conversation and prevents avoidance. The value is not the placement. The value is what you do after placement.

Card 35: Succession for Key Roles

The Number: Identified successor for every key role.

Context: Key person dependency is a risk that buyers discount. Succession planning creates organizational resilience and reduces that risk. For each critical role, there should be a name: ready now, ready in 12 months, or external hire required.

When It Applies: All leadership roles, plus specialized roles with unique knowledge. Particularly important for roles where departure would create operational disruption or loss of institutional knowledge.

When It Breaks: In very small organizations, succession may not be feasible for every role. The principle is to reduce single points of failure where possible and have contingency plans where succession is not realistic.

When to Use This Card: Use when preparing for exit, mitigating key person risk, or building organizational depth. Essential when a critical leader shows signs of departure or when buyers begin due diligence.

Diagnostic Question: If your CEO left tomorrow, who would step in? If the answer is "no one," that is a risk that should be priced. Run the same question for CFO, CRO, and any role where the answer creates anxiety.

Coaching Lesson: "What happens if X gets hit by a bus?" is crude but useful. If the answer is "we are in trouble," succession planning is urgent. Buyers will ask this question. Better to have an answer than to be exposed in diligence.

Card 36: The First Team Concept

The Number: Leadership team members' first loyalty is to the leadership team, not their function.

Context: From Patrick Lencioni, the first team concept means executives prioritize the enterprise over their function. The CEO's team, not the functional team, is the primary allegiance. When the CFO sits in the leadership meeting, they are an enterprise leader first and the finance leader second.

When It Applies: All leadership teams. The concept becomes critical when resource trade-offs require one function to sacrifice for enterprise benefit.

When It Breaks: Functional expertise matters. The goal is not to eliminate functional identity but to subordinate it to enterprise priority when they conflict. The CFO should still advocate for finance needs. But when the enterprise requires a different allocation, they should commit.

When to Use This Card: Use when diagnosing silo behavior, improving cross-functional collaboration, or building executive team cohesion. Particularly useful when budget discussions reveal functional advocacy over enterprise thinking.

Diagnostic Question: Do your executives advocate for the enterprise or for their function? Watch what they fight for in budget discussions. Listen for "my team needs" versus "the company needs."

Coaching Lesson: First team behavior prevents silos. It enables trade-offs where one function gives up something for enterprise benefit. Without first team mindset, the leadership meeting becomes a negotiation between functional advocates rather than a unified leadership body. The CEO must model and demand first team behavior.

Card 37: Annual Employee Engagement

The Number: Measure employee engagement at least annually.

Context: Engagement surveys provide signal about organizational health. Engagement predicts retention, productivity, and customer outcomes. Declining engagement is a leading indicator of future problems. Improving engagement is evidence of culture progress.

When It Applies: All organizations of meaningful size. For smaller organizations, pulse surveys or structured conversations may substitute for formal surveys.

When It Breaks: Surveys without action breed cynicism. Only conduct surveys if you will act on results. A survey followed by silence is worse than no survey at all.

When to Use This Card: Use when establishing baseline organizational health, predicting turnover risk, or demonstrating culture improvement to potential buyers. Engagement trends can become part of the exit narrative.

Diagnostic Question: Do you survey engagement and then act on results, or just survey? Can you point to three changes made based on employee feedback in the last year?

Coaching Lesson: Engagement is a leading indicator. Declining engagement predicts future turnover and performance problems. The trend matters more than the absolute score. A score of 65 improving to 72 is better than a score of 75 declining to 70. Watch the direction.

Exit and Value

Card 38: The Value Creation Bridge

The Number: Entry equity $\to$ EBITDA growth $\to$ multiple expansion $\to$ debt paydown $\to$ exit equity.

Context: The bridge visualizes how value is created over the hold period. It shows the contribution of each lever: how much comes from growing EBITDA, how much from improving the multiple, how much from paying down debt. It enables communication about value creation priorities and progress.

When It Applies: Every PE investment. The bridge should be built at close and updated quarterly to show actual versus plan.

When It Breaks: Distressed investments or special situations may have different bridge structures. But the principle of decomposing value creation into its components applies broadly.

When to Use This Card: Use when aligning leadership on value creation strategy, communicating investment thesis to management team, or evaluating which value levers deserve priority. The bridge answers "where is value coming from?"

Diagnostic Question: Can your CEO draw the bridge from entry to exit equity and explain each component? Can they show where you are versus plan?

Coaching Lesson: The bridge translates PE economics into operating terms. It answers: what creates value here? It enables prioritization. If EBITDA growth is the biggest bar, that is where attention should focus. If multiple expansion is key, that shapes different priorities. The bridge makes the abstract concrete.

Card 39: MOIC and IRR

The Number: MOIC = magnitude of return. IRR = speed of return.

Context: Both metrics matter, and they reveal different things. A 3x return is good. A 3x return in 3 years (42% IRR) is excellent. A 3x return in 7 years (17% IRR) is mediocre. MOIC tells you how big the win was. IRR tells you how efficiently capital was deployed over time.

When It Applies: All PE investments. Management should understand both metrics and how their work affects each.

When It Breaks: Early-stage investments may optimize differently, accepting lower IRR for larger MOIC. But the interplay of magnitude and speed applies to all PE-backed companies.

When to Use This Card: Use when coaching management on sponsor urgency, explaining why early wins matter disproportionately, or setting appropriate pace expectations. Essential when management questions why the sponsor pushes for speed.

Diagnostic Question: Does your operating team understand that time is literally money in PE? Do they act like it? When decisions stall for weeks, do they understand the IRR impact?

Coaching Lesson: IRR sensitivity to timing explains why sponsors push for early wins. Value created in year one compounds longer than value created in year three. A dollar of EBITDA improvement in month six is worth more than a dollar in month thirty. Time is money, literally. Management that understands this moves faster.

Card 40: The 2 and 20 Fee Structure

The Number: 2% management fee + 20% carried interest.

Context: The traditional PE fee structure. The fund charges 2% annually on committed capital as a management fee. The fund takes 20% of profits above a hurdle rate as carried interest. Understanding this helps management understand sponsor incentives.

When It Applies: Fund-level economics. Useful for management education about how their sponsor operates.

When It Breaks: Fee structures vary. Some funds have different management fees, different carry splits, or different hurdle rates. The principle of aligned incentives remains.

When to Use This Card: Use when educating management on PE economics, aligning incentives through equity participation, or explaining sponsor motivations. Helps management understand why the sponsor cares about returns.

Diagnostic Question: Does your management team understand how their equity connects to sponsor economics? Do they understand that successful exits benefit both parties?

Coaching Lesson: Understanding sponsor economics creates alignment. The sponsor makes money when investments succeed. Management equity participates in that success. When management understands this, they see the sponsor as a partner in value creation, not an adversary to be managed. Aligned incentives drive aligned behavior.

Card 41: Quality of Earnings Analysis

The Number: Third-party analysis of adjusted EBITDA.

Context: QofE examines every adjustment to reported EBITDA for defensibility. It tests revenue recognition, expense timing, one-time items, and run-rate assumptions. It is how buyers validate what they are paying for. Sell-side QofE identifies issues before buyers do.

When It Applies: Exit preparation and, proactively, midway through the hold period. A sell-side QofE at month 18-24 provides time to address findings.

When It Breaks: Very small transactions may not warrant formal QofE. But the discipline of clean, defensible adjustments applies to every PE-backed company.

When to Use This Card: Use when preparing for exit process, proactively identifying financial presentation issues, or coaching CFOs on EBITDA quality. Essential when adjustments are material or unusual.

Diagnostic Question: What would a sell-side QofE find that we have not already addressed? If you do not know, commission one.

Coaching Lesson: Sell-side QofE identifies problems before buyers do. Issues found early can be addressed: documentation improved, policies changed, adjustments removed. Issues found in buyer due diligence become price reductions or deal killers. The CFO who resists proactive QofE is usually the CFO with something to hide.

Card 42: Customer Concentration Risk

The Number: No single customer above 10-15% of revenue.

Context: Concentration creates risk. If one customer is 25% of revenue and leaves, the business is severely impacted. Buyers discount for concentration because it represents binary risk they cannot underwrite. The discount can be material: a turn of multiple or more.

When It Applies: All businesses, but particularly relevant for exit positioning. Concentration should be measured and tracked throughout the hold period.

When It Breaks: Some business models inherently have concentration: government contractors, specialized suppliers, companies serving a few large enterprises. The goal is to reduce concentration where possible and mitigate through contracts and relationships where it cannot be eliminated.

When to Use This Card: Use when assessing exit readiness, developing diversification strategy, or quantifying customer concentration risk for valuation purposes. Critical when top customer exceeds 15% of revenue.

Diagnostic Question: What percentage of revenue comes from your top customer? Your top five? What is the plan to reduce it? Is that plan working?

Coaching Lesson: Concentration reduction should be an explicit goal with a named owner and tracked progress. It requires deliberate effort to diversify the customer base: new customer acquisition, growth in smaller accounts, sometimes consciously limiting growth with dominant customers. Starting early provides time to make meaningful progress before exit.

Card 43: The 4-6x Leverage Ratio

The Number: Debt to EBITDA ratio typically in the 4-6x range for PE transactions.

Context: Leverage amplifies returns but also amplifies risk. At 5x leverage, a company with 20M EBITDA carries 100M of debt. The debt service on that 100M is non-negotiable. Cash must be managed to service it.

When It Applies: Leveraged buyouts. The specific ratio varies by deal structure, but the 4-6x range is common for sponsored transactions.

When It Breaks: Lower leverage for riskier or more cyclical businesses. Higher leverage where cash flows are very stable and predictable. The ratio should match the business's ability to service debt through cycles.

When to Use This Card: Use when educating management on capital structure, explaining why cash discipline matters, or contextualizing debt service requirements. Essential for management teams new to PE ownership.

Diagnostic Question: Does the operating team understand what leverage means for how they must manage cash? Do they understand that debt service comes before everything else?

Coaching Lesson: Operating teams must understand leverage. The company is not theirs to run as they wish. Debt service is contractual. Covenants are real. Cash generation matters because it services debt. Management that does not understand leverage makes decisions that create unnecessary risk.

Card 44: Exit Readiness Audit

The Number: Formal assessment across six dimensions: financial quality, operational excellence, strategic position, organizational capability, risk profile, growth story.

Context: The audit identifies gaps that would concern buyers before buyers find them. Conducted midway through the hold period, it provides time for remediation. Each dimension is assessed, gaps are identified, and remediation plans are developed.

When It Applies: Every PE investment, typically at the 18-24 month mark or when exit horizon becomes visible. The audit should involve external perspective for objectivity.

When It Breaks: Shorter holds may not have time for a formal audit. But the principle of proactive gap identification applies regardless of timeline.

When to Use This Card: Use when beginning exit preparation, identifying remediation priorities, or creating shared understanding of exit readiness gaps. The audit provides structure for pre-exit work.

Diagnostic Question: If a buyer arrived tomorrow, what would they find that we wish we had already fixed? Have we formally identified those gaps?

Coaching Lesson: What a buyer will find during due diligence is largely knowable. The exit readiness audit surfaces those findings early, enabling proactive improvement rather than reactive negotiation. The management team that has conducted an audit and addressed findings presents with confidence. The team that has not gets surprised.

Card 45: Proof Points

The Number: Concrete demonstrations of value creation capability.

Context: Proof points are evidence that the thesis is working. Customer wins. Margin improvements. Successful initiatives. Team upgrades. Product launches. Market share gains. Each proof point supports the narrative that this business creates value and will continue to do so.

When It Applies: Throughout the hold period, for board communication and exit preparation. Proof points should be tracked monthly and accumulated over time.

When It Breaks: Proof points are not spin. They must be genuine accomplishments that can withstand scrutiny. A proof point that collapses under buyer due diligence is worse than no proof point at all.

When to Use This Card: Use when developing exit narrative, tracking value creation progress, or ensuring quarterly board updates build cumulative evidence. By exit, there should be 30-50 meaningful proof points.

Diagnostic Question: What three proof points have we created in the last six months that support our exit narrative? What will we create in the next six months?

Coaching Lesson: Proof points accumulate over time. Each quarter should add to the evidence base. The CEO who tracks proof points monthly arrives at exit with a compelling portfolio of evidence. The CEO who does not arrives with a scramble to reconstruct what happened. Build the evidence as you go.

Additional Essential Heuristics

Card 46: The Fruitful Five Value Levers

The Number: Five primary levers: grow revenue, expand margins, execute M&A, accelerate debt paydown, expand exit multiple.

Context: All value creation flows through these five levers. They provide a framework for prioritizing initiatives and ensuring the value creation plan is complete. Every initiative should connect to at least one lever.

When It Applies: Value creation planning and execution. The levers should be referenced when evaluating any significant initiative.

When It Breaks: The relative importance of each lever varies by investment thesis. A platform with a buy-and-build thesis emphasizes M&A. A margin turnaround emphasizes efficiency. But all five should be considered.

When to Use This Card: Use when developing value creation plan, prioritizing initiatives, or ensuring balanced portfolio of value creation activities. The levers provide a checklist: are we working all five?

Diagnostic Question: Which of the five levers is getting the least attention? Is that intentional or accidental? What would change if we applied equal rigor to each?

Coaching Lesson: The Fruitful Five provides structure and completeness. Every initiative should connect to one or more levers. Initiatives that do not connect to levers may not belong in the plan. The framework prevents both gaps and drift.

Card 47: 5-12 Vital KPIs

The Number: The dashboard should contain 5-12 metrics, not more.

Context: Too few metrics leaves blind spots. Too many creates noise and diffuses attention. The 5-12 range forces prioritization and focus. These are the metrics reviewed weekly by the leadership team.

When It Applies: Operating dashboards for leadership and board. Functional teams may need more detailed metrics, but the leadership view should be focused.

When It Breaks: Complex businesses may need the higher end of the range. Simpler businesses may need fewer. But exceeding 12 metrics indicates failure to prioritize.

When to Use This Card: Use when designing dashboards, simplifying reporting, or coaching leaders to focus on what matters most. Essential when the current dashboard has 25 metrics that no one actually reviews.

Diagnostic Question: How many KPIs does your leadership team actually review weekly? If the answer is more than 12, you are not prioritizing. If the answer is "I don't know," you have a bigger problem.

Coaching Lesson: If everything is a priority, nothing is. The discipline of limiting KPIs forces clarity about what matters most. The debate about which metrics make the dashboard is itself valuable. It reveals what the leadership team believes drives the business.

Card 48: The Hypothesis Mindset

The Number: Treat the value creation plan as a set of hypotheses to be tested.

Context: Plans are built on assumptions. Assumptions may be wrong. The hypothesis mindset embraces this uncertainty and creates mechanisms for testing and adaptation. Rather than defending the plan, the team seeks evidence about whether it is working.

When It Applies: Value creation planning and execution. Particularly important when the business is entering new markets, launching new products, or executing unfamiliar initiatives.

When It Breaks: Core elements of strategy should not pivot constantly. But specific initiatives and assumptions should be treated as experiments that produce learning.

When to Use This Card: Use when coaching teams attached to failing plans, establishing learning culture, or creating permission to adapt based on evidence. Essential when results diverge from expectations.

Diagnostic Question: When did you last update the value creation plan based on something you learned? If it has been more than 90 days, the plan is becoming stale.

Coaching Lesson: Plan attachment kills learning. The hypothesis mindset enables the organization to recognize when assumptions are failing and adapt accordingly. The team that defends a failing plan loses money. The team that adapts based on evidence preserves it.

Card 49: Commitment to Outcomes, Flexibility on Path

The Number: Hold firm on goals, adapt on methods.

Context: The EBITDA target is the commitment. How you get there can evolve based on what is learned. This frame resolves the tension between accountability for results and permission to adapt approaches.

When It Applies: Managing the tension between plan adherence and adaptation. Useful when an initiative is failing but the underlying goal remains valid.

When It Breaks: If outcomes become genuinely unachievable due to external factors, they may need to be reset. But this should be exceptional, not routine, and should involve sponsor alignment.

When to Use This Card: Use when balancing accountability with adaptation, coaching leaders through plan pivots, or maintaining outcome focus while allowing tactical flexibility.

Diagnostic Question: Is your team defending a failing approach, or adapting based on evidence while maintaining commitment to the outcome?

Coaching Lesson: This frame resolves the paradox of planning. The plan matters. Commitments matter. But clinging to a failing approach in defense of the plan is worse than adapting. The outcome is sacred. The path is not.

Card 50: Care With Teeth

The Number: Combine safety for surfacing truth with accountability for performance.

Context: Safety without pressure creates comfort. Pressure without safety creates fear. Both kill performance. Care with teeth is the synthesis: genuine care for people combined with genuine accountability for results. The best PE coaches and the best CEOs operate in this mode.

When It Applies: Leadership style and culture-building. The frame applies to how the Coach works with the CEO, how the CEO works with the team, and how the organization operates.

When It Breaks: The balance point varies by situation. Crisis may require more teeth. Recovery may require more care. The art is reading the situation and calibrating appropriately.

When to Use This Card: Use when coaching leadership style, building high-performance culture, or diagnosing whether the organization has the right balance of support and accountability.

Diagnostic Question: Is your organization safe for surfacing problems? Is it also demanding about fixing them? You need both. Which is missing?

Coaching Lesson: Care with teeth is how the best PE coaches operate. They listen and support. They also demand and hold accountable. They create environments where people feel safe bringing bad news and also feel pressure to perform. The combination is rare. It is also what builds high-performing organizations.

Using the Canon

The Canon 50 is a reference, not a checklist. No single conversation or meeting will use all fifty cards. The skill is knowing which cards apply in the moment.

When discussing cash, reach for Cards 1-5. When discussing growth, Cards 6-12. When a decision is stalling, Cards 17-22. When preparing for exit, Cards 38-45.

The cards create shared language. When the Coach references the 70% rule, everyone knows what it means. When the CEO invokes care with teeth, the team understands. Common language enables faster communication and deeper alignment.

The cards also create accountability. When a commitment is made to implement a 13-week cash forecast, the card provides the standard. When decision velocity is lagging, Card 17 diagnoses the problem.

Print them. Save them. Carry them into meetings. Use them to diagnose, to challenge, to coach. They are tools that improve with use.

Coach Card Trigger Map

Symptoms → Root cause → Best card
category → Next meeting move

Symptom	Root cause	Card category	Move
Great deck, ugly reality	Truth gap	Reality & Metrics	Weekly KPI truth ritual
Growth ok, cash dying	Cash conversion blind spot	Cash & Working Capital	13-week actions
Strong CEO, weak team	Capability gap	Team & Accountability	Role resets + owners
We need a re-rate	Proof missing	Exit & Multiple	Proof-point roadmap

Coach Standard

⚠️ • One truth metric per lever

🧭 • One owner per initiative

☑️ • One deadline before next board

🏆 • Trophy icon for exit readiness

Field Drills

- **Select five cards most relevant to your current situation.** Use them in your next leadership meeting.
- **Audit your organization against the first ten cards.** Which standards are you meeting? Which are you missing?
- **Teach one card to your leadership team this week.** See if they can apply it before your next conversation.
- **Identify which cards you have never used.** Is that because they are not relevant, or because you have a blind spot?
- **Create a "card of the month" practice** where the leadership team focuses on one card's discipline for 30 days.

Clinic Questions

- Which of the Canon 50 are most critical for our current stage and situation?
- Which cards reveal gaps in our current operating discipline?
- How many of these numbers can our CEO state without looking them up?
- Which cards would surface the most important conversations if we used them in our next board meeting?
- Are there cards we should be using that we are ignoring?

Chapter 19

Clinic: Strong CEO, Weak Team

The sponsor partner was frustrated.

"The CEO is excellent. Strategic. Articulate. Great with the board. Understands the business deeply. But nothing is getting done. Every initiative stalls. Every deadline slips. And when I ask what is happening, he has good explanations but no results."

The operating partner nodded. "I have been watching the leadership team in meetings. The CEO carries every conversation. The CFO is passive. The CRO talks a good game but the pipeline is thin. The COO is overwhelmed. The CEO is essentially running the company alone."

"So the CEO is the problem?"

"No. The CEO is strong. The team is weak. And the CEO either does not see it, or sees it and is not acting."

This is one of the most common patterns in PE-backed companies: a capable CEO surrounded by an inadequate team. The CEO compensates through heroic effort, but heroics do not scale. The business underperforms not because of the leader at the top, but because of the layer below.

This clinic addresses how to diagnose the pattern, confront the CEO, and drive the team upgrade that unlocks performance.

Strong CEO, Weak Team

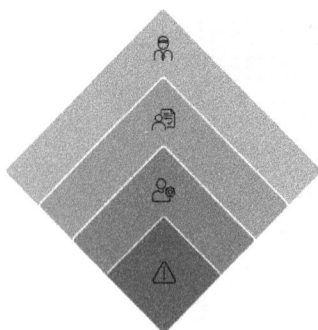

Coach action
Reset standards and rebuild bench

Role clarity gap
Unclear decision rights and scope

Capability gap
Skill shortages causing delays

Symptoms
CEO over-involved, handoffs missed

Recognizing the Pattern

The strong CEO with a weak team presents a characteristic set of symptoms.

The CEO is always in the room. Every important meeting includes the CEO. Every significant decision flows through the CEO. The CEO is the bottleneck because no one else can be trusted to handle critical matters.

Execution is inconsistent. Some things get done, typically the things the CEO personally drives. Other things languish, the things delegated to the team.

The CEO has explanations for everything. When results disappoint, the CEO can explain why. Market conditions. Customer delays. Resource constraints. The explanations are plausible, but they accumulate into a pattern of non-delivery.

Direct reports defer excessively. In leadership team meetings, the CEO talks 70 percent of the time. Others wait to hear the CEO's view before offering their own. Challenge is rare. The dynamic is presentation to the CEO rather than debate among peers.

The CEO is exhausted. Running the company alone is unsustainable. The CEO works excessive hours. They show signs of fatigue. Their strategic thinking suffers because they are consumed by operational detail.

The CEO defends the team. When weaknesses are raised, the CEO explains context. "The CFO is new to PE. Give him time." "The CRO just needs more support." "The COO is dealing with a lot." The defense prevents action.

Board meetings rely heavily on the CEO. Other executives present their sections, but substantive questions route to the CEO. The board interacts primarily with one person.

These symptoms may appear individually in many companies. When they cluster together, the pattern is strong CEO with weak team.

The Root Causes

Several dynamics can create this pattern.

The CEO built the team before PE. Founder CEOs often surround themselves with loyal lieutenants who grew with the company. These lieutenants may lack the capability to operate at PE pace and scale. The CEO is loyal in return and reluctant to make changes.

The CEO is a poor talent judge. Some leaders struggle to distinguish strong performers from weak ones. They hire based on chemistry rather than capability. They mistake confidence for competence.

The CEO avoids conflict. Upgrading the team means difficult conversations, terminations, and disruption. A CEO who avoids conflict will delay these actions indefinitely, hoping performance improves on its own.

The CEO enjoys being indispensable. Some leaders derive identity from being needed. Surrounding themselves with a strong team would diminish their centrality. Unconsciously, they prefer a weaker team that depends on them.

The CEO lacks a model for what good looks like. If the CEO has never worked with a high-performing executive team, they may not recognize what one looks like. Their standard is calibrated to mediocrity.

The sponsor did not assess team quality during diligence. Sometimes the team weakness was knowable before close but was not surfaced. The deal proceeded with an assumption of team adequacy that proved wrong.

Understanding the root cause shapes the intervention. A CEO who is loyal to legacy team members needs a different conversation than a CEO who enjoys being indispensable.

The Economics of Inaction

Leaving the pattern unaddressed has predictable costs.

Execution lag compounds. The team cannot deliver what the value creation plan requires. Initiatives fall behind. Milestones slip. A 90-day initiative becomes a 180-day initiative. The gap between plan and reality widens. At 15 million dollars of planned EBITDA improvement over three years, every quarter of delay costs roughly 1.25 million in unrealized value, plus the IRR impact of slower realization.

The CEO burns out. Heroic effort is not sustainable. Eventually the CEO's performance degrades, their health suffers, or they leave. The company loses its strongest asset because the load was never distributed. CEO turnover mid-hold typically costs 6 to 12 months of momentum.

Strong performers below the team leave. High performers in the next tier see the weak leadership team and conclude there is no path to advancement, or they simply do not want to work for weak bosses. Talent attrition compounds the problem. Replacing a strong director-level performer costs 12 to 18 months of productivity.

The sponsor loses patience. Board meetings become tense as results continue to disappoint. The sponsor starts to question the CEO, not because the CEO is weak, but because the CEO has not built the team needed to deliver.

Exit value suffers. Buyers assess team quality. A company dependent on one person is riskier than a company with a deep bench. The weak team becomes a multiple discount. Buyers routinely discount by 0.5 to 1.0 turns of multiple for key person risk.

The cost of inaction compounds over time. Early intervention is far less expensive than late intervention.

The Conversation with the CEO

Addressing the pattern requires a direct conversation with the CEO. This conversation is the Coach's most important contribution.

The conversation should be private. This is not a board discussion or a group critique. It is a one-on-one coaching conversation.

The conversation should be evidence-based. Not "I think your team is weak" but "Here is what I am observing. Initiatives X, Y, and Z are behind schedule. In leadership meetings, the discussion pattern is A. When I ask your CFO about B, the answer lacks depth. Help me understand what you are seeing."

The conversation should be curious, not accusatory. The goal is to help the CEO see what you see, not to attack. "What is your assessment of your leadership team? Where are the strengths and gaps?"

The conversation should connect to outcomes. "Given what we are trying to accomplish, do you have the team you need? If you were starting fresh, would you hire each of these people into their current roles?"

The conversation should name the dynamic. "I want to share an observation. You are carrying a very heavy load. You are in every meeting, every decision, every problem. That is not sustainable, and it may be a signal that you are compensating for gaps in the team."

The conversation should offer support. "I am not here to criticize. I am here to help you build the team that can deliver what we all want to achieve. What support would be useful?"

Most CEOs, when approached with curiosity and support, will acknowledge what they already know. They have been avoiding the problem, but they are not blind to it. The conversation gives them permission to act.

Mapping the Team

Following the initial conversation, the work of team assessment begins.

For each leadership team member, assess capability and fit.

Capability is whether the person can do the job. Do they have the skills, experience, and judgment required for the role at this company at this stage?

Fit is whether the person is right for this context. A capable executive might be wrong for PE pace, wrong for this industry, or wrong for this CEO's style.

The assessment should draw on multiple inputs.

Direct observation in meetings. How does the person contribute? Are they prepared? Do they challenge appropriately? Do they deliver crisp, clear communication?

One-on-one conversation. Meet with each executive individually. Ask about their priorities, challenges, and view of the business. Assess depth of thinking and self-awareness.

360 feedback. What do their peers and direct reports say? Patterns across multiple perspectives are more reliable than any single view.

Results. What has the person delivered? Are their commitments met? Is their function performing?

CEO perspective. What does the CEO see? Where does the CEO have concerns? Sometimes the CEO's assessment differs from external observation, and understanding why is important.

The assessment produces a view of each team member: strong and in the right role, capable but in the wrong role, developing but not yet ready, or not capable for this context.

The Upgrade Decision

With the assessment complete, decisions follow.

For each weak or misaligned team member, there are limited options.

Develop in place. If the gap is addressable with coaching, training, or support, invest in development. Set clear expectations and a timeline. This works when the gap is skill, not will, and when the timeline permits. Typical development window: 90 to 180 days with clear milestones.

Reassign. Sometimes a capable person is in the wrong role. The CFO who should be a VP of Finance. The CRO who should run a region rather than the whole commercial function. Reassignment preserves talent while addressing the gap.

Exit. If the person cannot succeed in any role at the required level, they must leave. This is difficult but necessary. Delayed exits compound the cost.

The decision should be made with the CEO, not for the CEO. The Coach's role is to help the CEO see clearly and decide well, not to dictate personnel actions. But the Coach should not accept indefinite delay.

What the Coach notices: The CEO who says "let me think about it" for the third consecutive meeting. The assessment conversation that happened two months ago with no action since. The weak performer who keeps getting defended despite mounting evidence.

What the Coach says: "We talked about the CFO gap eight weeks ago. You agreed the role needed to change. What has prevented action? What would need to be true for you to make the decision this week?"

Managing the Transition

Team upgrades create disruption. Managing the transition well determines whether the upgrade succeeds.

Timing matters. Too many changes at once destabilizes the organization. Too few changes too slowly leaves gaps unfilled. The typical pattern is one to two leadership changes per quarter until the team is complete.

Sequencing matters. Start with the role where the gap is most damaging. Often this is commercial leadership (CRO) or financial leadership (CFO), where weak performance has the most immediate impact.

Communication matters. The organization watches leadership changes closely. Handling departures with dignity and clarity maintains morale. Handling them poorly creates fear and distraction.

Interim coverage matters. Between departure and replacement, who handles the function? The CEO should not absorb all displaced responsibility, or the hero pattern continues. Interim solutions, whether internal stretch assignments or external interim executives, bridge the gap.

Search quality matters. The replacement must be right. A weak-to-weak swap solves nothing. Investing in a quality search, even if it takes longer, produces better outcomes than a rushed hire. Average search timeline for a strong executive: 90 to 120 days.

Onboarding matters. New executives fail at alarming rates. Industry data suggests 40 percent of new executives fail within 18 months. Structured onboarding with 30/60/90 plans, clear expectations, and coaching support increases success rates significantly.

Success Indicators

How do you know the team upgrade is working?

The CEO's load decreases. The CEO is no longer in every meeting. Decisions are made without CEO involvement. The CEO has time for strategic work.

Execution improves. Initiatives move forward. Milestones are hit. The gap between plan and results narrows.

Meeting dynamics change. Leadership team meetings feature genuine debate among peers. The CEO listens more and talks less. Decisions emerge from discussion rather than CEO pronouncement.

Board interactions broaden. Board members engage with multiple executives, not just the CEO. The bench is visible.

Talent attracts talent. Strong executives attract strong performers to their teams. The upgrade cascades through the organization.

The CEO acknowledges the change. The CEO reflects on how different the experience is with a capable team. "I did not realize how much I was carrying until I stopped carrying it."

CHAPTER 19 · CLINIC

60-Day Team Upgrade Plan

Stabilize execution without detonating morale

Days 1–30

Role clarity · Scorecard · Meeting cadence · 11 performance contracts

1

2

Days 31–60

Decisive upgrades (hire, move, exit) · Delegation model · Leadership routines

☐ Kindness is clarity delivered early

When the CEO Is the Problem

Sometimes the diagnosis shifts. What appeared to be a weak team is actually a CEO who cannot build or lead a team.

Signs that the CEO is the problem include:

Multiple team members have failed in succession. If the CRO, CFO, and COO have all turned over and the replacements are also struggling, the common factor is the CEO.

Strong executives leave. Capable people join, assess the situation, and depart. They are voting with their feet.

The CEO resists every upgrade. Despite evidence and coaching, the CEO defends weak performers, delays decisions, and blocks change.

The CEO undermines new executives. New team members are set up to fail through inadequate support, unclear authority, or active undermining.

If the CEO is the problem, the intervention must address the CEO, not the team. This may mean intensive coaching, a performance improvement plan, or ultimately a CEO change. The Coach must be honest with the sponsor when the diagnosis shifts.

Coach Cards Referenced

- **9-Box talent grid for assessment**
- **A-Players attract A-Players**
- **First Team concept**
- **30/60/90 onboarding for new executives**
- **Succession for key roles**
- **One decision maker per decision**

Field Drills

- **Assess your leadership team against role requirements.** For each member, rate capability and fit. Identify the one or two seats with the largest gaps.

- **Schedule a conversation with the CEO about team composition.** Use curiosity, not accusation. Ask: "Do you have the team you need to deliver the plan?"
- **For the weakest team member, define the options:** develop, reassign, or exit. Set a timeline for decision.
- **Review the last three leadership team meetings.** What percentage of airtime did the CEO take? What does that signal?
- **If you have made recent leadership changes, assess onboarding quality.** Are new executives set up to succeed?

Clinic Questions

- Is our CEO surrounded by a team capable of delivering the value creation plan?
- How much of the CEO's time is consumed by work that should be handled by the team?
- What would happen to this company if the CEO took a month off? Would it run smoothly or collapse?
- Which leadership team member, if upgraded, would have the biggest impact on performance?
- What is preventing the CEO from making necessary team changes?
- How does the board assess leadership team quality beyond the CEO?
- Are we developing future leaders, or are we dependent on externally hiring every upgrade?

Chapter 20

Clinic: Beautiful Board Pack, Ugly Reality

The board pack was impressive. Forty-two slides of polished content. Revenue trending up. EBITDA ahead of prior year. Customer count growing. Initiative milestones marked complete. A dashboard of green indicators.

The sponsor partner reviewed it on the plane to the board meeting, feeling cautiously optimistic.

Then she arrived at the company and walked the floor with the COO.

The warehouse was in chaos. Inventory was misallocated. Orders were shipping late. The team was stressed and frustrated. When she asked about the operational improvement initiative that was marked complete in the board pack, the COO hesitated. "Well, we finished the planning phase. Implementation is... taking longer than expected."

By the time the board meeting started, the sponsor knew the board pack was fiction.

This is the beautiful board pack, ugly reality pattern. The presentation tells one story. The business tells another. The gap between the two erodes trust, delays necessary action, and ultimately destroys value.

This clinic addresses how to recognize the pattern, confront it without destroying the management relationship, and install disciplines that keep reporting honest.

Beautiful Board Pack, Ugly Reality

Gap callouts
Identify and highlight
discrepancies or areas for
improvement.

Board pack narrative
Compile key insights and
data into a cohesive story.

Operational truth
Reflect the actual
performance and status of
operations.

The Anatomy of Disconnect

The disconnect between board pack and reality takes several forms.

Selective metrics. The pack highlights metrics that look good and omits or de-emphasizes those that look bad. Revenue is featured; cash is buried in an appendix. Customer count is prominent; churn rate is mentioned in passing.

Favorable framing. Results are presented in the most favorable light. A miss becomes "slightly below plan due to timing." A failure becomes "a learning that informed our revised approach." The framing is not technically false but obscures the truth.

Activity masquerading as progress. Initiatives are reported as "on track" because activities occurred, even though outcomes have not materialized. "Completed supplier negotiations" sounds like progress, even if savings have not appeared in the P&L.

Delayed bad news. Issues that are known are not surfaced until they become undeniable. The customer loss that happened six weeks ago appears in the pack only when the revenue impact hits. The leader who is failing is described as "developing" until termination becomes necessary.

Adjusted reality. EBITDA is heavily adjusted, with add-backs that are aggressive or recurring items that keep recurring. The adjusted number looks good; the underlying business does not.

Forward optimism. Projections show improvement, quarter after quarter, even as actuals continue to disappoint. The future is always brighter than the present turns out to be.

Each of these forms represents a gap between what is presented and what is true. The cumulative effect is a board that cannot govern effectively because it does not know what is happening.

Why It Happens

The disconnect is rarely intentional deception. More often, it emerges from understandable dynamics that are nonetheless destructive.

Fear of consequences. Management fears how the board will react to bad news. Will they lose credibility? Will the sponsor intervene? Will they lose their jobs? Fear drives softening.

Performance pressure. The board has expectations. Management wants to meet them. When reality falls short, there is temptation to narrow the gap through presentation rather than performance.

Optimism bias. Management genuinely believes things will improve. The revenue that slipped will come next quarter. The initiative that stalled will restart. The optimism is sincere but not justified.

Insufficient time. Preparing the board pack is time-consuming. Investigating issues thoroughly takes more time. When the deadline approaches, management may present what they have rather than what they should have.

Lack of integration. Finance produces financial data. Operations produces operational data. Commercial produces commercial data. No one integrates the picture or checks consistency. Disconnects go unnoticed.

Board behavior. If the board punishes bad news, management learns to hide it. If the board rewards polish over substance, management invests in polish. Board behavior shapes management behavior.

Understanding why the disconnect happens enables intervention that addresses root causes, not just symptoms.

The Economics of Disconnect

The disconnect has significant costs, even if it feels comfortable in the short term.

Delayed action. If the board does not know about problems, it cannot help solve them. The cash issue that could have been addressed in Q2 becomes a crisis in Q4. The market shift that should have prompted a pivot is ignored until too late. Every quarter of delayed action on a material issue typically costs 2 to 5 percent of enterprise value in foregone opportunity or avoidable damage.

Lost trust. When the gap is eventually discovered, trust collapses. The sponsor who learns that the board pack was misleading will never fully trust management again. The relationship shifts from partnership to surveillance. Rebuilding trust takes 12 to 18 months of consistent honest reporting.

Bad decisions. The board makes decisions based on information received. If the information is wrong, the decisions will be wrong. Resources are allocated to the wrong initiatives. Risks are not mitigated. Opportunities are missed.

Credibility damage at exit. Buyers conduct due diligence. If they discover that historical reporting was unreliable, they discount both the business and the management team. Quality of earnings concerns compound into multiple compression. A QofE that surfaces material discrepancies can reduce purchase price by 10 to 20 percent.

Cultural rot. When leadership hides truth from the board, the organization learns that hiding truth is acceptable. The behavior cascades. Frontline employees hide from middle managers. Middle managers hide from executives. The culture of truth erodes throughout the organization.

The disconnect is expensive. The short-term comfort of avoiding difficult conversations is vastly outweighed by the long-term costs.

Recognizing the Pattern

Several signals indicate a potential disconnect.

Consistent beating of expectations. If every quarter comes in slightly ahead of plan, something may be wrong. Either the plan is sandbagged, or the reporting is managed. Consistent outperformance can be as concerning as consistent underperformance.

Absence of bad news. Every business has challenges. If the board pack contains no problems, no misses, no concerns, it is likely not telling the full story.

Excessive adjustment. If adjusted EBITDA is dramatically higher than GAAP EBITDA, the adjustments warrant scrutiny.

Are they truly non-recurring? Are they defensible? A gap of more than 15 to 20 percent between GAAP and adjusted EBITDA should trigger questions.

Vague initiative updates. "Progress continues on the commercial transformation initiative" says nothing. What specifically happened? What measurable result occurred?

Optimistic forecasts that repeat. If Q2 forecast promised improvement in Q3, and Q3 forecast promises improvement in Q4, and this pattern repeats, forecasts are not grounded in reality.

Disconnect between financial and operational data. If revenue is growing but customer count is flat, where is the growth coming from? If EBITDA is improving but cash is declining, what explains the divergence?

Management discomfort with questions. If management becomes defensive when questioned, if answers are evasive or overly complex, there may be something they do not want to reveal.

These signals warrant investigation. Not accusation, but investigation.

CHAPTER 23 CLINIC

Board Pack Rebuild Template

Turn the board pack into a decision instrument

3 Decisions Needed	KPI Truth
What requires board input	Leading + lagging · Red/yellow/green with owners

Variance Root Causes + Actions	Cash + Runway + Triggers
What's off and who's fixing it	Liquidity truth

☐ If the pack can't drive decisions, it's theater

The Investigation

When disconnect is suspected, the Coach helps facilitate investigation without destroying the relationship.

Walk the floor. Visit the operation. Talk to people beyond the leadership team. Ask open-ended questions. "What is working well? What is challenging?" The ground truth often differs from the board room presentation.

Triangulate data. Compare the board pack numbers to other sources. The CRM should reconcile to reported pipeline. The ERP should reconcile to reported financials. Discrepancies warrant explanation.

Ask specific questions. Not "Is everything on track?" but "Show me the specific customer wins in Q3. Walk me through the exact savings achieved from procurement. Explain the bridge from EBITDA to cash."

Request supporting detail. For any claim that seems questionable, request the underlying data. If the detail cannot be produced, the claim is not well-founded.

Engage external perspective. An auditor, consultant, or advisor can provide independent assessment. They can ask questions that the board might find awkward.

The investigation should be conducted without prejudice. The goal is to understand, not to punish. Perhaps the disconnect is smaller than feared. Perhaps there are reasonable explanations. But investigation is necessary to know.

The Conversation

When disconnect is confirmed, a direct conversation with the CEO is required.

The conversation should be private and supportive. "I want to talk about something I am observing. I am not here to attack or accuse. I am here to understand and to help."

The conversation should present evidence. "Here is what I saw in the board pack. Here is what I observed in the operation. Here is the gap I am trying to understand."

The conversation should invite explanation. "Help me understand. Is my perception accurate? What am I missing?" Sometimes there are legitimate explanations. Sometimes the CEO acknowledges the gap.

The conversation should name the stakes. "The trust between management and the board is essential. If that trust erodes, everything becomes harder. I need to understand what is real so I can help."

The conversation should offer a path forward. "Let us talk about how we can ensure the board pack accurately reflects reality. What needs to change?"

Most CEOs, when approached with directness and support, will engage constructively. They know the disconnect exists. They may feel trapped by it. The conversation provides an exit.

What the Coach notices: The CEO who becomes defensive immediately. The explanation that keeps shifting. The promise to "look into it" that never produces follow-up. The pattern of deflection rather than engagement.

What the Coach says: "I am not looking for perfection. I am looking for truth. The board can handle bad news. What the board cannot handle is discovering that we have been operating on fiction. Help me understand what is actually happening so we can address it together."

If the CEO is defensive or dismissive, that is a more serious signal. It may indicate that the disconnect is intentional or that the CEO lacks the self-awareness to lead effectively.

Closing the Gap

Once the disconnect is acknowledged, the work of closing it begins.

Reset expectations. Management may believe the board expects perfection. The Coach helps calibrate: the board expects truth, not perfection. Bad news delivered early builds trust. Bad news discovered late destroys it.

Improve information quality. What systems, processes, or disciplines would produce more accurate information? Better forecasting. More rigorous initiative tracking. Clearer definitions of metrics. The operational infrastructure must support honest reporting.

Change the board pack structure. Remove the invitation to polish. Require explicit discussion of misses and risks. Include a "what went wrong" section. Make honest reporting the default format.

Model board behavior. When management delivers bad news, how does the board react? If the reaction is punishment, management will revert to hiding. The board must reward honesty, even when the news is unwelcome.

Install the no surprises discipline. The 24-hour surfacing norm, the 48-hour pre-alignment, the weekly triangle touchpoint. These disciplines create channels for truth to flow before it reaches the board pack.

Coach presentation skills. Sometimes management does not know how to deliver difficult messages effectively. They default to softening because they lack the skill to be direct. Coaching on communication helps.

The Board Pack Redesign

A well-designed board pack makes honest reporting easier.

Lead with reality, not celebration. The opening should present the state of the business clearly. What is working. What is not. What changed since last meeting.

Use consistent metrics. The same metrics, defined the same way, every meeting. Changes in definition must be disclosed. Consistency prevents gaming.

Show trends, not just snapshots. A single quarter can be noisy. Trends over four to six quarters reveal the real trajectory.

Require specific evidence. "Initiative on track" is not acceptable. "Completed X, delivered Y result, next milestone Z by date" is acceptable.

Include a risk register. What are the material risks? What is the mitigation? Risks should be discussed, not hidden.

Present cash clearly. Cash position, 13-week forecast, covenant headroom. Cash is not an afterthought. It is central.

Limit length. An 80-slide pack invites skimming. A 20-slide pack invites reading. Force prioritization through constraints. The discipline of brevity forces clarity.

Distribute early. Seven to ten days before the meeting. Early distribution signals control and enables preparation.

The redesigned pack becomes a tool for honesty rather than a canvas for performance.

Rebuilding Trust

If significant disconnect has damaged trust, rebuilding takes time and consistency.

Acknowledge the problem. The CEO may need to explicitly acknowledge to the board that prior reporting was inadequate. This is uncomfortable but cleansing. "I have not been giving you the full picture. I am committed to changing that."

Demonstrate change quickly. The next board pack must be demonstrably different. More honest. More complete. More accurate. The change must be visible immediately.

Accept increased scrutiny. For a period, the board will verify more. They will ask harder questions. They will triangulate more aggressively. Management must accept this as a consequence of prior behavior.

Deliver results. Ultimately, trust rebuilds through performance. When management says something will happen and it does, trust grows. When forecasts prove accurate, credibility rebuilds.

Maintain consistency. One honest board pack is not enough. The discipline must persist over multiple quarters. Trust builds slowly through repeated demonstration. Expect 12 to 18 months of consistent honest reporting before trust is fully restored.

The Coach supports the CEO through the rebuilding period. It is uncomfortable to operate under increased scrutiny. The Coach helps the CEO maintain perspective: the discomfort is temporary, and the alternative, continuing the disconnect, would be far worse.

When the Pattern Persists

Sometimes the conversation does not work. The CEO acknowledges the disconnect but reverts to prior behavior. The next board pack is just as polished and just as disconnected from reality.

Persistent disconnect is a serious problem. It indicates either that the CEO cannot change or that the CEO has chosen not to change.

The Coach must escalate. The sponsor needs to know that coaching has not worked. The intervention must shift from coaching to accountability.

Accountability might mean explicit performance requirements around reporting accuracy. It might mean increased board oversight. In severe cases, it might mean CEO change.

The Coach does not make these decisions. But the Coach must surface the reality that decisions are needed.

Prevention

The best approach is preventing the disconnect from developing in the first place.

Set expectations early. From the first board meeting, establish that honest reporting is expected and rewarded. Make clear that the board values truth over comfort.

Install disciplines from the start. The 13-week cash forecast. The weekly triangle touchpoint. The 24-hour surfacing norm. These disciplines create ongoing truth flow that prevents accumulation of disconnect.

Model behavior at the top. If the sponsor and board behave consistently, management learns what is expected. Punish hiding. Reward surfacing.

Review board packs with a critical eye. Do not accept polish at face value. Ask probing questions. Request supporting detail. Verify against other sources.

Conduct periodic reality checks. Walk the floor. Talk to customers. Engage with the operation directly. Supplement board pack information with direct observation.

Prevention is far less costly than remediation. The trust that is never broken does not need to be rebuilt.

Coach Cards Referenced

- **24-hour surfacing norm for material issues**
- **48-hour pre-alignment before board meetings**
- **Board pack 7-10 days early**
- **13-week cash forecast as the truth anchor**
- **One voice outward for consistent narrative**
- **Care with teeth for holding accountability without punishment**

Field Drills

- **Compare your last board pack to operational reality.** Walk the floor. Talk to frontline employees. Identify gaps between presentation and truth.
- **Review the last four board packs for patterns.** Are forecasts consistently optimistic? Is bad news absent? Are adjustments increasing?
- **Redesign your board pack template** to require explicit discussion of misses, risks, and challenges.
- **Conduct a conversation with your CEO about board pack accuracy.** Use curiosity, not accusation. Understand their perspective on what is presented.
- **Assess how the board reacts to bad news.** Is honesty rewarded or punished? What behavior does board reaction create?

Clinic Questions

- How confident are we that our board pack reflects reality? What would an independent observer find if they investigated?
- What topics are we softening or avoiding in board presentations?
- How does our board react when management delivers bad news? Does that reaction encourage or discourage honesty?
- What disciplines do we have that force accurate reporting? Are they working?
- If there is a gap between board pack and reality, what is causing it? Fear? Optimism? Insufficient systems?
- How would buyers react if they compared our board presentations to underlying data during due diligence?
- What would it take to create a board pack that tells the complete truth, comfortably?

Chapter 21

Clinic: Growth Fine, Cash Dying

The revenue chart looked excellent. Up 18 percent year over year. New customers acquired. Market share expanding. The commercial team was executing.

The cash chart told a different story. Operating cash flow was negative for the third consecutive quarter. The revolver was nearly maxed. Covenant headroom had shrunk from comfortable to concerning. The 13-week forecast showed the company would need to request a covenant amendment or find additional capital within 90 days.

The CEO was confused. "How can we be growing this fast and running out of cash?"

This is the growth fine, cash dying pattern. Revenue and EBITDA move in the right direction while cash moves in the wrong direction. The P&L tells a story of success. The bank account tells a story of stress. The disconnect creates danger because leadership focuses on the success story while the survival story unfolds in the background.

This clinic addresses how to diagnose the pattern, identify the cash drains, and restore cash health without killing the growth that makes the business valuable.

Understanding the Disconnect

Growth consumes cash before it generates cash. This is a fundamental dynamic that many operators underestimate.

When revenue grows, working capital grows with it. More sales mean more receivables. More production means more inventory. Payables may grow too, but often not enough to offset the receivables and inventory increase.

The cash math is unforgiving. If a company has a 60-day cash conversion cycle and grows revenue by 10 million dollars, it needs approximately 1.6 million dollars of additional working capital to fund that growth. This cash is consumed before the growth generates any return.

Capital expenditure may also increase. Growth may require capacity expansion, new equipment, additional locations, or technology infrastructure. These investments consume cash today for returns that arrive over years.

And growth often requires investment in people, systems, and overhead before the revenue materializes. The sales team hired in Q1 does not produce revenue until Q3. The implementation team scaled for expected volume consumes cash while volume ramps.

The result is that profitable growth can be cash-negative for extended periods. A company can grow itself into a liquidity crisis while reporting excellent financial performance.

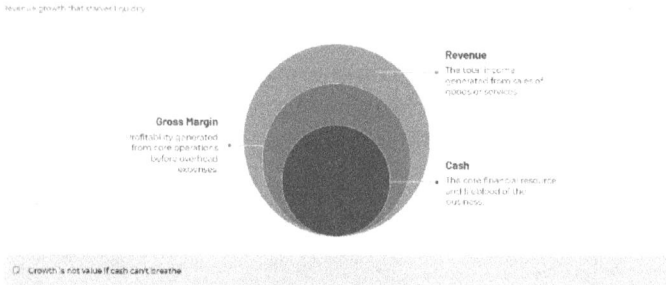

CHAPTER FIFTY-NINE

Growth Fine, Cash Dying

Revenue growth that chokes liquidity

Revenue
- The total income generated from sales of goods or services

Gross Margin
profitability generated from core operations before overhead expenses

Cash
- The core financial resource and lifeblood of the business

Growth is not value if cash can't breathe

The Warning Signs

Several signals indicate that cash is dying while growth is fine.

Receivables growing faster than revenue. If receivables are up 25 percent while revenue is up 18 percent, collection is slowing. Cash is getting trapped in customer balances.

Inventory growing faster than cost of goods sold. If inventory is up 30 percent while COGS is up 15 percent, inventory is building beyond what sales require. Cash is getting trapped in warehouses.

Operating cash flow negative despite positive EBITDA. If EBITDA is 5 million but operating cash flow is negative 2 million, something is consuming the profit before it becomes cash.

Revolver utilization increasing. If the company is drawing more on its credit facility quarter over quarter, it is consuming more cash than it is generating.

Covenant headroom shrinking. If leverage or coverage ratios are approaching limits, cash stress is building.

Cash forecast showing deterioration. If the 13-week forecast shows cash declining week over week, or shows a floor being approached, trouble is ahead.

The earlier these signs are recognized, the more options exist for response. The company that catches cash stress in month one can adjust gracefully. The company that catches it in month twelve faces hard choices.

Diagnosing the Drains

When cash is dying, the first task is understanding where it is going. The diagnosis requires tracing cash flow in detail.

Start with the bridge from EBITDA to operating cash flow. EBITDA is the starting point. Then adjustments for working capital changes, capital expenditures, interest, taxes, and other items produce actual cash flow. Each adjustment reveals where cash is being consumed.

Examine working capital components individually.

Receivables. What is DSO? How has it changed? Which customers are paying slowly? Is there a concentration issue? Are there disputed invoices holding up collection?

Inventory. What is DIO? How has it changed? What is the composition between raw materials, work in progress, and finished goods? Is there obsolete inventory? Is inventory being built in anticipation of demand that may not materialize?

Payables. What is DPO? How has it changed? Are we paying suppliers faster than we need to? Are there opportunities to extend terms?

The working capital analysis often reveals the largest cash drains. In growing companies, receivables and inventory are typically the culprits.

Examine capital expenditures. What is being spent? Is it maintenance capex (necessary to sustain the business) or growth capex (investment in expansion)? Is the spending aligned with the value creation plan? Is it delivering expected returns?

Examine other cash uses. Interest on debt. Tax payments. Distributions. One-time items. Each category should be understood.

The diagnosis produces a clear picture of where cash is going. This picture enables targeted intervention.

The Economics of the Pattern

The growth fine, cash dying pattern has specific economic consequences that compound over time.

Working capital as hidden leverage. Every day of DSO on 50 million of annual revenue represents approximately 137,000 dollars trapped in receivables. If DSO expands from 45 to 62 days during a growth phase, that is 2.3 million of cash consumed, roughly equivalent to adding debt without the benefit of the capital.

Covenant math. If the company's leverage covenant is 5.0x and current EBITDA is 8 million, the debt ceiling is 40 million. But if working capital consumption forces revolver draws from 5 million to 12 million, leverage moves from 3.75x to 4.6x. The company approaches breach not because EBITDA declined but because growth consumed cash.

IRR erosion. Cash consumed by working capital during the hold period reduces exit cash and delays debt paydown. A company that consumes 5 million in working capital to fund growth has 5 million less to show at exit. On a 30 million equity base, that is 17 percent less equity value, pure IRR destruction.

The economic stakes make early recognition and intervention essential.

The Cash Conversation

With diagnosis complete, the conversation with the leadership team must be direct.

Present the reality. "Our growth is strong, and that is valuable. But our cash position is deteriorating. If we do not change course, we will face a liquidity constraint within X months. This requires immediate attention."

Connect cash to survival. "Cash is not a finance issue. It is a survival issue. Companies do not die from low profits. They die from running out of cash. We need to treat this with appropriate urgency."

Assign ownership. "We are going to install a weekly cash discipline. The CFO will own the 13-week forecast. Each of you will own the cash drivers in your function. We will review weekly until we stabilize."

Resist the optimism. The natural response to cash stress is to believe it will resolve itself. "Revenue will catch up." "Collections will improve." "The big payment is coming next month." The Coach must resist this optimism and insist on conservative assumptions.

Create urgency without panic. The goal is focused action, not chaos. Cash stress is serious but manageable if addressed early. The tone should be urgent but not catastrophic.

What the Coach notices: The CFO who presents the cash problem as "temporary timing." The CRO who promises that "Q4 collections will normalize everything." The CEO who changes the subject to revenue growth whenever cash is raised.

What the Coach says: "I hear the optimism. But hope is not a cash flow strategy. Show me the specific actions, with owners and dates, that will generate 2 million of cash improvement in the next 60 days. We will track them weekly."

The Intervention Framework

Restoring cash health requires action on multiple fronts. The intervention framework has three components: stop the bleeding, improve the flow, and fund the gap.

Stop the bleeding means eliminating unnecessary cash consumption immediately.

Discretionary spending freeze. What spending can be paused without damaging the business? Travel, events, non-critical hiring, nice-to-have projects. This is not about cost cutting for EBITDA. It is about preserving cash.

Capital expenditure review. What capex is committed versus discretionary? Can discretionary projects be delayed? Can committed projects be renegotiated?

Inventory correction. Stop building inventory beyond immediate needs. Work down excess inventory through sales or liquidation. Convert inventory to cash.

Payment timing. Are we paying anything faster than required? Align payment timing with contractual terms.

Improve the flow means accelerating cash collection and optimizing working capital.

Receivables acceleration. Intensify collection efforts. Follow up on overdue accounts. Consider early payment incentives (1-2% discount for payment within 10 days can accelerate cash significantly). Tighten credit terms for new customers. Address disputed invoices blocking payment.

Inventory optimization. Improve demand forecasting to reduce safety stock. Accelerate inventory turns. Sell slow-moving inventory at discount if necessary.

Payables optimization. Renegotiate supplier terms where possible. Align payment timing to terms without damaging critical relationships.

Fund the gap means securing additional liquidity to bridge the cash shortfall.

Revolver draw. If capacity exists, drawing on the revolver provides immediate liquidity. Understand the covenant implications before drawing.

Covenant amendment. If covenants will be breached, proactive conversation with lenders is essential. Lenders prefer to work with borrowers who surface issues early and have credible plans.

Additional equity. In some cases, the sponsor may need to inject additional equity. This is expensive for returns but may be necessary.

Asset sales. Are there non-core assets that could be sold? The cash from a sale may exceed the earnings lost.

The three components work together. Stopping the bleeding buys time. Improving the flow addresses root causes. Funding the gap provides cushion while the other interventions take effect.

CHAPTER 21 - CLINIC

13-Week Cash "Action Board"

Weekly actions that move cash, not just forecast it

This Week Collections	Next Week	Blocked	Done
Customer A: $50K	Customer B: $75K	Customer C: $30K	Customer D: $40K
Owner: Sales	Owner: AR	Issue: Dispute	Collected Wed
Due: Fri	Due: Mon	Owner: CFO	

Escalation trigger: Runway < X weeks = sponsor alert + cost actions

☐ Forecast without action is false comfort

The 13-Week Cash Forecast Intensified

The 13-week cash forecast becomes the central management tool during cash stress.

Frequency increases. Weekly update is the minimum. During acute stress, daily visibility may be required.

Granularity increases. Not just total cash, but cash by source and use. Collections by customer. Disbursements by category. Each line item is managed.

Scenarios are required. Best case, base case, worst case. What if the big collection slips? What if sales come in below forecast? Stress scenarios reveal how fragile the position is.

Accuracy is tracked. Each week, compare forecast to actual. Understand variances. Improve forecasting. Accountability for forecast accuracy drives better information. Target: within 5 percent variance week over week.

The forecast is the weekly truth anchor. Every leadership team meeting during cash stress should begin with the 13-week update.

The Cash Huddle

The weekly cash huddle becomes essential during cash stress.

Attendees should include the CEO, CFO, and leaders of functions with significant cash impact: commercial (collections), operations (inventory and disbursements), procurement (payables).

The agenda is focused.

Last week versus forecast. What did we project? What actually happened? Why the variance?

Updated 13-week forecast. What does the new forecast show? Where is the stress point? What changed?

Intervention status. What actions are we taking to stop the bleeding and improve the flow? Are they working? What adjustments are needed?

Decisions required. Are there cash-related decisions for this week? Approve a collection incentive? Delay a payment? Pause a project?

The huddle creates visibility and accountability. Everyone knows the cash position. Everyone knows their role in improving it. Progress is tracked weekly.

Protecting Growth While Preserving Cash

The tension in this pattern is that cash preservation can kill growth, and growth is what makes the company valuable.

The goal is not to stop growing. The goal is to grow in a cash-efficient way.

Prioritize profitable growth. Growth that generates positive contribution margin and reasonable payback. Unprofitable growth, customers acquired at negative margin, products sold below cost, consumes cash without creating value.

Manage working capital with growth. As revenue grows, working capital discipline must grow with it. Tighter collection. Leaner inventory. The growth adds value only if the cash cycle does not expand.

Time growth investments carefully. Investments in capacity, people, and systems should match the pace of revenue realization. Investing ahead of revenue creates cash drag. The more severe the cash stress, the more closely investments should track realized revenue.

Make trade-offs explicit. The leadership team should understand: if we pursue this growth initiative, here is the cash impact. Is the expected value worth the cash consumption? Sometimes the answer is yes. Sometimes the answer is wait until cash health is restored.

The Coach helps the CEO hold this tension. Neither growth-at-all-costs nor cash-preservation-at-all-costs is the right answer. The right answer is disciplined growth that creates value without killing the company.

The Sponsor and Lender Conversations

Cash stress requires proactive communication with both sponsor and lenders.

The sponsor conversation:

Do not wait until crisis. If the 13-week forecast shows covenant risk or liquidity constraints, the sponsor should know early. Surprising the sponsor with a cash crisis destroys trust and reduces options.

Present the situation clearly. "Our growth is strong, and that is creating cash consumption that we need to manage. Here is the current position. Here is the forecast. Here is what we are doing about it."

Present what you need. If additional support is needed, whether covenant flexibility, additional capital, or other resources, ask clearly.

The lender conversation:

Proactive is better than reactive. A borrower who surfaces covenant risk with a plan maintains credibility. A borrower who breaches without warning loses credibility and negotiating leverage.

Present facts, not spin. The lender will see through optimism. Present the situation accurately: here is where we are, here is how we got here, here is what we are doing.

Request specific relief. If you need a covenant holiday, request it specifically. If you need amended terms, propose them. Vague requests generate vague responses.

Be prepared for consequences. The lender may require additional reporting, increased pricing, tighter terms, or other conditions. These are the cost of flexibility.

Recovery Indicators

How do you know cash health is being restored?

Operating cash flow turns positive. The business generates more cash than it consumes. This is the fundamental indicator.

Revolver utilization decreases. The company repays borrowings rather than increasing them.

Covenant headroom expands. The ratios move away from limits, providing cushion.

Working capital metrics improve. DSO decreases. DIO decreases. The cash conversion cycle shortens.

The 13-week forecast stabilizes. The weekly update stops showing deterioration. The forecast shows stability or improvement.

Recovery may take several quarters. The interventions do not produce instant results. Patience and consistency are required. But the trajectory should be visible early, even if the destination takes time to reach.

Structural Fixes

Once immediate cash stress is addressed, structural fixes prevent recurrence.

Working capital targets. Set targets for DSO, DIO, and DPO. Make them part of the operating rhythm. Review monthly. Tie compensation to achievement.

Cash-aware growth planning. Build cash impact into growth planning from the start. Model the working capital and capex requirements of growth initiatives. Ensure cash is available before committing.

Capex governance. Establish clear approval thresholds and return requirements for capital expenditures. Track actual returns against projected returns.

Forecasting discipline. Maintain the 13-week forecast as a permanent discipline, not just a crisis response. Accurate cash forecasting prevents future surprises.

Cash culture. Build awareness throughout the organization that cash matters. Commercial leaders should care about collection, not just booking. Operations leaders should care about inventory turns. The culture shift sustains the discipline.

Coach Cards Referenced

- **13-week cash forecast as the central management tool**
- **Cash conversion cycle (DSO + DIO - DPO)**
- **Weekly cash huddle**

- **Covenant headroom management (15-20% minimum)**
- **24-hour surfacing norm for material issues**
- **Stop the bleeding, improve the flow, fund the gap framework**

Field Drills

- **Calculate your current cash conversion cycle.** Compare to 12 months ago. What changed?
- **Build the bridge from EBITDA to operating cash flow** for the last four quarters. Identify the largest cash consumers.
- **Review your 13-week cash forecast for accuracy.** Compare last month's forecast to actuals. What was the variance?
- **Identify three actions you could take this week to improve cash.** Assign owners and deadlines.
- **If you do not have a weekly cash huddle, institute one.** If you do, assess whether it is driving real improvement.

Clinic Questions

- Is our growth creating or consuming cash? What is the cash cost of our growth?
- What is our cash conversion cycle, and how has it changed as we have grown?
- Where specifically is cash being trapped: receivables, inventory, capex, or other?
- How accurate is our cash forecasting? Would we see a problem coming 90 days in advance?
- What working capital discipline do we have? Are there targets for DSO, DIO, and DPO?
- If we faced a cash crisis, how quickly would we recognize it? How quickly could we respond?
- Does our organization understand the connection between their actions and cash impact?

Chapter 22

Clinic: The Plan Is Stale

The value creation plan was developed 14 months ago. It was thorough: market analysis, competitive positioning, initiative roadmaps, financial projections. The investment committee approved it. The board endorsed it. The leadership team committed to it.

Now, sitting in the quarterly review, the operating partner noticed something troubling. The initiatives being discussed were the same ones from the original plan. The metrics being tracked were the same. The targets were the same. But the world had changed.

A competitor had launched a disruptive product. Two key assumptions about market growth had proven wrong. A technology shift had altered unit economics. The regulatory environment had tightened. The supply chain had restructured.

The plan, which had been right 14 months ago, was now disconnected from reality. And no one seemed to have noticed.

"When did we last update the plan?" the operating partner asked.

Silence.

This is the stale plan pattern. The value creation plan, which should be a living document that evolves with reality, has become a historical artifact. The team continues to execute against it not because it is still right, but because no one has challenged it. The plan drifts further from relevance with each passing quarter.

CHAPTER 22 · CLINIC

The Plan Is Stale

When the plan stops matching reality

Signals	Root Causes
Repeated misses · Initiatives slipping · Market changes ignored · Team gaming KPIs · Board conversations looping	No re-baselining rhythm · Weak accountability · Overconfidence · Talent gaps

☐ A stale plan is a slow-motion value leak

How Plans Go Stale

Plans go stale through predictable mechanisms.

The world changes, but the plan does not. Markets shift. Competitors act. Customers evolve. Technology advances. Regulations change. The plan was built on a snapshot of the world at a moment in time. The world did not stop moving.

Assumptions decay without detection. The plan assumed 8 percent market growth. Actual growth was 4 percent. The plan assumed stable pricing. Competitors cut prices by 10 percent. These assumption failures accumulate, but without explicit tracking, they go unnoticed.

Initiatives complete without impact. The plan included an initiative to improve sales productivity. The initiative was declared complete because activities occurred: training was delivered, tools were deployed. But productivity did not actually improve. The plan shows green. The results show red.

New information is ignored. The team learns things during execution that should inform the plan. Customer feedback reveals the product needs changes. Pilot results show a market is not as attractive as expected. But the plan is not updated to reflect this learning.

Inertia favors the status quo. Updating the plan is work. It requires admitting that prior assumptions were wrong. It requires making new commitments. It is easier to continue executing the existing plan than to revise it.

Leadership changes break continuity. The CEO who developed the plan departs. The new CEO inherits it but does not own it. They execute mechanically rather than adapting strategically.

The staleness accumulates gradually. In month three, the plan is slightly dated. In month nine, it is noticeably misaligned. In month 18, it is fiction.

The Economics of Staleness

Executing a stale plan is expensive.

Resources flow to the wrong priorities. The plan allocates investment to initiatives that made sense 18 months ago. Those initiatives may no longer be the highest-value opportunities. A company that invests 2 million in an initiative that no longer creates value has consumed 2 million that could have funded a relevant initiative.

Opportunities are missed. While the team executes stale initiatives, new opportunities emerge that are not in the plan. Without a mechanism to incorporate new opportunities, they are ignored or under-resourced. The market share that could have been captured goes to a competitor who acted faster.

Threats are not addressed. The competitive response, the market shift, the technology disruption: these were not in the plan because they had not happened yet. If the plan is not updated, these threats are not addressed. By the time they are recognized, the damage is done.

IRR suffers. Every quarter spent executing a stale plan is a quarter not spent on the best path to value creation. On a typical PE timeline, six months of misdirected effort represents 15 to 20 percent of the hold period. The IRR impact of that delay compounds.

Exit story weakens. The value creation narrative requires a credible plan for continued value creation. A stale plan does not provide that. Buyers will see the disconnect during diligence. They will question whether management understands the business they are running.

Recognizing Staleness

Several signals indicate plan staleness.

The plan has not been formally updated in over six months. Some elements of any plan will remain stable. But if no aspect of the plan has changed in six or more months, it is likely stale.

Key assumptions have not been tested. The assumption register (if one exists) has not been reviewed. No one can articulate which assumptions are holding and which are failing.

Initiatives are tracked on activity, not outcome. "Completed supplier negotiations" is activity. "Achieved 2 million in savings reflected in Q3 actuals" is outcome. If reporting focuses on activity, outcomes may be diverging.

The external environment has changed materially. Competitive moves, market shifts, regulatory changes, technology developments. If these have occurred and the plan does not reflect them, the plan is stale.

Forecast accuracy has degraded. If projections consistently miss, the model underlying them may be based on outdated assumptions.

Leadership discussions feel repetitive. The same initiatives, the same challenges, the same talking points quarter after quarter. Nothing evolves.

When these signals cluster, staleness is likely.

The Staleness Conversation

Addressing staleness requires a direct conversation, typically with the CEO.

Name the observation. "I want to share something I am noticing. Our value creation plan was developed 14 months ago. The world has changed since then. I am not sure the plan still reflects our best path to value creation."

Ask the diagnostic question. "When did we last fundamentally revisit the plan? Not update a slide, but actually challenge whether our priorities are still right?"

Invite reflection. "What has changed in our market, with our competitors, or in our business that should inform our plan? What assumptions have proven wrong? What have we learned that should redirect us?"

Propose action. "I think we need a formal plan refresh. Not a complete restart, but a rigorous review of assumptions, initiatives, and priorities. Can we schedule time for this?"

Most CEOs, when the staleness is named, will recognize it. They have been too busy executing to step back and question whether they are executing the right things. The conversation gives permission to pause and reassess.

What the Coach notices: The CEO who deflects the conversation. The leadership team that cannot name which assumptions have been invalidated. The initiative tracker that shows green on everything while financial results show red.

What the Coach says: "We have been executing this plan for 14 months. What have we learned that should change it? If nothing, that would be remarkable. If something, I want to understand what and why it has not been incorporated."

The Plan Refresh Process

A plan refresh is not a complete replanning. It is a structured review and update that incorporates learning and changed conditions.

Step one: Reassess the external environment. What has changed in the market, competitive landscape, regulatory environment, technology context, and macroeconomic conditions since the plan was developed? What new information do we have?

This reassessment should be fact-based. Market data. Competitive intelligence. Customer feedback. Regulatory developments. Not opinion, but evidence.

Step two: Test the assumptions. Review the key assumptions underlying the plan. For each assumption, assess: is it still valid? What evidence do we have? If the assumption has failed, what are the implications?

The assumption register is the tool for this. If one does not exist, create one during the refresh.

Step three: Evaluate initiative performance. For each initiative in the plan, assess: what was the expected outcome? What has actually been achieved? Is the initiative on track to deliver value? Should it continue, be modified, or be stopped?

This evaluation should be honest. Activity completion is not the same as value delivery. Focus on outcomes.

Step four: Identify new opportunities and threats. What opportunities have emerged that were not in the original plan? What threats have materialized? Should these be incorporated?

The plan should not only defend the original thesis but also adapt to new realities.

Step five: Reprioritize. Given the reassessment, what should change? Which initiatives should be accelerated? Which should be slowed or stopped? What new initiatives should be added? What is the new priority order?

Reprioritization is the hardest part. It requires releasing attachment to the original plan and embracing what is now the best path.

Step six: Update the financial model. Refresh the projections to reflect updated assumptions and priorities. What is the new expected EBITDA trajectory? What is the new expected exit value?

The updated model becomes the new baseline against which performance is measured.

Step seven: Communicate the refresh. Share the updated plan with the leadership team, the board, and (at appropriate level of detail) the organization. Explain what changed and why.

Communication ensures alignment around the updated direction.

The Refresh Cadence

A one-time refresh addresses immediate staleness. Preventing recurrence requires ongoing discipline.

Quarterly assumption reviews. Each quarter, explicitly review the key assumptions underlying the plan. Are they still valid?

What evidence do we have? This becomes a standing agenda item in quarterly reviews.

Semi-annual initiative assessments. Twice per year, rigorously evaluate each initiative against expected outcomes. Make continue, modify, or stop decisions.

Annual plan refresh. Once per year, conduct a comprehensive refresh: external reassessment, assumption testing, initiative evaluation, reprioritization, model update. This is a deeper exercise than the quarterly and semi-annual reviews.

Continuous hypothesis testing. Treat the plan as a set of hypotheses. Test them continuously. When evidence accumulates that a hypothesis is wrong, act on it rather than waiting for the formal refresh.

This cadence ensures the plan remains current. Staleness cannot accumulate if the plan is regularly revisited.

Building the Adaptive Muscle

Beyond process, the goal is to build organizational capability for adaptation.

Intellectual honesty is foundational. The willingness to acknowledge when assumptions are wrong, when initiatives are failing, when the plan needs change. Without intellectual honesty, no process will overcome the human tendency to defend prior commitments.

Curiosity drives learning. The interest in understanding what is happening in the market, what customers are saying, what competitors are doing, what the data shows. Curiosity generates the information that enables adaptation.

Speed enables responsiveness. The ability to recognize a changed condition and respond quickly, before the window closes. Slow organizations see the change but cannot act in time.

Psychological safety enables truth. People must be able to say "this initiative is not working" or "this assumption was wrong" without fear of punishment. Safety enables the surfacing that drives adaptation.

The Coach models these capabilities and helps the CEO build them in the organization. Adaptation is not just a process. It is a culture.

The Sponsor Perspective

Sponsors want plans that work, not plans that are defended.

If the plan needs updating, communicate proactively. "We have learned things over the past six months that inform our plan. We are proposing these adjustments based on what we now know."

Frame updates positively. Plan updates are evidence of learning, not evidence of failure. The organization that updates is smarter than the one that clings to outdated assumptions.

Maintain commitment to outcomes. The EBITDA target may still be achievable, but through different means. Or the target may need adjustment because of factors beyond management control. Either way, the commitment is to creating value, not to executing a specific playbook.

Demonstrate rigor. The sponsor should see that updates are based on evidence and analysis, not whim or avoidance. The assumption register, the initiative evaluation, the external reassessment: these demonstrate that the update is rigorous.

Most sponsors appreciate adaptive management. They have seen too many management teams defend failing plans until failure became undeniable. A team that adapts proactively is a team they can trust.

Re-Baselining Sprint

Fast reset without chaos · 2 weeks

Days 1-3
Reality pack: market · customer · ops · cash

Days 4-7
Refresh hypotheses · Reprioritize levers

Days 8-10
Owners · Milestones · KPIs

Days 11-14
Board pre-wire · Commit

☑ Re-baseline early. Don't defend a dead plan.

When the Plan Cannot Be Saved

Sometimes the plan is not just stale. It is fundamentally broken.

The thesis was wrong. The market opportunity does not exist as assumed. The competitive position is weaker than believed. The growth that was projected is not achievable.

When the thesis is wrong, refreshing the plan is not enough. A fundamental rethink is required. What value can be created from this asset? What is the realistic path?

This is a harder conversation. It may involve resetting expectations with the sponsor. It may involve significant strategic pivots. It may involve changes in leadership or approach.

The Coach helps distinguish between a stale plan (which can be refreshed) and a broken thesis (which requires fundamental rethink). The interventions are different.

A stale plan needs updating. A broken thesis needs reinvention.

Preventing Staleness

The best approach is preventing staleness from developing.

Build adaptation into the operating rhythm. The quarterly assumption reviews, semi-annual initiative assessments, annual plan refresh. Make these non-negotiable calendar items.

Create the assumption register at the start. Document key assumptions from day one. Assign owners. Establish review cadence. The assumption register prevents invisible decay.

Track outcomes, not just activities. Report on whether initiatives are delivering expected value, not just whether activities occurred. Outcome focus reveals disconnects early.

Maintain external awareness. Stay connected to the market, competitors, customers, and technology. The organization that stops watching the environment will be surprised by changes it should have anticipated.

Model adaptation from the top. The CEO who is willing to say "I was wrong about this, and here is what we are doing instead" creates permission for the entire organization to adapt.

Prevention is far less costly than remediation. The organization that stays current does not need crisis refreshes.

Coach Cards Referenced

- **Assumption register for tracking key hypotheses**
- **90-day hypothesis review cycle**
- **Quarterly assumption reviews**
- **Semi-annual initiative assessments**
- **Annual plan refresh**
- **Commitment to outcomes, flexibility on path**
- **Hypothesis mindset**

Field Drills

- **Review when your value creation plan was last fundamentally updated.** If it has been more than six months, schedule a refresh.
- **Create or update your assumption register.** List the ten most important assumptions. Assess which are holding and which are failing.
- **Evaluate each initiative in your plan against expected outcomes, not just activities.** Identify which are delivering and which are not.
- **Assess your external environment.** What has changed since the plan was developed? How should the plan reflect those changes?
- **Establish a quarterly assumption review as a standing agenda item.** Make it non-negotiable.

Clinic Questions

- When did we last fundamentally revisit our value creation plan? Are we executing a current plan or a historical artifact?
- What key assumptions underlie our plan, and which have been validated or invalidated by evidence?
- Are we tracking initiatives on outcomes or activities? Do we know which initiatives are actually creating value?
- What has changed in our external environment that our plan does not yet reflect?
- Do we have a regular cadence for plan review and update? If not, why not?

- How does our organization respond when evidence contradicts the plan? Do we adapt or defend?
- If we conducted a rigorous plan refresh today, what would change?

Chapter 23

Clinic: We Need a Re-Rate, Not Just EBITDA

The exit preparation meeting started with the investment banker's assessment.

"Your EBITDA has grown nicely. From 12 million at entry to 19 million today. That is solid execution. But I need to be direct with you: your multiple is going to be challenged."

The CEO looked confused. "We grew EBITDA by 58 percent. Why would buyers not pay up for that?"

The banker pulled up a comparable transaction list. "Look at the peer set. Companies with your profile are trading at 7 to 8x. Your entry multiple was 7.5x. If we exit at 7.5x, your equity value increase comes entirely from EBITDA growth. You captured operating value but no multiple expansion."

"What would get us to 9x or 10x?"

"That is the question. You need a re-rate. You need buyers to see this company differently than they saw it at entry. Not just bigger, but better. Not just more profitable, but more valuable per dollar of profit."

This is the re-rate challenge. EBITDA growth is necessary but not sufficient for exceptional returns. The multiple at which the company sells determines whether the investment is good or great. A company that grows EBITDA by 50 percent but sells at the same multiple as entry has created value. A company that grows EBITDA by 50 percent and expands its multiple by 25 percent has created significantly more value.

This clinic addresses how to diagnose whether you need a re-rate, what drives multiple expansion, and how to build the company that commands a premium.

CHAPTER 21 CLINIC

We Need a Re-Rate, Not Just EBITDA

Multiple expansion requires the buyer to re-rate, not only earnings

Today	Risk	Exit
Baseline metrics; proof point required	Reduction; proof point required	Systems & leadership proof point required

EBITDA	Growth
Improvements; proof point required	Quality of growth; proof point required

The market pays only for durability and repeatability

The Multiple Math

The value creation bridge makes the math clear.

Entry equity value equals entry EBITDA times entry multiple, minus entry debt.

Exit equity value equals exit EBITDA times exit multiple, minus exit debt.

The three sources of equity value growth are: EBITDA growth, multiple expansion, and debt paydown.

Consider two scenarios for a company bought at 10 million EBITDA, 7x multiple, with 40 million of debt.

Entry equity: $(10 \times 7) - 40 = 30$ million.

Scenario A: EBITDA grows to 15 million. Multiple stays at 7x. Debt is paid down to 25 million.

Exit equity: (15 × 7) - 25 = 80 million. **Return: 2.7x.**

Scenario B: EBITDA grows to 15 million. Multiple expands to 9x. Debt is paid down to 25 million.

Exit equity: (15 × 9) - 25 = 110 million. **Return: 3.7x.**

The difference is 30 million of equity value, entirely from multiple expansion. Same EBITDA. Same debt paydown. Different multiple. Dramatically different outcome.

This is why re-rating matters. EBITDA is the engine. Multiple is the multiplier. Both must be managed.

What Drives Multiples

Multiples are not arbitrary. They reflect buyer assessment of risk and return. Understanding what drives multiples enables action to improve them.

Growth rate is the most powerful multiple driver. Buyers pay for future earnings, not just current earnings. A company growing at 15 percent commands a higher multiple than one growing at 5 percent because more of the buyer's return will come from future growth.

The coaching implication: sustainable revenue and EBITDA growth support multiple expansion. One-time improvements do not. The growth must be believable and repeatable.

Predictability reduces risk, and reduced risk supports higher multiples. Recurring revenue, long-term contracts, sticky customers, stable margins: these create predictability that buyers value.

The coaching implication: revenue mix matters. Shifting from transactional to recurring revenue improves multiples. Improving customer retention improves multiples. Reducing revenue volatility improves multiples.

Quality of earnings affects how buyers value EBITDA. Heavily adjusted EBITDA, with numerous add-backs and normalizations, gets scrutinized and often discounted. Clean EBITDA, with minimal adjustments, trades at a premium.

The coaching implication: reduce adjustments over time. Run the business cleanly. Eliminate non-recurring items. Build credible, defensible earnings.

Customer concentration creates risk. If one customer represents 25 percent of revenue, buyers worry about what happens if that customer leaves. Concentration risk depresses multiples.

The coaching implication: diversify the customer base. No single customer should exceed 10 to 15 percent of revenue. This takes time and intentional effort.

Management team depth reduces key-person risk. If the business depends on one or two individuals, buyers see vulnerability. A deep bench signals that the business can perform under new ownership.

The coaching implication: build the team. Develop succession. Demonstrate that the organization, not just the CEO, creates value.

Competitive position determines sustainability. Market leaders with defensible moats command premiums. Commoditized players in fragmented markets trade at discounts.

The coaching implication: strengthen market position. Build brand. Create switching costs. Deepen customer relationships. Develop differentiated capabilities.

Operational excellence signals scalability. Efficient processes, documented systems, strong metrics, proven scalability: these tell buyers the business can grow without breaking.

The coaching implication: professionalize operations. Document processes. Build systems. Demonstrate operational discipline.

Technology capability is increasingly valued. Modern systems, data capabilities, digital presence: these suggest the business is positioned for the future.

The coaching implication: invest in technology appropriately. Address technical debt. Build capabilities that buyers will value.

Each of these factors contributes to the multiple. Improving across multiple dimensions creates cumulative re-rating potential.

The Economics of Re-Rating

The economics of multiple expansion are asymmetric and powerful.

Each turn of multiple on exit EBITDA creates substantial equity value. On 20 million of EBITDA, moving from 7x to 8x creates 20 million of additional enterprise value. After debt, most of that flows to equity. On a 50 million equity base, that single turn of multiple improvement adds 40 percent to returns.

Multiple expansion compounds with EBITDA growth. If EBITDA grows from 15 million to 20 million while multiple expands from 7x to 9x, the combined effect is dramatic. At 7x on 15M: 105M enterprise value. At 9x on 20M: 180M enterprise value. The 75 million of value creation came roughly half from EBITDA growth and half from multiple expansion.

IRR benefits from multiple expansion disproportionately. Because multiple expansion typically materializes at exit, it creates a large terminal value increase. On a 4-year hold, an additional 30 million of exit value from multiple expansion adds roughly 400 basis points to IRR.

The asymmetry means that re-rating deserves explicit attention, not as a lucky outcome but as a managed objective.

Diagnosing the Re-Rate Need

Not every company needs to focus on re-rating. Some are already well-positioned. The diagnosis determines where you stand.

Compare your current multiple to entry multiple. If you bought at 8x and peer transactions suggest you would sell at 8x, there is no multiple expansion in the base case. Re-rating requires intentional action.

Compare your profile to higher-multiple peers. What do companies trading at 10x have that you lack? Faster growth? More recurring revenue? Less concentration? Better margins? The comparison reveals the gaps.

Assess your strengths and weaknesses against the multiple drivers. For each driver, rate yourself: strong, average, or weak. The weak areas represent re-rating opportunities.

Talk to buyers and advisors. Bankers, M&A advisors, and potential buyers can provide perspective on how the market views your company. Their feedback reveals what is valued and what is discounted.

Project the exit value under different multiple scenarios. What is the equity value at 7x, 8x, 9x, 10x? Understanding the sensitivity motivates action.

The diagnosis produces a clear view: this is where we stand on multiple, these are the gaps, and this is what would need to change to re-rate.

What the Coach notices: The leadership team that focuses exclusively on EBITDA without understanding multiple dynamics. The CEO who assumes growth will automatically translate to premium valuation. The board that has not discussed what would drive multiple expansion.

What the Coach says: "Walk me through your exit math. What multiple are you assuming, and why? What would need to change for buyers to pay a turn higher?"

The Re-Rating Roadmap

Re-rating does not happen by accident. It requires a deliberate plan executed over time.

Identify the highest-impact opportunities. Not all multiple drivers are equally addressable. Focus on the two or three where improvement is most feasible and impactful.

Set specific targets. "Improve growth" is not actionable. "Accelerate revenue growth from 8 percent to 15 percent through geographic expansion and product extension" is actionable.

Develop initiatives for each target. What specific actions will move the metric? Who owns them? What resources are required? What is the timeline?

Build the proof points. Each initiative should generate evidence. Customer wins. Market share gains. Margin improvement. Retention metrics. The proof points accumulate into a narrative.

Track progress rigorously. Re-rating initiatives are long-duration efforts. Progress must be tracked quarterly to ensure momentum.

Integrate into the value creation plan. Re-rating is not separate from value creation. It is part of value creation. The initiatives belong in the mVMS alongside EBITDA improvement efforts.

Accelerating Growth

Growth is the most powerful re-rating lever, but also the hardest to manufacture.

Organic growth acceleration requires investment. New products, new markets, new channels, new capabilities. The investment consumes cash before generating returns. The timing and magnitude must be managed.

The Coach helps the CEO identify growth opportunities with favorable economics. What is the market size? What is the competitive intensity? What is the expected return on investment? What is the risk?

M&A can accelerate growth and support re-rating. Acquiring a faster-growing company improves the blended growth rate. Acquiring capabilities or market access enables organic growth acceleration.

The Coach helps ensure M&A is strategic, not just additive. Acquisitions must improve the profile, not just increase size. A bad acquisition at a high multiple destroys value even if it increases EBITDA.

Growth must be sustainable. Buyers discount growth that appears temporary or artificial. Sustainable growth comes from durable competitive advantages, not one-time circumstances.

Improving Predictability

Predictability often requires business model evolution.

Shifting to recurring revenue. Subscription models, maintenance contracts, long-term agreements. Each shift increases the portion of revenue that is predictable.

The transition can be challenging. Existing customers may resist new models. Revenue recognition timing may shift unfavorably. The investment in transition must be managed.

Improving retention. High retention makes existing revenue predictable. Retention improvement requires understanding why customers leave and addressing those causes.

The Coach helps diagnose churn. Is it product quality? Service quality? Price? Competitive displacement? Each cause requires different intervention.

Reducing volatility. Diversifying revenue across customers, products, and markets reduces the impact of any single disruption. Less volatility means more predictability.

Cleaning Up Earnings Quality

Earnings quality is within management control.

Reduce adjustments over time. Each year, the add-backs should decrease. Non-recurring items should actually not recur. The path from GAAP to adjusted should be simple and defensible.

Eliminate related-party transactions. Buyers scrutinize related-party transactions. They create questions about whether EBITDA is real or manufactured. Clean them up before exit.

Simplify accounting where possible. Complex structures, unusual recognition policies, and aggressive interpretations all create risk. Simplicity builds confidence.

Prepare for quality of earnings scrutiny. Commission a sell-side QofE analysis midway through the hold period. Identify issues proactively. Address them before buyers find them.

Addressing Concentration

Customer concentration takes time to address.

Diversification requires growth. To reduce concentration from 25 percent to 15 percent without losing the large customer, the rest of the business must grow substantially. This is multi-year work.

The Coach helps set realistic timelines. If the largest customer is 30 percent of revenue, reducing to 15 percent while growing the base requires doubling non-concentrated revenue. The plan must reflect this math.

Mitigate where diversification is slow. If concentration will persist at exit, mitigate the risk through long-term contracts, strong relationships, and demonstrated stickiness. Buyers discount concentration, but evidence of durability reduces the discount.

CHAPTER 23 · CLINIC

Re-Rate Playbook

What to build so buyers pay a premium — The 5 Proof Buckets

Revenue Quality	Margin Durability	Cash Conversion
Retention · Mix · Concentration	Process · pricing power	Working capital discipline

Management Depth	Digital Confidence
Bench · Succession · Accountability	Data · Controls · Dashboards

☐ A re-rate is engineered, not negotiated

Building Team Depth

Team depth signals organizational maturity.

Succession for key roles. Every critical role should have an identified successor, either internal or a defined external profile. Succession depth reduces key-person risk.

Leadership development. Invest in developing the next tier of leaders. The bench should be visible and credible.

Reduce CEO dependency. If the business runs through the CEO, buyers see risk. Distribute authority and capability. Demonstrate that the organization performs, not just the individual.

Document institutional knowledge. The expertise that lives in people's heads should be captured in processes, systems, and training. This reduces dependency and supports scalability.

The Narrative Dimension

Re-rating requires narrative as well as performance.

Buyers must understand why this company deserves a premium. The performance must be packaged in a story that creates confidence.

The narrative should highlight what has changed. "This was a 7x company at entry. Here is what we did to make it a 9x company." The improvement must be articulated.

The narrative should emphasize durability. "These changes are structural, not temporary. The growth is sustainable. The improvements are embedded in the business."

The narrative should project the future. "Here is the roadmap for the next owner. Here is the continued value creation potential." Buyers pay for the future, and the narrative must paint it.

The Coach helps the CEO develop the re-rating narrative. What is the story of transformation? What evidence supports it? How will it be delivered to buyers?

Timing the Exit

Re-rating initiatives take time. The exit must be timed to capture their value.

Exiting too early leaves re-rating potential unrealized. The initiatives are underway but not yet reflected in results. Buyers see the work in progress but do not pay for it.

Exiting too late risks market changes. The multiple environment may shift. The initiatives may plateau. The opportunity may pass.

The Coach helps assess exit timing. Are the re-rating initiatives reflected in results? Is there compelling evidence for the narrative? Is the market receptive?

The best exit timing captures both EBITDA growth and demonstrated re-rating, with a credible story of continued improvement for the next owner.

When Re-Rating Is Not Achievable

Sometimes the re-rate is not realistic.

The business is fundamentally a commodity. No amount of effort will create differentiation that buyers will pay for. The multiple is what it is.

The market has shifted. Sector multiples have compressed. What would have been a re-rate at entry is now just maintaining position.

Time has run out. Re-rating initiatives require years. If exit is imminent, there is not enough runway.

In these cases, the focus shifts to maximizing EBITDA and optimizing the exit process. A well-run sale process can capture value even without multiple expansion. And EBITDA growth still creates returns, even at a flat multiple.

The Coach helps the CEO face this reality. Not every deal will achieve multiple expansion. The goal is to create maximum value given the circumstances, not to pretend circumstances are different than they are.

The Final Truth

There is a moment in many PE deals when the room gets honest. It usually happens after the easy work has been done. Margins have improved. Costs have been cut. A few quick wins landed. The company is more disciplined than it was at close. EBITDA is up.

And yet, the equity value is not where it needs to be.

The sponsor runs the math quietly, then says it out loud: "Even if we hit the EBITDA plan, we still do not get the outcome we want unless the multiple improves."

That sentence changes everything. Because EBITDA growth is familiar. It is the muscle memory of PE. Multiple expansion is different. It is not only performance. It is perception. It is risk. It is quality. It is narrative. It is buyer appetite. It is a set of signals the market rewards.

A re-rate is not negotiated at exit. It is built over the hold period. It is earned through discipline. Through growth that is sustainable. Through earnings that are clean. Through customers that are diversified. Through teams that are deep. Through operations that are excellent. Through stories that are credible.

The company that earns a re-rate has done something harder than growing EBITDA. It has changed what buyers believe about the business. It has made the business undeniable.

That is the final lesson of the PE Coach. Not just to grow the profits. But to build a company that commands a premium. Not by hope. By design.

Coach Cards Referenced

- **Multiple drivers: growth, predictability, quality, concentration, team depth, competitive position, operational excellence, technology**
- **Value creation bridge: EBITDA growth + multiple expansion + debt paydown**
- **Quality of earnings analysis**
- **Customer concentration under 10-15%**
- **Succession for key roles**
- **Exit readiness framework**
- **LTV/CAC and net revenue retention for recurring revenue businesses**

Field Drills

- **Calculate your entry multiple and estimate your current exit multiple** based on comparable transactions. Is there multiple expansion in your base case?
- **Rate yourself on each multiple driver:** growth rate, predictability, earnings quality, concentration, team depth, competitive position, operational excellence, technology. Identify your two weakest areas.
- **Develop a re-rating roadmap.** For your two weakest areas, define specific targets, initiatives, and timelines.
- **Talk to a banker or M&A advisor** about how the market views your company. What would it take to command a premium multiple?
- **Project your exit value under different multiple scenarios** (current multiple, +1 turn, +2 turns). Understand the sensitivity.

Clinic Questions

- Do we have multiple expansion in our base case, or are we relying entirely on EBITDA growth for returns?

- What do higher-multiple peers have that we lack? What would we need to change to trade at their level?
- Is our growth rate sufficient to support multiple expansion? If not, what would accelerate it?
- How predictable is our revenue? What would increase predictability?
- What is our customer concentration, and what is the realistic timeline to improve it?
- How would a buyer assess our management team? Where are the gaps?
- What is our re-rating narrative? Can we articulate why this company deserves a premium?

APPENDIX

PE COACHING FRAMEWORKS

Innovative Frameworks to Differentiate PE Coaching from Traditional Coaching

Overview

This appendix presents 12 innovative frameworks that starkly differentiate PE Coaching from traditional executive coaching. Traditional coaching focuses on person, potential, and patience. PE Coaching focuses on outcome, equity value, and velocity.

These frameworks are designed to be 'light and simple' in presentation but conceptually heavy in impact, providing coaches, operating partners, and PE professionals with practical tools to drive measurable value creation within compressed timeframes.

Framework Summary

The following table provides a quick reference to all 12 frameworks and their core differentiators:

#	Framework Name	Core Differentiator	Recommended Placement
1	Coach's Triangle	Structural (Triad vs. Dyad)	Chapter 1-2
2	Velocity vs. Capacity Matrix	Speed (Fast & P&L vs. Slow & Personal)	Chapter 2-3
3	Exit-Back Coaching Roadmap	Temporal (Deadline-driven)	Exit Planning Chapter
4	Cash Conversion Coaching Clock	Quarterly Focus (12 Quarters to Exit)	PE Coaching Rules Chapter
5	EBITDA-or-Exit Scorecard	Metric-Driven (P&L or Kill)	Chapter 2 or Appendix
6	Board Cadence Coaching Calendar	Governance Rhythm	Stakeholder Management
7	Founder-to-CEO Transition Ladder	Behavioral Shift (Founder → CEO Mode)	CEO Development
8	KPI Coaching Cascade	Data-Driven (Numbers First)	Performance Management

#	Framework Name	Core Differentiator	Recommended Placement
9	Multiple Expansion Mindset Map	Valuation Focus (EV > Growth)	Redefining Success
10	Urgency Gradient	Time-Based Intensity	Hold Period Management
11	Tension Triangle of Accountability	Productive Tension (Board-Coach-CEO)	Coaching Relationship
12	No-Bullshit Coaching Playbook	Tactical Tools (One-Pagers)	Appendix

PE Coaching Frameworks (Toolkit Index)

12 models that separate PE coaching from traditional coaching

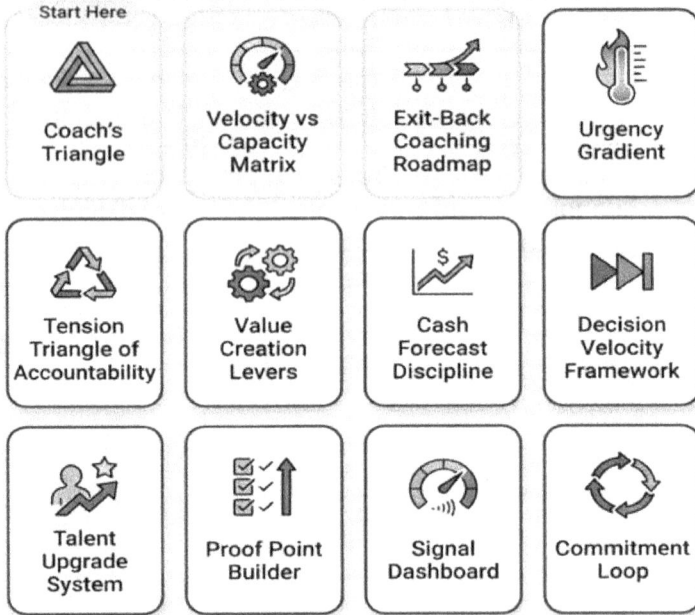

Start Here

Coach's Triangle

Velocity vs Capacity Matrix

Exit-Back Coaching Roadmap

Urgency Gradient

Tension Triangle of Accountability

Value Creation Levers

Cash Forecast Discipline

Decision Velocity Framework

Talent Upgrade System

Proof Point Builder

Signal Dashboard

Commitment Loop

How to Use This Appendix

- Pick 1 framework to explain the situation
- Pick 1 metric that proves reality
- Pick 1 cadence loop to stabilize execution
- Pick 1 conversation you are avoiding
- Pick 1 proof point for exit readiness
- Repeat quarterly

Foundation / Execution / Exit

Framework 1: The Coach's Triangle

The Structural Differentiator: Triad vs. Dyad

Core Concept: Traditional coaching is a dyad. PE coaching is a triad.

Traditional Executive Coaching	The PE Coach Framework
Structure: Coach + Executive **Goal:** 'Unlock potential' **Metric:** Self-reported growth, 360 feedback **Timeline:** Indefinite/Ongoing **Analogy:** A therapist or personal trainer	**Structure:** Coach + CEO + Sponsor (Board/Owner) **Goal:** 'Unlock Enterprise Value (EV)' **Metric:** EBITDA Growth, Multiple Expansion **Timeline:** The Hold Period (3-5 years) **Analogy:** A sports coach whose contract depends on winning this season

The Triangle of Tension

In PE coaching, there are no secrets that endanger the equity. The coach serves the exit, not just the person. This creates three critical relationships:

- Coach ↔ CEO: Building capability and addressing blind spots
- CEO ↔ Board: Delivering measurable value creation
- Coach ↔ Board: Providing honest assessment and accountability

Key Insight

Traditional coaching = 'The Confidential Void.' PE coaching = 'The Value Triangle.' The coach's loyalty is to the exit outcome, which requires transparent accountability to all stakeholders.

Framework 2: The Velocity vs. Capacity Matrix

The Speed Differentiator: Fast & P&L vs. Slow & Personal

Core Concept: Traditional coaching builds capacity. PE coaching forces velocity.

	Long-term Development	Immediate Impact
P&L Impact	**Management Consultant** (Strategy decks, 10-year plans)	**THE PE COACH** (Quarterly EBITDA, 100-Day Plans)
Individual Growth	**Life Coach / Therapist** (Not for PE)	**Executive Coach** (Fixing 'presence' or 'conflict')

The PE Coaching Zone

PE coaches operate exclusively in the top-right quadrant: Fast & P&L. Every intervention must answer the question: 'Does this move the needle on EBITDA in the next 90 days?'

Coaching Mantra

"We don't have 6 months to 'find your why.' We have 2 weeks to fix the sales pipeline."

Framework 3: The Exit-Back Coaching Roadmap

The Temporal Differentiator: Coaching with a Deadline

Core Concept: Traditional coaching is open-ended. PE coaching has a deadline - the exit.

Phase	Timeline & Focus	Goal	Coaching Style
Phase 1	**The 'Jolt'** Year 1 - Value Creation Focus: Pace & Alignment	Break 'founder mode' inertia. Install the 'PE Operating System' (KPIs, Cadence, 13-week cash)	Directive, High-Intensity *'Drill Sergeant'*
Phase 2	**The 'Build'** Years 2-3 - Growth Focus: Capability & Scale	Build the team that can run the bigger company. Remove the CEO as the bottleneck	Socratic, Strategic *'Architect'*
Phase 3	**The 'Sprint'** Years 4-5 - Exit Prep Focus: Narrative & Proof	Polish the story. Ensure the data room is bulletproof. Coach the CEO on 'the pitch'	Refining, Precise *'Editor'*

The Coach's Timeline

Instead of 'Month 1, Month 2...', the PE coach thinks in '12 Quarters to Exit.' The coaching topic changes based on the remaining runway:

- Q1: Coach on Cash Flow
- Q12: Coach on Presentation Skills for the buyer

The exit isn't the end of coaching—it's the organizing principle from day one.

Framework 4: The Cash Conversion Coaching Clock

Core Concept: Traditional coaching measures 'growth.' PE coaching measures 'cash velocity to exit.'

The coaching clock is divided into 12 quarters (3-year hold period), with each quarter labeled by a Cash Conversion Question:

- **Q1-Q3:** 'Did we stop the bleeding?' (Stabilize)
- **Q4-Q6:** 'Can we prove the model?' (Validate)
- **Q7-Q9:** 'Can we scale it?' (Multiply)
- **Q10-Q12:** 'Can we sell the story?' (Exit Prep)

Coaching Mantra: "*We don't have time to 'explore.' We have 12 quarters to create proof.*"

Before jumping my throat, for some the Q could be M or even W (month or week). It is up to you to choose.

Framework 5: The EBITDA-or-Exit Scorecard

Core Concept: In traditional coaching, 'success' is subjective. In PE coaching, success is EBITDA growth or you're fired.

Coaching Intervention	EBITDA Impact (90 Days)	Keep or Kill?
Executive presence training	+$0	✖ Kill
Sales process overhaul	+$500K	☑ Keep
'Finding your purpose' workshop	Unknown	✖ Kill
13-week cash flow system	+$300K	☑ Keep

The Rule: If a coaching session doesn't connect to a P&L metric within 90 days, it's not PE coaching—it's therapy.

Framework 6: The Board Cadence Coaching Calendar

Core Concept: Traditional coaching follows the coach's schedule. PE coaching follows the board meeting cadence.

The 12-week board cycle determines coaching intensity:

- **Week 1-2 (Post-Board):** Reflection mode - 'What did the board say? What must change?'
- **Week 3-8 (Pre-Board Prep):** Execution mode - 'Can we show measurable progress?'
- **Week 9-11 (Pre-Board Sprint):** Performance mode - 'Do the numbers tell the story?'
- **Week 12 (Board Week):** Presentation mode - 'Can the CEO deliver the pitch?'

PE Coaches don't work on 'personal growth timelines'—they work on governance rhythms.

Framework 7: The Founder-to-CEO Transition Ladder

Core Concept: PE coaching forces the founder out of 'founder mode' and into 'CEO mode' in 6 months, not 6 years.

Rung	Founder Mode (Before)	CEO Mode (After)	Coaching Focus
1	'I approve everything'	'I approve only 3 things'	Delegation System
2	'I know every customer'	'We have a CRM'	Process > Personality
3	'I feel good about Q3'	'Here's the 13-week cash forecast'	Data Literacy
4	'We're a family'	'We have an org chart'	Role Clarity
5	'We do great work'	'Here's our equity story'	Exit Language

PE coaches ask: 'Which rung are you on, and how fast can you climb?' Not 'What kind of leader do you want to be?'

Framework 8: The KPI Coaching Cascade

The Decision Tree:

1. What does the KPI dashboard say? (Data, not feelings)
2. Which KPI is red? (Problem, not symptom)
3. What behavior caused the red KPI? (Accountability, not excuses)
4. What coaching conversation fixes the behavior? (Action, not theory)
5. Did the KPI turn green in 30 days? (Proof, not promises)

Every coaching conversation must be traceable back to a red KPI or it's wasted time.

Framework 9: The Multiple Expansion Mindset Map

Traditional Coaching Mindset	PE Coaching Mindset
'You have unlimited potential'	'You have 3 years to 2x EBITDA'
'Personal mastery is the goal'	'Enterprise value is the goal'
'Leadership is a journey'	'Leadership is a deliverable'
'Be authentic'	'Be predictable (for buyers)'
'Follow your passion'	'Follow the value creation plan'

Question: 'How does today's conversation increase the multiple we'll get at exit?'

Framework 10: The Urgency Gradient

Coaching intensity increases as the exit approaches:

- **Year 1 (36-48 months to exit):** 🔥 Low urgency - 'We're building the foundation'
- **Year 2-3 (24-36 months to exit):** 🔥 🔥 Medium urgency - 'We're scaling the model'
- **Year 4 (12-24 months to exit):** 🔥 🔥 🔥 High urgency - 'We're polishing the story'
- **Final Year (0-12 months to exit):** 🔥 🔥 🔥 🔥 Maximum urgency - 'We're in the data room'

Traditional: 'Take all the time you need.'

PE: 'You have 6 weeks before the next board meeting.'

The Urgency Gradient

Coaching intensity increases as time-to-exit compresses.

0-12
months

Data room mode

12-24
months

Polish the story

24-36
months

Scale the model

36-48
months

Build the foundation

Coach Moves by Urgency

- Shorten cycles
- Raise standards
- Kill weak initiatives
- Tighten cash controls
- Make owners visible
- Convert 'plans' to proof
- Reduce surprises to zero
- Rehearse the narrative

0:00
Zero

Time-to-exit

Framework 11: The Tension Triangle of Accountability

Three Forces Creating Healthy Tension:

- **CEO ↔ Board:** 'Am I delivering what they want?'
- **Coach ↔ CEO:** 'Am I being honest with myself?'
- **Coach ↔ Board:** 'Is the CEO coachable or replaceable?'

The PE coach serves the exit, not the ego. Confidentiality is conditional, not absolute.

Tension Triangle of Accountability

Healthy tension creates speed and truth

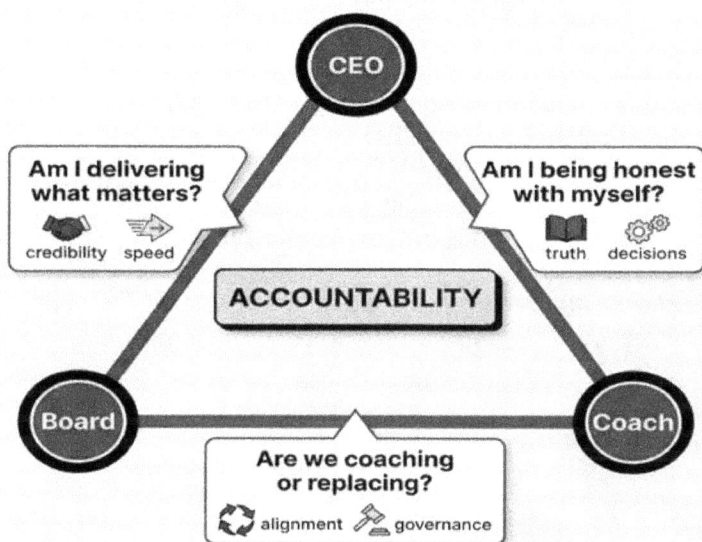

CEO

Am I delivering what matters?

credibility speed

Am I being honest with myself?

truth decisions

ACCOUNTABILITY

Board

Coach

Are we coaching or replacing?

alignment governance

Non-Negotiables

- The goal is enterprise value
- Truth travels fast
- Commitments beat discussion
- Confidentiality has limits when value is at risk
- No surprise rule
- Follow-through is visible

Framework 12: The No-Bullshit Coaching Playbook

Twelve One-Page Tactical Tools:

1. The 100-Day CEO Reset Checklist
2. The EBITDA Breakdown Coach
3. The Board Presentation Scorecard
4. The Delegation Diagnostic
5. The Sales Pipeline Coaching Script
6. The Org Chart Audit
7. The Cash Flow Coaching Session
8. The Founder-to-CEO Transition Checklist
9. The Pre-Exit CEO Prep
10. The 'Bad News' Delivery Coach
11. The KPI Coaching Cascade
12. The Exit Narrative Rehearsal Guide

Traditional coaches have 'reflective exercises.' PE coaches have tactical one-pagers that solve specific problems in 30 minutes.

Conclusion: The Undeniable Difference

By the time someone finishes reviewing these frameworks, they should be able to say:

"I now understand that PE coaching is not traditional coaching with a finance twist. It's a completely different discipline with different rules, different metrics, different relationships, and different outcomes. And I have 12 frameworks to prove it."

Key Differentiators Summarized

- **Structural:** Triad (Coach-CEO-Board) vs. Dyad (Coach-Executive)
- **Speed:** 90-day cycles vs. open-ended development
- **Metrics:** EBITDA & EV vs. self-reported growth
- **Timeline:** Exit-driven (3-5 years) vs. indefinite
- **Focus:** Enterprise value vs. personal potential
- **Accountability:** Transparent to stakeholders vs. confidential
- **Tools:** Tactical one-pagers vs. reflective exercises
- **Outcomes:** Multiple expansion vs. personal mastery

APPENDIX A

The Hard Conversations: Scripts That Work

The Coach earns their fee in the conversations no one else will have. These are not theoretical exercises. They are the exact moments where value is created or destroyed based on whether the truth gets spoken.

Below are battle-tested scripts for the hardest conversations in PE-backed leadership. Each has been refined through actual use. Each works because it follows principles that create openness rather than defense.

Hard Conversations (The First Sentence)

The Coach earns the fee in the conversations no one wants to start

Founder-CEO transition

The skills that built this are different from what's needed now.

CEO performance unacceptable

The board sees a gap between commitments and results.

Sponsor plan unrealistic

The model assumes outcomes we haven't proven we can deliver.

Toxic high performer

This person delivers results but damages the team's ability to scale.

Team is inadequate

We need different capabilities to hit the exit multiple.

Board member undermining CEO

There's a trust issue that's slowing decisions and creating confusion.

Why these work

- Observation before judgment
- Acknowledge what is true
- Clarity is kindness
- Preserve dignity with choices
- End with a question + next step

SLOW   FAST

Telling the Sponsor Their Value Creation Plan Is Unrealistic

This conversation is career-defining. Get it wrong, and you lose credibility or create an adversarial relationship. Get it right, and you become the trusted voice the sponsor relies on for the next decade.

The Setup: The value creation plan assumes 20 percent revenue growth for three consecutive years. The market is growing at 6 percent. The sales team has four reps when the plan requires twelve. The commercial infrastructure does not exist. The plan is fiction, and everyone in the room suspects it but no one will say it.

The Wrong Approach: "I think the plan might be a little aggressive." This is weak. It invites dismissal. The sponsor hears hedging and moves on.

The Script:

"I want to share something that I think serves us both. I have been pressure-testing the revenue assumptions in the plan against what I am seeing in the business.

The model assumes 20 percent growth in a market growing at 6 percent. That implies we capture 14 points of share annually from entrenched competitors. We would need to do that with a sales team of four that the plan assumes becomes twelve, but without a recruiting pipeline, a sales ops function, or a CRO who has built at this scale before.

I am not saying it is impossible. I am saying the plan as written has a low probability of success. My estimate is below 20 percent. And if we staff and spend against it, we will burn 3 to 4 million in cash and significant credibility before we adjust.

Here is what I think is achievable with high confidence: 12 percent growth in year one, accelerating to 15 percent by year three if we execute the commercial build correctly. That still creates substantial value. At 15 million entry EBITDA and a 12 percent growth rate, we are looking at 21 million by year three versus the plan's 26 million. The difference is meaningful, but 21 million is real and 26 million is hope.

I would rather we commit to a plan we can beat than defend a plan we will miss. What is your reaction?"

Why It Works: You lead with service ("serves us both"). You bring specific evidence (market data, team reality, probability estimate). You quantify the risk (3-4 million cash burn). You offer a credible alternative with numbers. You invite dialogue rather than demanding agreement.

The Economics: A plan miss in year one does not just affect that year. It triggers board concern, lender scrutiny, and management distraction that compounds through the hold period. The credibility cost of a 20 percent miss often exceeds the direct financial impact by 2 to 3x.

Firing a Founder-CEO Who Has Hit Their Ceiling

This is among the most painful conversations in PE. The founder built something real. They are emotionally invested. They may have significant equity. And they can no longer lead what the company must become.

The Setup: The founder-CEO was effective at 20 million in revenue. The company is now 60 million and needs to be 150 million. The founder cannot delegate, cannot build a leadership team, and cannot operate at the pace PE requires. Three consecutive quarters have missed plan. Two strong executives have resigned citing the founder's management style. The board has decided to make a change.

The Wrong Approach: A long buildup that buries the message. Or a cold, HR-scripted termination that treats the founder like a stranger they never met.

The Script:

"I need to have a direct conversation with you, and I want to start by saying this is hard for me because I have genuine respect for what you built. You took an idea and turned it into a 60 million dollar business. That is rare. That matters.

The company has reached a stage where it needs a different kind of leadership than it needed when you started. This is not about effort or commitment. You have given more of both than anyone could ask. It is about fit between what you do best and what the company now requires.

The board has decided to bring in a new CEO to lead the next phase. I want to be clear: this decision is made. What is not decided is how we handle it together.

You have options. You can stay involved in a different capacity. Perhaps as a board advisor, which would preserve your voice in strategy. Perhaps in a customer-facing role that leverages the relationships you built over fifteen years. Or you can make a clean transition with a separation package that reflects your contribution.

Either way, we will treat you with the respect you have earned, and we will protect your equity position. Your ownership does not change. Your vesting continues. You will participate in the exit you helped make possible.

I know this is not what you wanted to hear. What questions do you have?"

Why It Works: You honor what they built with specifics (60 million, fifteen years). You are clear the decision is made. No false hope, no ambiguity. You offer choices that preserve dignity and agency. You address the equity question directly because that is what they are worried about. You invite questions rather than ending abruptly.

Critical Follow-Up: Have the next steps ready before you walk in the room. Transition timeline (typically 60-90 days). Communication plan for employees, customers, board. Severance terms in writing. Interim leadership coverage. Do not leave them in limbo wondering what happens Monday.

Confronting the High-Performing Toxic Executive

This executive delivers results. They also destroy culture, hoard information, undermine peers, and create fear. The CEO tolerates them because the numbers are good. But the damage compounds invisibly until it becomes undeniable.

The Setup: The CRO hit 108 percent of quota last year. The CRO also has 40 percent annual turnover on their team (versus 15 percent company average). Two strong peers have resigned citing inability to work with the CRO. The finance team dreads forecast meetings. Three high-potential sales managers have left in the past year, two to competitors.

The Script (to the CEO):

"I want to talk about something uncomfortable. It is about your CRO.

I know the numbers are strong. 108 percent of quota. That is real. I also know what is happening underneath the numbers.

Forty percent turnover on the sales team. That is roughly 400,000 in recruiting and ramp costs annually, plus the revenue leakage from territories in transition. Two executives gone in the past year who cited the CRO as a primary factor. Three high-potential managers who left to competitors. The finance team spending hours reworking forecasts because the CRO refuses to follow the process.

Here is what I have learned about high-performing toxic executives: they are the most expensive people in your company. Not because of their compensation. Because of the talent they drive away, the collaboration they prevent, and the organizational debt they accumulate.

Every quarter you keep them, you are making a trade. You are trading short-term revenue for long-term organizational health. At some point, that trade stops working. Usually when you need to scale, integrate an acquisition, or prepare for exit, and you discover you have built a revenue function around one person's dysfunction.

I am not telling you to fire them tomorrow. I am asking you to look clearly at the full cost. Not just the quota attainment. The full cost.

What do you see when you look at that full picture?"

Why It Works: You acknowledge the results first, which establishes credibility. You present evidence of the hidden cost with specific numbers (40 percent turnover, 400K cost, two executives, three managers). You frame it as a trade-off with a time horizon, not a moral judgment. You ask them to reach their own conclusion.

If the CEO Still Resists: "Let me ask it differently. If this person left tomorrow, what would you feel? Relief or panic? If the answer is relief, that tells you something important about what you already know."

The Economics: A toxic CRO at 400K total compensation who drives 400K in annual turnover costs, loses two executives worth 500K each in replacement and ramp, and prevents cross-functional collaboration that costs another 300K in inefficiency is actually a net negative contributor despite hitting quota. The math often surprises CEOs who have not done it.

Telling a CEO Their Leadership Team Is Inadequate

This conversation is addressed fully in Chapter 19 (Clinic: Strong CEO, Weak Team). Here is the specific opening script that creates dialogue rather than defense.

The Script:

"I want to share an observation, and I am genuinely curious about your reaction.

When I watch your leadership team operate, I see you carrying most of the weight. You are in every meeting. Every decision flows through you. When I ask your direct reports substantive questions about their functions, the answers lack depth, or they defer to you.

I counted last week. You were in 23 meetings. Your CFO made one decision without checking with you first. Your CRO could not answer a basic question about pipeline conversion rates.

That is not sustainable. It is also not how high-performing PE-backed companies operate. The companies that exit well have CEOs who work 50 hours a week and leadership teams that run their functions independently. You are working 70 hours a week and running everyone else's function too.

Help me understand: Do you see the same thing? And if you do, what is preventing you from making changes?"

Why It Works: You describe what you observe with specifics (23 meetings, one decision, could not answer). You contrast with what good looks like (50 hours, independent functions). You invite their perspective, which creates dialogue rather than defense.

The Intervention When the CEO Is in Denial About Performance

The business is missing plan. The CEO keeps explaining why it is not their fault. External factors. Timing. Market conditions. The pattern has repeated for three quarters. The explanations are plausible individually but damning collectively.

The Script:

"I need to share something difficult with you.

For three quarters, we have had this conversation. Results come in below plan. Q1 was supply chain. Q2 was the delayed product launch. Q3 was competitive pricing pressure. You explain the variance. We adjust the forecast. And then it happens again.

I am not questioning your effort or your intelligence. I am questioning whether we are being honest with ourselves about what is actually happening.

Here is the pattern I see: consistent optimism in forecasting, followed by external attribution after the fact. Each explanation is plausible on its own. Taken together, they suggest something structural we are not addressing.

The cost is compounding. We have lost credibility with the board. The lender is asking harder questions. We have consumed 18 months of a 48-month hold period without hitting a single quarterly target. That is time we cannot recover.

I need you to sit with a hard question: Is this a temporary situation that will self-correct, or is there something structural we are not addressing? And if it is structural, what would need to change? Not in the market. In us."

Why It Works: You establish the pattern with specifics (three quarters, specific excuses). You separate effort from outcomes. You name the compounding cost (credibility, lender, time with specific numbers). You ask them to diagnose rather than defend. The final line ("Not in the market. In us.") redirects from external to internal.

Telling a CEO Their Forecast Is Fiction

The CEO presents another optimistic forecast. The board approves it. Three months later, the miss is explained with external factors. This has happened four consecutive quarters. The forecast has become a wish dressed up as a commitment.

The Script:

"I want to talk about forecasting, and I am going to be direct.

Over the last four quarters, we have set forecasts that we have not achieved. Q1: forecast 5.2 million EBITDA, actual 4.4 million. Q2: forecast 5.5 million, actual 4.7 million. Q3: forecast 5.8

million, actual 4.9 million. Q4: forecast 6.2 million, actual 5.1 million. Each quarter, we explain the gap with factors we did not anticipate.

But the pattern suggests the problem is not external factors. The problem is how we forecast.

I am not questioning your intentions. I am questioning our process.

Here is what I think is happening: we forecast what we hope will happen rather than what we believe will happen. We anchor on the plan number and work backward to justify it. We do not stress-test assumptions. We do not build in contingency. We do not ask what would have to go wrong for us to miss. The forecast becomes a wish rather than a commitment.

The cost is significant. We have lost credibility with the board. We are creating unrealistic expectations with the lender, which affects our covenant flexibility. We staff and spend against a fiction, then adjust in panic when reality hits.

I want to propose something different. For next quarter, let us build a forecast we are 80 percent confident we can hit. Not 50/50. Not best case. Eighty percent. Then let us track what actually happens.

If we beat it, we rebuild credibility. If we miss even a conservative forecast, we have learned something important about what is actually broken.

What is your reaction to that approach?"

Why It Works: You establish the pattern with actual numbers (four quarters of specific forecast versus actual). You diagnose the cause (hope over belief, anchoring on plan). You name the cost (credibility, lender, spending). You propose a specific change (80 percent confidence) with a clear benefit (rebuild credibility). You invite response.

Telling a Board Member They Are Undermining the CEO

The board member is well-intentioned but damaging. They go around the CEO to talk to executives directly. They offer conflicting direction. They second-guess decisions publicly. The CEO is frustrated but afraid to confront a board member. The operating partner or Coach must do it.

The Script (Coach to Board Member):

"I want to share an observation, and I hope you will receive it in the spirit it is intended, which is making this company work better.

I have noticed that you have been engaging directly with several of the CEO's direct reports. Calling the CFO to ask about specific deals. Emailing the CRO with suggestions on the pipeline. Giving the COO direction on the warehouse project.

I understand the instinct. You have built companies. You see things. You want to help. And your pattern recognition is valuable.

But I am seeing an unintended consequence. The CFO is confused about whether to prioritize your questions or the CEO's priorities. The CRO is getting conflicting signals about which deals matter. The COO is not sure whose direction to follow on the warehouse.

More importantly, the CEO feels undermined. Not because you intend to undermine them. Because the organization cannot tell whose voice matters most.

In a well-functioning governance model, the board's relationship is with the CEO, and the CEO's relationship is with the team. When board members engage directly with the team, even with good intentions, it blurs accountability and creates confusion.

I have a specific ask. Would you channel your observations and suggestions through the CEO, or through me? That way we can ensure they land constructively rather than create confusion.

Can we agree on that approach?"

Why It Works: You assume positive intent explicitly (wants to help, pattern recognition is valuable). You describe the specific behaviors (calling CFO, emailing CRO, directing COO). You name the unintended consequence (confusion, undermining). You reference the governance principle. You make a specific request. You ask for agreement.

Confronting a CEO About Micromanagement

The CEO cannot let go. They review every decision. They are in every meeting. They second-guess their executives. The result is slow decisions, disempowered leaders, CEO exhaustion, and an organization that cannot scale.

The Script:

"I want to share something I am noticing, and I am curious about your perspective.

Last week, I tracked your calendar and your decision involvement. You were in 27 meetings across five days. You approved 14 decisions that your direct reports could have made. You reviewed three documents that did not require CEO review. You spent four hours on a vendor selection that your procurement lead should own.

From the outside, it looks like this organization cannot move without you. That might feel like engagement or quality control. From where I sit, it looks like a bottleneck that is limiting what this company can become.

Here is the cost I am seeing. Decision velocity is slow. Your executives are not developing judgment because they do not get to make mistakes and learn. You are exhausted and do not have time for the strategic work only you can do. And buyers will see a company that depends on one person, which depresses the multiple.

I have a hypothesis about what might be driving this. I think you care deeply about getting things right. I think you have been burned before by delegation that went wrong. And I think you may not fully trust that others will get things right without you.

The problem is, as long as you are always there, they will not develop the judgment you wish they had. And you will remain the bottleneck.

I want to propose an experiment. Pick one area this month. Let someone else own it completely. No checking in. No reviewing their work. No overriding their decisions. Let them make mistakes if they make mistakes.

One area. One month. Then we assess. What area could you let go of?"

Why It Works: You describe the behavior with specific data (27 meetings, 14 approvals, 4 hours on vendor selection). You name the cost (velocity, development, exhaustion, multiple impact). You offer a hypothesis about the motivation (care about quality, trust issues). You propose a small, low-risk experiment (one area, one month). You end with a concrete question.

Ending a Coaching Relationship That Is Not Working

Sometimes the CEO is not coachable. They take feedback defensively. They do not act on insights. They agree in the room and change nothing afterward. The engagement is not creating value.

The Script:

"I want to step back and assess our work together honestly.

We have been meeting for four months. In that time, we have discussed the same issues repeatedly. The CFO gap. The forecast accuracy problem. The leadership team's lack of accountability. Each conversation, you agree these are priorities. Each month, I come back and find nothing has changed.

A coaching relationship only works if it creates value. That requires openness to feedback, willingness to experiment, and visible change over time.

I am not seeing that. When we discuss challenges, I hear agreement in the moment but I do not see changes in behavior afterward. When I offer observations, I sense defense rather than curiosity. When I push, you explain why the suggestion will not work rather than trying it.

I am not placing blame. It is possible I am not the right coach for you. It is possible the timing is wrong. It is possible you need a different kind of support than coaching.

But I do not want to continue a relationship that is not serving you. That is not fair to either of us, and it is not fair to the sponsor who is investing in this engagement.

What is your honest assessment of whether this is working?"

Why It Works: You are specific about the pattern (four months, same issues, no change). You own your part (maybe not the right fit). You describe what you observe without attacking. You give them an exit that preserves dignity. You invite their assessment, which creates shared ownership of the conclusion.

Using These Scripts

These scripts are not magic words. They work because they follow principles:

Lead with observation, not judgment. Describe what you see before drawing conclusions. "I noticed you were in 27 meetings" is observation. "You are a micromanager" is judgment. Observation creates openness. Judgment creates defense.

Acknowledge what is true. The founder did build something valuable. The CRO does hit quota. The board member does have valuable experience. Starting with acknowledgment creates the space for difficult truth.

Be clear that difficult decisions are made. When a decision is final, say so. "The board has decided" is clear. "We are thinking about" invites negotiation. Clarity is kindness. Ambiguity prolongs suffering.

Offer choices where possible. People accept difficult news better when they retain some agency. The founder can choose their role going forward. The CEO can choose which area to delegate. Choice preserves dignity.

Invite response. End with a question, not a pronouncement. "What is your reaction?" creates dialogue. "That is all" creates distance. Dialogue is more productive than monologue.

Have the next step ready. Hard conversations without clear next actions create anxiety, not progress. Know what happens after the conversation before you start it.

The Coach who masters these conversations becomes indispensable. These are the moments when trust is built, when value is created, when the fee is earned.

Opening Lines: The First Sentence That Changes Everything

The hardest part of a hard conversation is starting. Once you begin, momentum carries you forward. But finding the first words can paralyze even experienced leaders.

Below are opening lines for the most difficult conversations in PE-backed leadership. These are not complete scripts. They are starters. Use them to break the silence, then let the conversation flow.

Firing a Founder-CEO

Primary: "John, I need to have a direct conversation with you about your role, and I want you to know that what I am about to say comes from respect for what you have built."

Alternative: "This is one of the hardest conversations I have had to have. The company you built has reached a stage where it needs something different at the top."

Telling a CEO Their Performance Is Unacceptable

Primary: "I need to talk to you about something difficult, and I am going to be direct because I think you deserve honesty, not comfort."

Alternative: "We have had this conversation indirectly a few times. Today I need to have it directly."

Telling a Sponsor Their Value Creation Plan Is Unrealistic

Primary: "I want to share something with you that I think serves our shared interest, even though it might not be what you want to hear."

Alternative: "I have been pressure-testing the plan, and I have concerns I need to put on the table before we commit resources against it."

Confronting a High-Performing Toxic Executive

Primary (to CEO): "I want to talk about someone on your team, and I need to share some observations that might be uncomfortable."

Alternative: "Can we talk about the full cost of keeping [Name] in their current role? Not just the upside. The full cost."

Telling a CEO Their Team Is Inadequate

Primary: "I have been watching your leadership team operate, and I want to share what I am seeing. I am curious whether you see the same thing."

Alternative: "I need to ask you a direct question: Do you have the team you need to deliver this plan?"

Telling a CEO They Are the Problem

Primary: "This is a hard thing to say, and I have thought carefully about whether to say it. But I think not saying it would be a disservice to you."

Alternative: "I want to talk about patterns I am observing, and I need you to hear me out before you respond."

Telling a Board Member They Are Undermining the CEO

Primary: "I want to share an observation about governance, and I hope you will receive it as it is intended: in service of the company working well."

Alternative: "I have noticed something happening that I think has unintended consequences. Can I share it with you?"

Ending a Coaching Relationship That Is Not Working

Primary: "I want to step back and honestly assess whether our work together is creating value."

Alternative: "I think we owe each other an honest conversation about whether this coaching engagement is working."

Telling a CEO Their Forecast Is Fiction

Primary: "I want to talk about forecasting, and I am going to be direct because I think the pattern we are in is costing us more than we realize."

Alternative: "We have missed forecast four quarters in a row. I think we need to talk about what is actually happening."

Confronting a CEO About Micromanagement

Primary: "I want to share an observation about how you are spending your time, and I am curious about your reaction."

Alternative: "I have been watching the decision-making pattern in this company, and I want to talk about what I see."

Telling a CEO They Need to Resign

Primary: "This is the hardest conversation I have ever had to have. I need to talk to you about whether this role is still right for you."

Alternative: "I am going to say something that I wish I did not have to say. The board has lost confidence, and I think you need to hear that from me directly before you hear it from them."

General Principles for Opening Lines

Start with intent, not content. Signal that you are about to say something difficult. "I need to have a direct conversation" prepares them emotionally before you deliver the substance.

Acknowledge the difficulty. Saying "this is hard" is not weakness. It is humanity. It signals that you are not enjoying this, which makes it easier to receive.

Establish your motive. Make clear you are speaking from care, not attack. "I think you deserve honesty" or "in service of the company" frames your intent before they can assume the worst.

Be direct after the opening. The opening buys you permission. Then deliver the message clearly. Do not bury the point in caveats after a strong opening.

Pause after you speak. Let the words land. Do not rush to fill silence. Do not immediately start explaining or justifying. They need time to absorb what you said.

The first sentence is the key that unlocks the conversation. Get it right, and the rest flows. Get it wrong, and defenses rise before you reach the point.

Appendix B

The 30 Rules of Leadership

A PE Coach Perspective

Leadership in a PE-backed company is not a personality contest. It is behavior under pressure. It is judgment when information is incomplete. It is the discipline to tell the truth early, to choose coherence over cleverness, and to build a system that performs when the room gets tense.

The PE environment does not forgive two things for long: denial and drift. Denial creates surprises. Drift creates politics. Both destroy speed. Both leak cash. Both turn strong plans into slow-motion disappointments. The market does not care why it happened. Buyers do not pay premiums for excuses.

A PE Coach sits inside that reality with one job: keep the operating system anchored. Not by grabbing the wheel. Not by becoming the shadow CEO. By strengthening the triangle of trust, installing cadence, forcing signal, and making decisions move. A coach turns standards into habits, habits into culture, and culture into compounding performance.

These rules are not inspirational posters. They are field rules. They are written for leaders who want to win without losing themselves, who want to build value without burning people, and who understand that the best exits are earned long before the process starts.

Use these rules like a pre-flight checklist. Re-read them when the board pack looks good but the business feels off. Revisit them when growth is loud and cash is quiet. And if you only remember one thing, remember this: pressure does not create character. It reveals it.

Rule 1: Tell the Truth Early

Speed of truth beats speed of spin.

In PE, truth has a shelf life. If you wait, it rots into a surprise. A covenant concern surfaced in week one is a problem to solve. The same concern surfaced the day before the board meeting is a crisis that destroys trust.

Your job is to surface reality before it becomes damage. Do not manage impressions. Manage the system. The best leaders treat bad news like a perishable item: they move it quickly, clearly, and without drama.

The 24-hour rule exists for a reason. Material issues reach the sponsor within 24 hours. Not because the sponsor demands it. Because truth delayed is trust destroyed. The CEO who calls with bad news on Tuesday builds more credibility than the CEO who hides it until the board pack reveals it on Friday.

Trust is built in those moments. Not when things go well. When things go wrong and you say so anyway.

Rule 2: Coherence Is a Growth Strategy

One company, one story, one set of priorities.

Most performance problems are not capability problems. They are coherence problems. Too many priorities, too many narratives, too many agendas running in parallel. The sales team chasing one number. The operations team optimizing for another. The board hearing a third story entirely.

A leader's first act is simplification. If you cannot say the plan in two minutes, you do not have a plan. If your leadership team cannot name the same three priorities without looking at notes, you do not have alignment.

The Vital Few concept exists because coherence creates leverage. Five initiatives done well beat fifteen initiatives done poorly. Every additional priority dilutes focus, consumes management attention, and creates coordination overhead.

Coherence turns effort into momentum. Chaos turns effort into heat. The difference between a 2x return and a 4x return is often not strategy. It is coherence.

Rule 3: Never Become the Shadow CEO

Influence without ownership is sabotage, even when it is well intentioned.

A PE Coach can help a CEO see around corners, but should not take the wheel. An operating partner can provide pattern recognition and network access, but should not run the business through back channels.

When you work through the CEO, you strengthen the organization. The CEO grows. The team sees consistent leadership. Accountability is clear.

When you work around the CEO, you weaken everything. The CEO loses authority. The team gets confused about who actually decides. Information starts flowing through side channels. Politics fill the space you created.

The shadow CEO pattern creates dependency, resentment, and confusion. It feels helpful in the moment. It is corrosive over time. Strong leadership builds leaders. It does not replace them.

The test is simple: if the CEO left tomorrow, would the organization be stronger or weaker for your involvement? If the answer is weaker, you have become a crutch, not a coach.

Rule 4: Pre-Alignment Is Not Politics

It is respect for the room and protection for the company.

Boardroom drama is rarely spontaneous. It is almost always a failure of preparation. The CEO who surprises the board with a miss. The sponsor who raises a concern no one anticipated. The board member who asks a question that exposes a gap no one discussed.

Pre-align sensitive topics 48 hours before the meeting. Not to hide truth. To sequence truth so it lands and converts into action rather than erupting into conflict.

The 48-hour rule is not about managing the sponsor. It is about respecting the governance process. A board meeting should be a decision forum, not a discovery forum. When everyone walks in informed, the conversation is productive. When anyone walks in surprised, the conversation becomes emotional.

Pre-alignment is how professionals operate. It is how trust is maintained. It is how decisions actually get made.

Rule 5: Cadence Beats Charisma

Rhythm is what makes performance repeatable.

Charisma can rally a team once. Cadence builds a team that wins every week.

Install a meeting architecture that forces clarity. The weekly leadership meeting: what happened, what matters, what we do next, who owns it. The monthly operating review: are we on track, where are we off, what are we doing about it. The quarterly board meeting: here is reality, here are decisions needed, here is what we are asking for.

Cadence reduces anxiety because people know when issues will be raised and how decisions will be made. They do not have to guess. They do not have to politic for airtime. The system handles it.

In PE, cadence is culture. It signals what matters. It creates accountability without drama. It builds the muscle memory that makes execution automatic.

The CEO who relies on charisma exhausts themselves and creates dependency. The CEO who installs cadence builds an organization that performs whether they are in the room or not.

Rule 6: Cash Is the Lie Detector

Profit is an opinion. Cash is a fact.

A leader who cannot face cash cannot face reality.

Revenue can be pulled forward with aggressive deals. EBITDA can be massaged with creative adjustments. The board pack can tell whatever story management wants to tell. But cash does not negotiate. Cash is what is actually in the bank account. Cash is what services the debt. Cash is what funds the payroll.

Treat cash as the company's truth serum. When the 13-week forecast shows deterioration, do not debate narratives. Go find the operational cause. Is it receivables aging? Inventory build? Spending ahead of revenue? Find it and fix it.

Cash discipline buys you three things. Time, because you see problems before they become crises. Credibility, because you can tell the lender exactly where you stand. And optionality, because you can fund opportunities when they appear.

A company can be profitable on paper and still die. It cannot run out of cash and survive.

Rule 7: Standards Are Care With Teeth

Being kind is not the same as being soft.

High standards are a form of respect. They tell people: I believe you can rise to this. I will not insult you by expecting less.

The opposite of standards is not freedom. It is confusion. When expectations are unclear, people guess. When performance varies without consequence, high performers leave and mediocrity becomes normal.

When a leader tolerates mediocrity, they punish the high performers. They signal that effort does not matter. They create resentment among the people who are carrying the load.

Standards must be visible, consistent, and enforced. The same standard for everyone. The same consequence for missing it. No exceptions for tenure, for relationships, for political convenience.

In PE, standards protect value and dignity at once. They create the clarity that lets people succeed and the accountability that lets the business perform.

Care with teeth. That is the frame. You can be demanding and supportive. You can hold people accountable and still have their back. The best leaders do both.

Rule 8: People First Means Truth First

You cannot protect people by hiding reality.

Leaders sometimes confuse kindness with concealment. They keep issues quiet to avoid discomfort. They delay difficult conversations to preserve feelings. They manage around underperformers rather than addressing them.

That is not protection. That is delay. And delay has costs.

Truth early allows teams to adapt early. It creates the chance to win. A sales team that knows they are behind in Q2 can still recover. A sales team that discovers in Q4 that leadership knew all along and said nothing loses trust permanently.

If you want a coachable culture, make truth honorable. Reward surfacing, not spinning. Thank the person who raises the uncomfortable question. Promote the leader who delivers bad news early rather than the one who delivers good news late.

The best teams are not fearless. They are forthright. They have learned that truth is safe, that problems shared become problems solved, that the organization can handle reality if leadership will share it.

Rule 9: Decisions Must Have Owners

If everyone is responsible, no one is responsible.

Leadership is the art of making ownership unambiguous.

Every decision needs a single owner. Not a committee. Not a working group. One person who will make the call, live with the consequences, and be accountable for the outcome.

The owner can gather input. They should gather input. But when the input is gathered, one person decides. That clarity is what creates velocity.

When decisions float, execution stalls and politics fill the space. People wait for someone else to move. They hedge their positions. They avoid commitment because commitment without clarity is risk without reward.

Give people the dignity of clarity. Who decides. Who contributes. When we move. That is how velocity is built.

The question "who decides this?" should have an immediate, unambiguous answer. If it takes more than three seconds to answer, ownership is unclear.

Rule 10: Move Fast on Reversible Decisions

Speed is a habit, not a mood.

The business does not need perfect decisions. It needs timely decisions and fast learning.

Most decisions are reversible. If a decision is reversible, treat it like an experiment and move. You will learn more from trying than from analyzing. You will create more value from iterating than from perfecting.

The 70 percent rule: when you have 70 percent of the information you wish you had, decide. The marginal value of additional information rarely exceeds the cost of delay.

Delay is a hidden cost. It drains energy as people wait. It slows execution as dependencies stack up. It invites second-guessing as new opinions emerge. It creates frustration as momentum stalls.

Leaders who build velocity create confidence. The organization learns that decisions happen, that movement is normal, that waiting is not rewarded.

Leaders who build hesitation create fear. The organization learns that commitment is risky, that delay is safe, that politics matter more than action.

Choose action, then adjust. That is how learning happens. That is how value is created.

Rule 11: Slow Down on Irreversible Decisions

When the door locks, take a longer look.

Some decisions change the company's trajectory permanently. CEO changes. Major acquisitions. Market exits. Strategic pivots. Existential financing moves.

Here, speed without depth is negligence.

Slow down. Pressure-test assumptions. Insist on clean data. Seek disconfirming evidence. Ask what would have to be true for this to fail.

The goal is not to avoid risk. PE is a risk business. The goal is to avoid unforced errors. The acquisition that looked good until you discovered the customer concentration. The CEO hire that seemed perfect until you checked the references properly. The market entry that made sense until you understood the competitive dynamics.

Mature leaders know when urgency is real and when it is theater. They know when speed matters and when diligence matters more. They do not let artificial deadlines force permanent mistakes.

The two-way door versus one-way door framework exists for this reason. Speed up two-way doors. Slow down one-way doors. Know which is which.

Rule 12: Write to Think

Leaders who still write see patterns others miss.

Writing is not communication. It is cognition.

If you cannot write the issue clearly, you do not understand it. The act of writing forces precision. What is true. What is assumed.

What is unknown. What we will do. Writing exposes fuzzy thinking that sounds reasonable in conversation.

The Amazon memo culture exists because writing creates rigor. A six-page narrative memo forces the author to think through the argument completely. It forces the reader to engage with the logic rather than the charisma of the presenter.

In PE, writing is also governance hygiene. Written plans create accountability. Written decisions create records. Written analysis creates the ability to learn from what worked and what did not.

Clear writing is clear leadership. The leader who can write a one-page summary of the situation, the options, and the recommendation demonstrates mastery. The leader who cannot is still working through their own confusion.

Rule 13: Questions Create Value

Control creates compliance. Questions create thinking.

The board's job is not to run the company. It is to improve the company's thinking.

Great leaders welcome sharp questions because they want signal, not comfort. They do not confuse questioning with disrespect. They use it to tighten the plan, expose blind spots, and accelerate choices.

The quality of questions determines the quality of governance. "How did we do?" is a weak question. "What surprised us this quarter, and what does it tell us about our assumptions?" is a strong question. "Are we on track?" is reporting. "What would have to change for us to miss, and how would we know early?" is strategy.

In PE, the highest-value board meetings feel like strategy sessions, not reporting sessions. The CEO leaves with better thinking, not just approval. The board leaves with confidence, not just information.

Questions are gifts. They reveal what the questioner cares about. They surface what the answerer has not considered. They create the dialogue that produces better decisions.

Rule 14: Protect the Credibility Bank

Credibility is earned slowly and lost in one sentence.

In PE, credibility is your currency. It buys you benefit of the doubt when things go wrong. It buys you support when you need resources. It buys you time when execution takes longer than planned.

Spend it wisely.

Do not over-promise. The forecast you cannot hit. The timeline you cannot meet. The capability you do not have. Each miss withdraws from the credibility bank.

Do not hide. The issue you knew about and did not surface. The risk you saw and did not mention. The truth you softened until it was unrecognizable. Each concealment withdraws from the credibility bank.

Do not bluff. The confidence you do not feel. The certainty you do not have. The knowledge you are faking. Each bluff withdraws from the credibility bank.

Say what you know, what you do not know, and what you will do next. That is how deposits are made.

When a leader becomes unreliable, the system becomes political. People start managing around the leader rather than through them. Information flows through back channels. Trust erodes everywhere.

When a leader is credible, the system becomes fast. People believe what the leader says. Decisions stick. Execution follows.

Credibility buys you forgiveness and time. It is the most valuable asset you have. Protect it.

Rule 15: Make the Uncomfortable Visible

What stays unspoken becomes expensive.

Silence is not peace. Silence is debt. Every issue that stays unspoken accumulates interest.

The unspoken issues are where value leaks. Customer dissatisfaction that no one wants to discuss. The weak manager everyone works around. The broken process that creates rework. The cultural toxicity that drives turnover. The cash games that mask reality.

Leaders who avoid discomfort pay for it later with drama and turnover. The conversation they did not have in January becomes the crisis they manage in September. The feedback they did not give becomes the termination they have to execute.

Bring the friction into the open. Convert it into decisions. Move.

Your job is not to keep the room calm. It is to keep the system honest. Sometimes honesty creates temporary discomfort. That discomfort is the price of avoiding permanent damage.

The leader who can say "we need to talk about the thing no one wants to talk about" creates more value than the leader who keeps the meeting pleasant.

Rule 16: Do Not Confuse Activity With Traction

Busy is not a metric.

High-performing teams can still be misdirected teams. Effort without alignment is just heat.

Leaders must separate motion from momentum. Ask: what moved enterprise value this month? What created durable capability? What reduced risk? What improved cash?

The initiative tracker can show green on every item while the business underperforms. Activities completed. Milestones achieved. Meetings held. None of it matters if the outcomes do not follow.

In PE, everything is eventually reconciled to outcomes. Revenue. EBITDA. Cash. Multiple. The work either creates value or it does not.

If work does not translate into value, it is theater. Cut it, refocus, and protect the team's energy for work that matters.

The question "what did we accomplish?" is different from "what did we do?" Strong leaders ask the first question. Weak leaders accept answers to the second.

Rule 17: Build a Bench, Not a Hero Story

Depth is the only scalable form of leadership.

A company that depends on one person is not strong. It is fragile. It is also worth less.

Buyers discount key-person risk. If the CEO is the system, if the sales come from one relationship, if the operations depend on one expert, buyers see vulnerability. They price that vulnerability into the multiple. The discount can be 0.5 to 1.0 turns.

PE-backed businesses need depth. Leaders who can run functions independently. Owners who can drive initiatives without constant oversight. Successors who can step up if someone leaves.

Bench strength is not optional. It is an exit requirement.

Invest early in talent upgrades. Invest in coaching and development. Invest in succession planning. The 9-box grid exists to force this conversation. Use it.

The hero story feels good. The founder who built it all. The CEO who carries everything. The sales leader who closes every deal. But hero stories do not scale. And they do not sell at premium multiples.

Build an organization that performs because of its system, not because of its heroes.

Rule 18: Culture Is a Financial Lever

Culture is not soft. It is the operating logic of the company.

Culture decides how truth travels through the organization. Does bad news surface quickly or get hidden? Culture decides how decisions are made. By consensus, by authority, by politics? Culture decides how people behave when no one is watching. Do they cut corners or maintain standards?

Those decisions determine execution speed and cash discipline. They determine whether the organization can scale or whether it breaks under pressure. They determine whether talent stays or leaves.

In PE, culture is not a vibe. It is an asset or a liability. Strong culture attracts talent, enables speed, and supports change. Weak culture repels talent, creates friction, and resists improvement.

The best leaders design culture through standards, cadence, and consequences. They do not outsource it to HR. They do not treat it as secondary to strategy. They understand that strategy without culture is a plan without an army.

Culture shows up in the numbers. Turnover rates. Time to decision. Forecast accuracy. Customer retention. The numbers reveal what the culture actually is, not what the values poster claims it to be.

Rule 19: Kill the Illusion of Control

Leaders who bend reality for power eventually lose the system.

Control feels safe. Knowing everything. Approving everything. Being in every meeting. Having every decision flow through you.

But control is often a mask for fear. Fear that others will make mistakes. Fear that you will be surprised. Fear that you are not needed.

Leaders who need to control everything suffocate initiative. People stop bringing ideas because the ideas always get overridden. They hide risk because surfacing it invites micromanagement. They optimize for the leader's comfort rather than the business's needs.

The irony is brutal: the more you tighten control, the less you know what is true. People tell you what you want to hear. Information gets filtered. Reality becomes invisible until it explodes.

Mature leaders build control through transparency, not intimidation. They create systems where truth is rewarded, not punished. They trust the process rather than controlling every step. They know that real control comes from seeing clearly, not from gripping tightly.

Rule 20: Align Incentives With Behaviors

People do what gets rewarded, especially under pressure.

If your compensation, promotions, and praise reward the wrong things, do not act surprised when behavior follows.

The sales team compensated only on bookings will pull forward revenue and discount aggressively. The operations team measured only on cost will defer maintenance and create quality problems. The leadership team with no equity will optimize for personal career rather than company value.

Leaders must design incentives that reinforce the operating system. Reward truth early, not just good news. Reward ownership, not just participation. Reward collaboration, not just individual achievement. Reward cash discipline, not just EBITDA. Reward customer outcomes, not just customer count.

In PE, misaligned incentives create internal games that buyers smell instantly during diligence. The patterns are visible in the data. The culture is visible in the behavior. The misalignment becomes a risk factor that depresses the multiple.

Align the system, and you reduce politics. Misalign it, and you manufacture friction. The choice is that direct.

Rule 21: Separate Signal From Noise

Most meetings fail because leaders let noise win.

Noise is performance theater. Slides that impress with complexity. Stories that soothe with narrative. Metrics that flatter with selective presentation. Answers that sound good but do not address the question.

Signal is uncomfortable. Churn rate. Quality defects. Pipeline reality. Cash timing. Capacity constraints. Talent gaps. The things that reveal what is actually happening rather than what we wish was happening.

A leader's job is to insist on signal.

Ask: what is changing? What is breaking? What is at risk? What is the next decision? What would have to be true for us to miss? What are we not talking about that we should be?

Signal creates value. It enables decisions. It reveals problems while they can still be fixed. It builds the shared reality that enables coordinated action.

Noise delays value. It consumes time. It obscures problems until they become crises. It creates the illusion of alignment while people leave the room with different understandings.

The meeting where everyone leaves feeling good but nothing changes is a noise meeting. The meeting where people leave uncomfortable but aligned on action is a signal meeting. Know the difference.

Rule 22: Coach the CFO and You Coach the Company

Finance is the nervous system of execution.

When finance is strong, the company sees clearly. Forecasts are reliable. Variances are explained. Cash is managed. The board gets truth.

When finance is weak, the company guesses. Forecasts miss. Variances are rationalized. Cash surprises. The board loses confidence.

Leaders must turn finance into a truth engine.

Clean forecasts built on operational reality, not hope. Honest variance analysis that diagnoses causes rather than excuses them. Rigorous cash management with weekly visibility. EBITDA-to-cash bridges that explain where the money actually goes.

Do not let finance become a compliance function that produces reports no one uses. Make it a leadership function that drives decisions.

The CFO who can explain the business in numbers, who can project forward with confidence, who can surface problems before they become crises, is worth their weight in gold. The CFO who produces board packs full of data but cannot answer basic questions about cash destroys value invisibly.

In PE, finance credibility shapes everything. Board trust. Lender trust. Buyer trust. The quality of earnings analysis at exit will reveal what kind of finance function you actually built.

Rule 23: Own the Hard Conversations

The leader's job is to say what others will not.

Avoidance is expensive.

If someone is not performing, the system already knows. Their peers know. Their team knows. Often they know themselves. The only person pretending everything is fine is the leader who will not have the conversation.

Silence does not protect anyone. It punishes the high performers who pick up the slack. It enables the underperformer to continue failing. It signals to the organization that standards are negotiable.

Leaders must address underperformance fast, privately, and with clarity.

Be direct. Name the gap between expectation and reality. Do not soften it into meaninglessness.

Be fair. Give specific examples. Explain what success looks like. Offer support for improvement.

Be decisive. Set a timeline. Define consequences. Follow through.

Compassion without clarity is cruelty. Clarity with respect builds trust.

This is how strong cultures protect themselves. By having the conversations that weaker cultures avoid.

Rule 24: Build a System That Keeps Changing

Transformation is not a project. It is a capability.

Most companies treat change like an event. There is a transformation initiative with a name, a budget, a timeline, and an end date. When the initiative ends, change ends.

PE demands change as a habit.

The value creation plan is a hypothesis. The market will evolve. Assumptions will be invalidated. New opportunities will emerge. The company that cannot adapt will fall behind.

Install a rhythm of review, prioritization, and follow-through. Quarterly assumption testing. Semi-annual initiative assessments. Annual plan refreshes. Continuous learning.

Make learning fast and visible. When something works, scale it. When something fails, kill it. Do not let initiatives linger in zombie status, consuming resources without creating value.

The goal is not constant disruption. The goal is constant adaptation. Small adjustments continuously rather than large transformations occasionally.

Businesses win when they can evolve without breaking. That is what buyers pay for: an organization that can keep improving after the exit. An organization that does not depend on the current owner to drive change.

Rule 25: Technology Must Create Speed, Not Slides

Digital is a lever, not a costume.

Leaders waste money when they chase shiny tools without clear economic intent.

The AI strategy that cannot explain what problem it solves. The digital transformation that has transformed nothing except the org chart. The dashboard project that produced dashboards no one uses. The ERP implementation that took three years and still does not work.

Technology should shorten cycles, reduce errors, improve visibility, and unlock capacity. If it does not, it is theater.

Make every technology initiative answer one question: what decision will this improve, and what cash outcome will follow?

The 13-week cash forecast in a spreadsheet is more valuable than a million-dollar BI platform that produces reports no one reads. The simple CRM that salespeople actually use is more valuable than the sophisticated system they work around.

In PE, technology premium is earned through execution, not ambition. Buyers will ask what capabilities actually exist, not what capabilities are planned. They will ask what the technology enables the business to do that it could not do before.

Technology is a means, not an end. Keep that clear.

Rule 26: Presence Beats Prediction

When the map is wrong, awareness becomes the advantage.

In complex environments, prediction is fragile. The forecast assumes conditions that may not hold. The plan assumes competitors will behave as expected. The model assumes customers will respond as projected.

Presence is powerful. The leader who observes deeply sees weak signals early. Morale shifts before turnover spikes. Customer hesitation before churn materializes. Operational strain before quality collapses. Political drift before alignment breaks.

They do not panic. They do not overreact. They adjust.

Presence is not softness. It is situational mastery. It is the ability to sense what is happening rather than relying entirely on what the reports say is happening.

Walk the floor. Talk to frontline employees. Listen to customer calls. Watch how decisions actually get made versus how the process says they should be made.

In PE, the leader who can stay calm and perceptive under pressure becomes the stabilizer of the system. When others are reactive, they are responsive. When others are panicked, they are clear. That presence is worth more than any forecast model.

Rule 27: Earned Confidence, Not Performative Certainty

"I do not know" can be the start of winning.

The most dangerous leader is the one who pretends to know.

Certainty can be a cover for ego. The leader who cannot admit uncertainty creates an organization where uncertainty cannot be admitted. People fake confidence. Risks get hidden. Problems fester because no one will say they do not know what to do.

Strong leaders admit uncertainty fast. They define what must be learned. They create a plan to learn it. They move from not knowing to knowing as quickly as possible.

"I do not know, but here is how we will find out by Friday" builds more trust than false certainty that collapses under scrutiny.

The room does not need your perfection. It needs your honesty and your judgment. Confidence is earned by facing reality, not by denying it. The leader who can say "I was wrong about this, and here is what we are doing instead" builds more credibility than the leader who never admits error.

Earned confidence. Not performed certainty. Know the difference.

Rule 28: Trust Is Built in Small Deposits

Big speeches do not build trust. Repeated behavior does.

Trust is an accumulation. It grows slowly through small moments.

It grows when leaders do what they said they would do. When they show up prepared. When they share the truth early rather than late. When they protect people from politics rather than creating politics. When they take blame and give credit.

It collapses when leaders blame others for their failures. When they surprise people who should have been informed. When they disappear during difficulty. When they say one thing and do another.

The grand gesture does not build trust. The consistent behavior does.

In PE, trust is the lubricant of velocity. Without it, every interaction requires verification. Every commitment requires hedging. Every decision requires politics. Everything slows.

With trust, commitments stick. Decisions move. People tell the truth because they believe it will be received well. The system accelerates because friction is low.

Trust is built in small deposits. Protect each one.

Rule 29: The Narrative Starts on Day One

Buyers do not buy your process. They buy your proof.

Exit value is not a story you invent at the end. It is a story you earn over time.

Leaders must build proof points deliberately. Not just financial results, but the evidence that explains why those results are durable and replicable.

Recurring revenue quality that shows customer stickiness. Margin durability that shows pricing power and cost discipline. Customer outcomes that show value delivery. Team depth that shows organizational capability. Clean governance that shows management maturity. Reliable cash that shows operational control.

Each proof point is a deposit in the exit narrative. By year three, you should have 30 to 50 meaningful proof points. Customer wins. Initiative completions. Retention improvements. Margin gains. Team upgrades. Each one supports the story of a business that creates value systematically.

When the time comes, the narrative should feel inevitable. Not manufactured. Not spun. Inevitable. The natural conclusion of what the evidence demonstrates.

In PE, multiple expansion is rarely a mystery. It is the reward for credibility built over three to five years. The work starts on day one.

Rule 30: Choose Legacy Over Optics

Optics impress the moment. Legacy compounds over years.

Leaders are tempted to manage perception. The polished deck that hides the reality. The confident presentation that masks the uncertainty. The curated story that omits the problems.

That is short-term thinking. It optimizes for the meeting at the expense of the business.

The best leaders build something that outlasts the meeting. A strong team that performs when they are not in the room. A culture of truth that surfaces problems early. A system of execution that delivers results consistently. A business that works without drama.

In PE, legacy is not sentimental. It is value.

Buyers pay premiums for companies that feel adult. That have their systems in order. That have depth beyond the CEO. That have a culture where truth flows and decisions move. That have the boring operational excellence that produces reliable results quarter after quarter.

The leader who builds for legacy creates more value than the leader who optimizes for optics. They build something worth buying. Something worth owning. Something that continues creating value long after they are gone.

That is the job. Not to look good. To be good. To build something good that lasts.

References

Private equity, ownership, and value creation

Acharya, Viral V., Oliver F. Gottschalg, Moritz Hahn, and Conor Kehoe. "Corporate Governance and Value Creation: Evidence from Private Equity." *Review of Financial Studies* 26, no. 2 (2013): 368–402.

Appelbaum, Eileen, and Rosemary Batt. *Private Equity at Work: When Wall Street Manages Main Street*. New York: Russell Sage Foundation, 2014.

Bain & Company. *Global Private Equity Report 2025*. Bain & Company, 2025.

Cendrowski, Harry, Louis W. Petro, James P. Martin, and Adam A. Wadecki. *Private Equity: History, Governance, and Operations*. 2nd ed. Hoboken, NJ: Wiley, 2012.

Coffey, Adam. *The Private Equity Playbook*. Revised and expanded ed. Cheval Press, 2024.

Davis, Steven J., John C. Haltiwanger, Kyle Handley, Ron S. Jarmin, Josh Lerner, and Javier Miranda. *Private Equity, Jobs, and Productivity*. NBER Working Paper No. 19458, 2013.

Davis, Steven J., John C. Haltiwanger, Ron S. Jarmin, Josh Lerner, and Javier Miranda. *Private Equity and Employment*. NBER Working Paper No. 17399, 2011.

Davis, Steven J., John C. Haltiwanger, Kyle Handley, Ben Lipsius, Josh Lerner, and Javier Miranda. *The (Heterogenous) Economic Effects of Private Equity Buyouts*. NBER Working Paper No. 26371 (rev. April 2024).

Ecock, Tony, ed. *The Operating Partner in Private Equity*, Vols. 1–2 (package). London: PEI Books / Private Equity International, 2015.

Gadiesh, Orit, and Hugh MacArthur. *Lessons from Private Equity Any Company Can Use (Memo to the CEO)*. Boston: Harvard Business Review Press, 2008.

Kaplan, Steven N., and Per Strömberg. "Leveraged Buyouts and Private Equity." *Journal of Economic Perspectives* 23, no. 1 (2009): 121–146.

Lanier, John. *Value-Creation in Middle Market Private Equity*. New York: Routledge, 2015.

Lerner, Josh, Morten Sørensen, and Per Strömberg. "Private Equity and Long-Run Investment: The Case of Innovation." *Journal of Finance* 66, no. 2 (2011): 445–477.

The Private Equity CEO Playbook: Best Practice Lessons from 350 CEOs. PDF report / playbook, 2025.

Dealcraft, valuation, and capital markets

Burrough, Bryan, and John Helyar. *Barbarians at the Gate: The Fall of RJR Nabisco*. New York: Harper & Row, 1989.

Carey, David, and John E. Morris. *King of Capital: The Remarkable Rise, Fall, and Rise Again of Steve Schwarzman and Blackstone*. New York: Crown Business, 2010.

Koller, Tim, Marc Goedhart, and David Wessels. *Valuation: Measuring and Managing the Value of Companies*. 8th ed. Hoboken, NJ: Wiley, 2025.

Rosenbaum, Joshua, and Joshua Pearl. *Investment Banking: Valuation, Leveraged Buyouts, and Mergers and Acquisitions*. 2nd ed. Hoboken, NJ: Wiley, 2013.

Execution, leadership, governance, and operating standards

Doerr, John. *Measure What Matters.* New York: Portfolio/Penguin, 2018.

Goldratt, Eliyahu M., and Jeff Cox. *The Goal: A Process of Ongoing Improvement.* Great Barrington, MA: North River Press, 1984.

Grove, Andrew S. *High Output Management.* New York: Vintage, 1995.

Institutional Limited Partners Association (ILPA). *ILPA Principles 3.0: Fostering Transparency, Governance and Alignment of Interests for General and Limited Partners.* 2019.

ISO. *ISO 31000:2018 Risk management — Guidelines.* Geneva: International Organization for Standardization, 2018.

NIST (National Institute of Standards and Technology). *The NIST Cybersecurity Framework (CSF) 2.0.* NIST CSWP 29, 2024.

OECD. *G20/OECD Principles of Corporate Governance 2023.* Paris: OECD Publishing, 2023.

OECD. *OECD Corporate Governance Factbook 2023.* Paris: OECD Publishing, 2023.

PMI (Project Management Institute). *A Guide to the Project Management Body of Knowledge (PMBOK® Guide).* 7th ed. Newtown Square, PA: Project Management Institute, 2021.

COSO (Committee of Sponsoring Organizations of the Treadway Commission). *Enterprise Risk Management: Integrating with Strategy and Performance.* 2017.

IFRS Foundation / IASB. *IFRS 16 Leases*. Issued January 2016; effective for annual reporting periods beginning on or after 1 January 2019.

Afterword

If this book did its job, you did not come away with a bag of tricks. You came away with a different standard.

Private equity does not reward activity. It rewards outcomes. And outcomes, in the end, are not philosophical. They are visible in cash, in execution speed, in decision quality, in the credibility of the team, and in the confidence of the next buyer.

The idea of "coaching" can sound soft in a hard business. But you now know what PE coaching really is. It is not therapy. It is not motivation. It is not vague leadership talk. It is a disciplined practice of installing behaviors that protect value and build value under time pressure.

The best leaders in PE-backed companies are not the smartest people in the room. They are the clearest. They can name the few things that matter, translate them into operating cadence, and keep the organization honest when emotion and noise try to take over. They do not let problems hide. They do not let meetings become theater. They do not let teams confuse explanation with progress.

That is the Coach's job. To raise the standard. To make reality discussable. To connect the human system to the economic system, without turning the organization into a spreadsheet.

If you are a CEO, your edge is not that you have answers. Your edge is that you can create the conditions where the right answers surface early, decisions get made fast, and accountability stays clean.

If you are a board member or sponsor, your edge is not pressure. Your edge is precision. You do not need louder urgency. You need sharper questions, clearer expectations, and a cadence that prevents drift.

And if you are the Coach, your edge is that you can hold the line without becoming the story. You build the system. You reinforce the behaviors. You shut down the patterns that kill value. Then you let the team own it.

Value creation is not purely financial. It is deeply human. Businesses improve when people understand the game, tell the truth faster, and act with discipline when it counts.

The work is never finished. But it becomes much simpler when you stop chasing "best practices" and start building a repeatable operating standard.

www.ingramcontent.com/pod-product-compliance
Lightning Source LLC
Chambersburg PA
CBHW061230220326
41599CB00028B/5387